PRENTICE HALL WRITING AND GRAMMAR

Formal Assessment Blackline Masters

Grade Seven

Boston, Massachusetts,
Upper Saddle River, New Jersey

Copyright © by Pearson Education, Inc., publishing as Pearson Prentice Hall, Boston, Massachusetts, 02116. All rights reserved. Printed in the United States of America. This publication is protected by copyright, and permission should be obtained from the publisher prior to any prohibited reproduction, storage in a retrieval system, or transmission in any form or by any means, electronic, mechanical, photocopying, recording, or likewise. For information regarding permission(s), write to: Rights and Permissions Department, One Lake Street, Upper Saddle River, New Jersey 07458.

Pearson Prentice Hall™ is a trademark of Pearson Education, Inc.
Pearson® is a registered trademark of Pearson plc.
Prentice Hall® is a registered trademark of Pearson Education, Inc.

ISBN 0-13-361517-0

4 5 6 7 8 9 10   10 09

Contents

PART 1: WRITING
For Chapters 4–14, Test 1 is Easy, Test 2 is Average, and Test 3 is Challenging.

Chapter 1: The Writer in You	3
Chapter 2: A Walk Through the Writing Process	6
Chapter 3: Paragraphs and Compositions	9
Chapter 4: Narration: Autobiographical Writing	12
Test 1 ...... 12 Test 2 ...... 15 Test 3 18	
Chapter 5: Narration: Short Story	21
Test 1 ...... 21 Test 2 ...... 24 Test 3 27	
Chapter 6: Description	30
Test 1 ...... 30 Test 2 ...... 33 Test 3 36	
Chapter 7: Persuasion: Persuasive Essay	39
Test 1 ...... 39 Test 2 ...... 42 Test 3 45	
Chapter 8: Exposition: Comparison-and-Contrast Essay	48
Test 1 ...... 48 Test 2 ...... 51 Test 3 54	
Chapter 9: Exposition: Cause-and-Effect Essay	57
Test 1 ...... 57 Test 2 ...... 60 Test 3 63	
Chapter 10: Exposition: How-to Essay	66
Test 1 ...... 66 Test 2 ...... 69 Test 3 71	
Chapter 11: Research: Research Report	75
Test 1 ...... 75 Test 2 ...... 78 Test 3 81	
Chapter 12: Response to Literature	84
Test 1 ...... 84 Test 2 ...... 87 Test 3 90	
Chapter 13: Writing for Assessment	93
Test 1 ...... 93 Test 2 ...... 96 Test 3 99	

PART 2: GRAMMAR, USAGE, AND MECHANICS

Grammar, Usage, and Mechanics: Cumulative Diagnostic Test	105
Chapter 14: Nouns and Pronouns	113
Chapter 15: Verbs	117
Chapter 16: Adjectives and Adverbs	120
Chapter 17: Prepositions	123
Chapter 18: Conjunctions and Interjections	127
Chapter 19: Basic Sentence Parts	130
Chapter 20: Phrases and Clauses	134
Chapter 21: Effective Sentences	139
Chapter 22: Using Verbs	144
Chapter 23: Using Pronouns	148
Chapter 24: Making Words Agree	151
Chapter 25: Using Modifiers	155
Chapter 26: Punctuation	158
Chapter 27: Capitalization	162
Grammar, Usage, and Mechanics: Cumulative Mastery Test	165

PART 3: ACADEMIC AND WORKPLACE SKILLS

Chapter 28: Speaking, Listening, Viewing, and Representing	175
Chapter 29: Vocabulary and Spelling	181
Chapter 30: Reading Skills	185
Chapter 31: Study, Reference, and Test-Taking Skills	190

ANSWERS 194

About the Tests

This Formal Assessment booklet contains one test for each chapter in the *Writing and Grammar* student textbook. To provide you with the greatest flexibility, the tests utilize a number of different formats and may be administered in one or more class periods, depending on your classroom needs and your students' abilities. The complete Formal Assessment program is also available on a Computer Test Bank CD-ROM.

Tests for Part 1: Writing

- With the exception of the tests on the Research chapter, the tests on the modes of writing ask students to write a brief paper, applying the skills taught in the chapter. The questions on the tests are designed to lead the students through the writing process. Depending on your students' abilities, you may assign the tests to be done in one class period or as an extended assignment. Three tests (1—easy, 2—average, and 3—challenging) are provided for each mode of writing, the difference in the levels of difficulty being the complexity of the assignment and of some of the tasks students are asked to complete.

- Using multiple-choice and short-answer formats, the tests for Chapters 1, 2, and 3 and for the Research chapter ask students to recognize, respond to, and evaluate the material taught in the chapters.

Tests for Part 2: Grammar, Usage, and Mechanics

- Part 2 contains extensive objective tests on all the grammar, usage, and mechanics topics taught in the student textbook. Each test ends with a question bank in one of several standardized-test formats. In the answer key at the back of the booklet, you will find a level designation—easy, average, or challenging—for each question. These designations, together with the ample number of questions provided, give you the flexibility of customizing the tests for individual students or classes.

- In addition to the chapter tests, Part 2 contains a Cumulative Diagnostic Test at the beginning and a Cumulative Mastery Test at the end. These long tests, which may be given in sections, are designed to help you evaluate your students' needs and progress.

Tests for Part 3: Academic and Workplace Skills

- The tests for the chapters in Part 3 use multiple-choice and short-answer formats to help you assess your students' mastery of the material.

Part 1: Writing

Name _____

 # Assessment for Chapter 1: The Writer in You

1. Give three specific examples of how people use writing in everyday life.
   _____
   _____
   _____

2. Give an example of a possible purpose for writing.
   _____
   _____

3. Write the letter of the definition on the line next to the qualities of good writing.

   _____ ideas   a. your unique writing personality
   _____ organization   b. general topics that get you started
   _____ voice   c. a smooth, connected flow
   _____ word choices   d. the rules that govern grammatical correctness in writing
   _____ sentence fluency   e. the order in which details are arranged
   _____ conventions   f. the building blocks of writing; must be precise and vivid

4. Name a way that you can keep track of ideas about which you might want to write. Explain your answer.
   _____
   _____
   _____

5. State a way that you can keep track of interesting facts, quotations, or opinions that you might have read during the day.
   _____
   _____

6. Place a number next to each item below to show the usual order of the writing process.
   _____ Improving and changing your draft
   _____ Writing a final copy
   _____ Listing ideas and notes
   _____ Writing a rough draft
   _____ Putting your notes in a logical order
   _____ Publishing your writing
   _____ Finding a topic

7. What kind of surroundings would be helpful to a writer as he or she prepares to work?
   _____
   _____
   _____

Name _____

8. List three items that a writer should have readily available before sitting down to write.
   _____
   _____
   _____

9. Since writing can be a long process, it is important to "budget your time." Explain, in your own words, what this phrase means.
   _____
   _____
   _____

10. Imagine you are writing an essay on your favorite sport, and that you have two weeks to complete the assignment. Use the calendar below, and fill in the following information:
    1) Choose subject and begin research;
    2) Finish research;
    3) Organize notes and write draft;
    4) Review draft with peers;
    5) Revise draft;
    6) Hand in final copy.

    NOVEMBER

1	2	3	4	5	6
7	8	9	10	11	12	13
14	15	16	17	18	19	20

11. Give a reason why it might be useful for writers to work together.
    _____
    _____
    _____

12. Give a specific example of how a student writer, like you, can publish his or her work for an audience beyond the classroom.
    _____
    _____

Name _____

13. Choose two examples listed below of professionals who use writing in their jobs. On the lines, write a sentence about how these two professionals might use writing in their careers.
    a jazz musician
    a fund-raiser for a homeless shelter
    an accountant
    a health-food store owner
    a math teacher
    a zoo director

    _____
    _____
    _____
    _____
    _____

Reflect on your own writing preferences and challenges by completing the sentences below.

14. My favorite kind of writing is _____
    _____
    _____
    _____
    _____

15. The kind of writing I find most difficult is _____
    _____
    _____
    _____
    _____

© Prentice-Hall, Inc.

Name _____ Date _____

 Assessment for Chapter 2: A Walk Through the Writing Process

1. When you write *reflexively*, you choose what to write about, and you are writing for yourself. When you write *extensively*, you are assigned a topic, and you are writing for a general audience. Give an example of each kind of writing.
   _____
   _____

2. Fill in the timeline, showing the following stages of the writing process in their correct order: Publishing and Presenting; Drafting; Prewriting; Revising; and Editing and Proofreading.

   Timeline of the Writing Process

   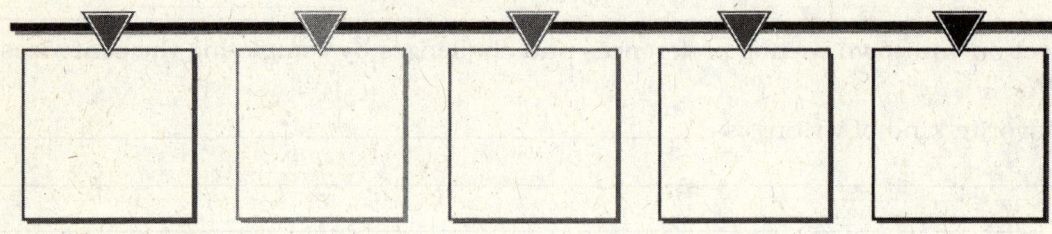

3. Explain the difference between *drafting* and *revising*.
   _____
   _____
   _____

4. Narrow the broad topic *pets* into a smaller topic that you could use for a short essay.
   _____
   _____

5. What is meant by the term *audience* with respect to a piece of writing?
   _____

   Who would represent an appropriate audience for an essay that describes your family's photo album? Explain your answer.
   _____
   _____

6. Apply the "reporter's formula" of *Who, What, Where, When,* and *Why* to write five questions about your favorite food.
   _____
   _____
   _____
   _____
   _____
   _____

Name _____

7. Read the paragraph below. On the line, write an enticing lead for the paragraph.

   I dreamed that I was in a ship, being tossed about by the waves. When I awakened, I discovered that I was lying in a reversed position, with my head located where my feet should be.

   _____
   _____
   _____
   _____

8. Use the SEE Method to write an *extension* and an *elaboration* for the statement below:

   STATEMENT: I wish I could go to the moon.

   EXTENSION: _____
   _____
   _____

   ELABORATION: _____
   _____
   _____

9. Read the paragraph. Then, use the information to fill out the application.

   Duke is my best friend. A ten-year-old golden mutt, he's thin and a little mangy. He sleeps most of the day on my bed. When I come home from school, he springs up like he's a puppy again, runs to the door, and licks my face and hands. He wants to go for a walk with me. Most days, that's just what we do.

   Read the application form. Next to *Job*, write the purpose of the paragraph. Under *Qualifications*, give two facts or examples from the paragraph that support the purpose.

   Paragraph Application

   Job: _____

   Qualifications:

   1. _____
      _____
      _____

   2. _____
      _____
      _____

© Prentice-Hall, Inc.

Chapter 2: A Walk Through the Writing Process • 7

Name _____

10. Read the sentence below. On the line, add a phrase to the beginning of the sentence so that it no longer starts with *I*.

    I like to walk outside.

    _____, I like to walk outside.

11. Circle the *to be* verb in the sentence below. Then, on the line, rewrite the sentence using an action verb, with NASA as the subject.

    Astronauts are chosen by NASA for their strength and intelligence.
    _____
    _____

12. Give an example of a question or comment you might make to a writer during a peer review.
    _____
    _____
    _____

13. Name a specific kind of error you should be looking for when you are *proofreading* your writing.
    _____
    _____
    _____

14. Why is it important for your writing to be both neat and accurate?
    _____
    _____
    _____

15. Why is it useful for students to keep a portfolio of their writing? What is its purpose?
    _____
    _____
    _____
    _____
    _____
    _____
    _____
    _____
    _____
    _____
    _____

Name _____   Date _____

 **Assessment for Chapter 3: Paragraphs and Compositions**

1. Write the correct letter of the definition on the line next to the term it describes.

   _____ paragraph   a. a suggested, but not stated, important idea

   _____ topic sentence   b. a group of related sentences

   _____ implied main idea   c. a detail that supports the main idea

   _____ supporting sentence d. a direct statement of the main idea

2. Circle the topic sentence in this paragraph, and underline the supporting sentences. Then, on the line, write an additional supporting sentence.

   Baking brownies for your friends is as easy as 1–2–3. First, you buy a brownie mix at the store. Second, you carefully follow the directions on the box. Third, you throw away the box so that everyone will think you baked brownies from scratch!

   _____

3. Circle the statistic in the following passage. Then, on the lines, write a statistic about your class or school.

   I've always wanted to visit Hawaii. It is a chain of islands over 1,900 miles long. In the photographs, it looks like a beautiful paradise, all green and lush and flowering.

   _____

   _____

4. Write three supporting sentences that illustrate the following topic sentence: Our school offers a variety of nonathletic activities.

   a. _____

   _____

   b. _____

   _____

   c. _____

   _____

5. Read the paragraph below. On the line, write the sentence that does not contribute to the unity of the paragraph.

   In the modern age, you can hear the radio through your computer. If you download certain files, you can actually use your mouse or keyboard as a sort of tape or CD player, starting and stopping the sound. My family just got a new computer, which I can't wait to use. You can even "rewind" the sound, if you need to hear something again.

   _____

6. Write the letter of the paragraph topic next to the type of organization that is most appropriate.

   _____ chronological order   a. a description of a beautiful mountain

   _____ spatial order   b. a reason for why I failed my history test

   _____ order of importance   c. a story about how I broke my leg

   _____ cause-and-effect order d. an essay about how to prevent floods

Name _____

7. Show that you understand the parts of a composition by completing these sentences:

   The *introduction* contains _____
   _____.

   The *body* contains _____
   _____.

   The *conclusion* contains _____
   _____.

8. Read the topical paragraph below. Then, on the lines, write two or three sentences that could serve as a follow-up functional paragraph.

   The adventurers hadn't eaten for days, and the sky was getting dark. The island seemed to hold little promise for survival. Then, all of a sudden, they walked into a clearing and spotted a giant coconut tree.

   _____
   _____
   _____
   _____

9. Name one of the purposes of a functional paragraph.
   _____

   Read the paragraph, and use it to answer the next three items.

   The day was <u>cloudy</u>. Winter was over. Spring wasn't here yet. Mud was everywhere. Nothing was green. No birds sang. It wasn't <u>hot</u>. It wasn't <u>cold</u>. I felt bored.

   _____
   _____
   _____

10. Rewrite the paragraph, making the underlined words more intensely negative in connotation.
    _____
    _____
    _____
    _____

11. Choose two of the sentences in the paragraph. Rewrite them, adding variety to their length or style.
    _____
    _____

12. How would you describe the tone of the paragraph?
    _____
    _____

13. Name one of the conventions of formal English.
    _____

Name _____

14. Read these two passages. Circle the one that is written using informal English. On the lines, explain your choice.

   Blueberry pie. My all-time favorite. It's warm. It's gooey and sweet.

   Blueberry pie is my favorite dessert because it is sweet, gooey, and delicious.

   _____
   _____
   _____
   _____

15. Read the sentence below. On the line, rewrite it in formal English.

   First, we scored some tunes, then we hung out at Tony's place.

   _____
   _____
   _____

Name _____ Date _____

Assessment for Chapter 4: Narration: Autobiographical Writing
Test 1

In this test, you will be asked to draft an autobiographical story of three paragraphs about something that happened to you. It can be a celebration, an adventure, or a surprise. Your story should include a conflict and a lesson that you learned. Use "I" to tell your story. Write your topic on the line.

_____

Prewriting

1. Use looping to narrow your topic. Choose an event for your general subject, and write freely about it on the lines below. Then, circle a phrase or sentence that will be your main focus.

   _____
   _____
   _____
   _____

2. Describe your purpose and your audience.

   In my autobiographical account, my purpose is to _____.

   My readers will probably include _____.

3. List three ideas connected to your topic.

   _____
   _____
   _____

   Now, choose the most important idea of the three. Add one detail to it to form a sentence that you can use in your autobiographical story.

   _____

Drafting

4. Describe the conflict that your story will show by naming the conflict in the center box of the conflict map and filling in the blanks and boxes with details about the cause of the conflict.

   Who? _____   **What?** _____

   CONFLICT:

   Why? [   ]   **How?** [   ]

12 • Chapter 4: Narration: Autobiographical Writing   © Prentice-Hall, Inc.

Name _____

5. Describe how the conflict is resolved in your story.
   _____
   _____
   _____
   _____

6. On a separate sheet of paper, use your notes and information from the graphic organizer to draft your autobiographical story.

Revising

7. Go back and read your draft. Find an unnecessary sentence or a phrase that you can delete. Remember that sentences should contain details related to the conflict. On the line, write the sentence or phrase that you deleted.
   _____

8. Choose a transition word from below, and use it to connect two sentences from your draft. On the lines below, write the new version of your sentences.

first	since	but	therefore
next	because	although	so
finally	if	however	then

   _____
   _____
   _____
   _____

9. Underline the vague noun in the sentence below. Then, on the line, rewrite the sentence, using a more precise noun.

   Mr. Solomon brought over a lot of stuff for the garage sale.
   _____

10. Find one vague noun in your draft. Write the sentence that contains it, and circle the vague noun.
    _____

    Now, rewrite the sentence using a more precise noun.
    _____

Editing and Proofreading

11. Find four errors in capitalization in the sentences below and correct them, using proofreading marks.

    In our game against middletown, the score was tied. only ten seconds were on the clock. All of a sudden, i got the ball and shot. It seemed like an Hour before it reached the basket.

12. Now, review your draft for any similar errors. Write the errors and corrections on the lines. If your draft does not contain capitalization errors, write *none*.
    _____
    _____

Name _____

13. Evaluate your draft based on the criteria in the rubric below. List any changes that you may need to make in your story.

	Score 4	Score 3	Score 2	Score 1
Audience and Purpose	Contains an engaging introduction; successfully entertains or presents a theme	Contains a somewhat engaging introduction; entertains or presents a theme	Contains an introduction; attempts to entertain or to present a theme	Begins abruptly or confusingly; leaves purpose unclear
Organization	Creates an interesting, clear narrative; told from a consistent point of view	Presents a clear sequence of events; told from a specific point of view	Presents a mostly clear sequence of events; contains inconsistent points of view	Presents events without logical order; lacks a consistent point of view
Elaboration	Provides insight into character; develops plot; contains dialogue	Contains details and dialogue that develop character and plot	Contains details that develop plot; contains some dialogue	Contains few or no details to develop characters or plot
Use of Language	Uses word choice and tone to reveal story's theme; contains no errors in grammar, punctuation, or spelling	Uses interesting and fresh word choices; contains few errors in grammar, punctuation, and spelling	Uses some clichés and trite expressions; contains some errors in grammar, punctuation, and spelling	Uses uninspired word choices; has many errors in grammar, punctuation, and spelling

_____
_____
_____
_____
_____
_____

Publishing and Presenting

14. How or where could you publish or present your autobiographical story?
_____
_____
_____
_____
_____
_____
_____

15. What did you learn from writing your autobiographical account?
_____
_____
_____
_____
_____
_____
_____

Name _____ Date _____

Assessment for Chapter 4:
Narration: Autobiographical Writing
Test 2

In this test, you will be asked to draft an autobiographical narrative of three paragraphs about yourself and an animal. Your narrative should include a conflict. It could show an experience with a family pet or a creature at the zoo. Write your topic on the line.
_____

Prewriting:

1. Use looping to narrow your topic. Write for 2–3 minutes about your general subject, and then circle a phrase or sentence that could become your main topic.
   _____
   _____
   _____
   _____
   _____

2. Describe your purpose and your audience.

   My purpose is to _____.

   I am writing for an audience of _____.

3. List three ideas connected to your topic.
   _____
   _____
   _____

   Now, choose the most important idea of the three. Add two details to it to form a sentence that you can use in your narrative.
   _____

Drafting

4. Describe the conflict that your story will show by naming it in the center box of the conflict map and filling in the blanks and boxes with details about the conflict.

Who? _____   What? _____

CONFLICT: _____

Why? [   ]   How? [   ]

Name _____

5. Below, list four details that characterize the animal you have chosen as your subject. Think about both behavior and appearance.
   _____
   _____
   _____
   _____

6. On a separate sheet of paper, use your notes and information from the graphic organizer to draft your autobiographical narrative.

Revising

7. Find two sentences about events in your narrative. Connect them by using a transition that shows *sequence*. Write the new version of the sentences below.
   _____
   _____

8. Compare the animal you've chosen to a person you've known. Write a sentence about both of them, using a transition to show a *comparison*. Circle the transition.
   _____
   _____

9. Underline the vague nouns in the sentence below. Then, on the line, rewrite the sentence, using more precise nouns.

   I told Mr. Wilson that I really wanted to help him build a place that his new pet could live in.
   _____
   _____

10. Find two vague nouns in your draft. Write the sentences that contain them, and circle the vague nouns.
    _____
    _____

    Now, rewrite the sentences using two precise nouns to replace the vague nouns.
    _____
    _____

Editing and Proofreading

11. Find six errors in capitalization and correct them, using proofreading marks.

    My dog, duke, is the best pet in the World. We got him at the shelter on tremont street. When we first went in, dogs were barking and yelping everywhere. Duke was quietly curled up in the corner of his cage. when his eyes met mine, i knew he would be my friend for life.

12. Now, review your draft for any similar errors. Write the errors and corrections on the lines. If your draft does not contain similar errors, write *none*.
    _____
    _____

16 • Chapter 4: Narration: Autobiographical Writing © Prentice-Hall, Inc.

Name _____

13. Evaluate your draft based on the criteria in the rubric below. List any changes that you may need to make in your narrative.

	Score 4	Score 3	Score 2	Score 1
Audience and Purpose	Contains an engaging introduction; successfully entertains or presents a theme	Contains a somewhat engaging introduction; entertains or presents a theme	Contains an introduction; attempts to entertain or to present a theme	Begins abruptly or confusingly; leaves purpose unclear
Organization	Creates an interesting, clear narrative; told from a consistent point of view	Presents a clear sequence of events; told from a specific point of view	Presents a mostly clear sequence of events; contains inconsistent points of view	Presents events without logical order; lacks a consistent point of view
Elaboration	Provides insight into character; develops plot; contains dialogue	Contains details and dialogue that develop character and plot	Contains details that develop plot; contains some dialogue	Contains few or no details to develop characters or plot
Use of Language	Uses word choice and tone to reveal story's theme; contains no errors in grammar, punctuation, or spelling	Uses interesting and fresh word choices; contains few errors in grammar, punctuation, and spelling	Uses some clichés and trite expressions; contains some errors in grammar, punctuation, and spelling	Uses uninspired word choices; has many errors in grammar, punctuation, and spelling

_____
_____
_____
_____
_____
_____

Publishing and Presenting

14. Give an example of the kind of tone you might use to present your narrative if you were to read it aloud.

_____
_____
_____
_____
_____
_____
_____
_____

15. How did focusing on a conflict help you to write this narrative?

_____
_____
_____
_____
_____
_____
_____
_____

Name _____   Date _____

Assessment for Chapter 4:
Narration: Autobiographical Writing
Test 3

In this test, you will be asked to draft an autobiographical sketch of three or four paragraphs about a time when you felt proud of a personal accomplishment. For example, it may be a "personal best" in sports, academics, the arts, or community service. Your sketch should include a conflict, either external or internal. Write your topic on the line.

_____

Prewriting

1. Use looping to get started. Write for 2-3 minutes about your general subject. Then, circle a phrase or sentence that will be your topic focus.
   _____
   _____
   _____
   _____
   _____

2. Describe your purpose and your audience.

   What is the purpose of my sketch? _____

   Who is my audience? _____

3. List four ideas connected to your topic.
   _____
   _____
   _____
   _____

   Now, select the most important idea of the four. Add two details to it to form a sentence that you can use in your autobiographical sketch.
   _____

Drafting

4. Describe the conflict that your sketch will show by writing a question in the middle of this conflict map and filling in the blanks and boxes.

   Who? _____   What? _____

   CONFLICT:

   Why? [_____]   How? [_____]

18 • Chapter 4: Narration: Autobiographical Writing   © Prentice-Hall, Inc.

Name _____

5. Your sketch should also include a moment of insight. What will it be?

   In my narrative, I learn that _____
   _____
   _____

6. On a separate sheet of paper, use your notes and information from the graphic organizer to draft your autobiographical sketch.

Revising

7. Write a sentence that sums up the conflict in your autobiographical sketch.
   _____
   _____

   Check the summary sentence above against each paragraph in your draft. If there is a sentence that does not support the summary sentence above, revise it. Write the new sentence or sentences below. If none of your sentences is in conflict with the summary sentence, write *none*.
   _____
   _____

8. Go back and read your draft. Find a weak or unnecessary sentence or phrase that you can delete. Write the phrase or sentence below, and explain why it is unnecessary.
   _____
   _____
   _____

9. Add one these transitions to your draft. Write the new version of the sentence, and circle the transition.
   - a transition that shows *sequence*
   - a transition that shows *cause and effect*
   - a transition that *identifies your conclusion*
   _____
   _____
   _____

10. Find three vague nouns in your draft. Write the sentences that contain them, and circle the vague nouns.
    _____
    _____
    _____

    Now, write three precise nouns to replace the vague nouns. _____
    _____

Editing and Proofreading

11. Find six errors in capitalization and correct them, using proofreading marks.

    It didn't matter that i didn't win the race. six months before, I couldn't run three miles without stopping. Now, I could run ten. When I crossed the Finish Line, I felt as though I'd won the boston marathon.

Name _____

12. Now, review your draft for any similar errors of capitalization. Write the errors and corrections on the line. If your draft does not contain capitalization errors, write *none*.

   _____
   _____

13. Evaluate your draft based on the criteria in the rubric below. List any changes that you may need to make in your sketch.

	Score 4	Score 3	Score 2	Score 1
Audience and Purpose	Contains an engaging introduction; successfully entertains or presents a theme	Contains a somewhat engaging introduction; entertains or presents a theme	Contains an introduction; attempts to entertain or to present a theme	Begins abruptly or confusingly; leaves purpose unclear
Organization	Creates an interesting, clear narrative; told from a consistent point of view	Presents a clear sequence of events; told from a specific point of view	Presents a mostly clear sequence of events; contains inconsistent points of view	Presents events without logical order; lacks a consistent point of view
Elaboration	Provides insight into character; develops plot; contains dialogue	Contains details and dialogue that develop character and plot	Contains details that develop plot; contains some dialogue	Contains few or no details to develop characters or plot
Use of Language	Uses word choice and tone to reveal story's theme; contains no errors in grammar, punctuation, or spelling	Uses interesting and fresh word choices; contains few errors in grammar, punctuation, and spelling	Uses some clichés and trite expressions; contains some errors in grammar, punctuation, and spelling	Uses uninspired word choices; has many errors in grammar, punctuation, and spelling

_____
_____
_____
_____
_____
_____

Publishing and Presenting

14. Describe the kind of magazine that might be interested in publishing an autobiographical sketch on your topic.

   _____
   _____
   _____
   _____
   _____

15. Reflect on an insight that you gained while you were writing this sketch.

   _____
   _____
   _____
   _____
   _____
   _____
   _____

Name _____ Date _____

 # Assessment for Chapter 5: Narration: Short Story
Test 1

In this test, you will be asked to draft a short story of three paragraphs, in which a bicycle, a car, or a train plays an important role. Plan to include some dialogue in your story.

Prewriting

1. Begin by freewriting for 2–3 minutes on the lines below. When you have finished, circle the words or phrases that are the most interesting ideas for a story.
   _____
   _____
   _____

2. What is the purpose of this story?
   _____
   _____
   _____

3. Write two details about the mode of transportation in the story.
   _____
   _____
   _____

4. What is the problem—or conflict—in your story? Describe it in one or two sentences.
   _____
   _____
   _____
   _____

Drafting

5. Plan what will happen in your story by filling in the plot diagram below.

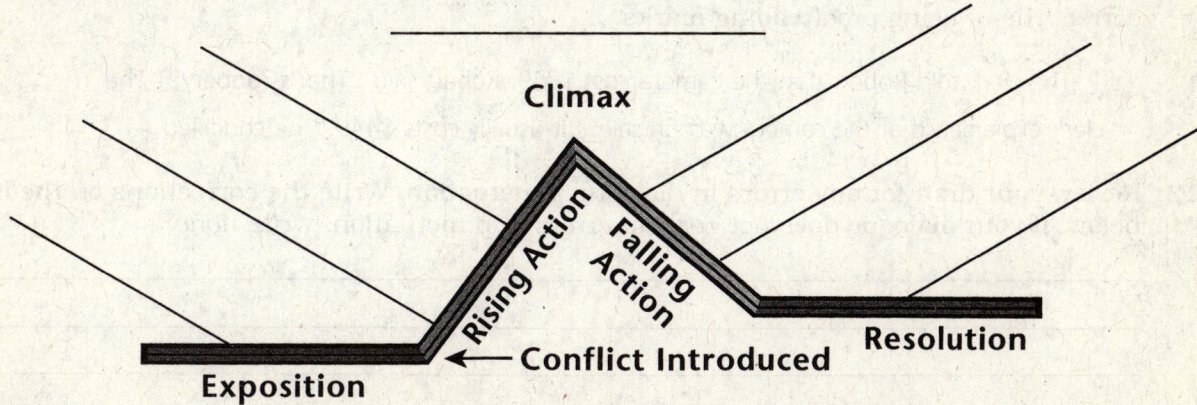

6. On a separate sheet of paper, use your notes and information from the plot diagram to draft your short story. Be sure to *show* rather than *tell* what happens.

© Prentice-Hall, Inc.   Chapter 5: Narration: Short Story • 21

Name _____

Revising

7. Find a sentence in your story that describes a character. Write it below.
   _____
   _____

   Now, rewrite the sentence, adding a descriptive phrase that will give the reader more information about the character's personality or behavior.
   _____
   _____

8. Add or subtract words to combine the sentences below into one sentence. Write it on the line.

   Simon went to the store. In the store, he bought a top hat. The hat was too big.
   _____
   _____

9. Find two short sentences in your draft that could be combined into a longer sentence. Underline them in your draft. On the lines below, write a sentence that combines them.
   _____
   _____
   _____
   _____

10. Circle three verbs in your story. Below, write two that are "colorless." Beside them, write two vivid verbs that could replace the ones in your draft.

Colorless Verbs	Vivid Verbs
_____	_____
_____	_____

Editing and Proofreading

11. Proofread this passage for errors in punctuation of dialogue. Find the three errors and correct them, using proofreading marks.

    The clerk told Robert that the camera cost $349. Robert said "That's robbery"! The clerk explained that the camera was on sale. "It usually costs $449." he chuckled.

12. Review your draft for any errors in dialogue punctuation. Write the corrections on the lines below. If your dialogue does not contain errors in punctuation, write *none*.
    _____
    _____
    _____
    _____
    _____

Name _____

13. Evaluate your draft based on the criteria in the rubric below. List any changes that you may need to make in your short story.

	Score 4	Score 3	Score 2	Score 1
Audience and Purpose	Contains an engaging introduction; successfully entertains or presents a theme	Contains a somewhat engaging introduction; entertains or presents a theme	Contains an introduction; attempts to entertain or to present a theme	Begins abruptly or confusingly; leaves purpose unclear
Organization	Creates an interesting, clear narrative; told from a consistent point of view	Presents a clear sequence of events; told from a specific point of view	Presents a mostly clear sequence of events; contains inconsistent points of view	Presents events without logical order; lacks a consistent point of view
Elaboration	Provides insight into character; develops plot; contains dialogue	Contains details and dialogue that develop character and plot	Contains details that develop plot; contains some dialogue	Contains few or no details to develop characters or plot
Use of Language	Uses word choice and tone to reveal story's theme; contains no errors in grammar, punctuation, or spelling	Uses interesting and fresh word choices; contains few errors in grammar, punctuation, and spelling	Uses some clichés and trite expressions; contains some errors in grammar, punctuation, and spelling	Uses uninspired word choices; has many errors in grammar, punctuation, and spelling

_____
_____
_____
_____
_____

Publishing and Presenting

14. Name a school publication in which you might be able to publish your short story. _____
_____
_____
_____

15. What did you learn about writing a short story that you can pass on to someone who is about to write one?
_____
_____
_____
_____
_____
_____
_____
_____
_____
_____
_____
_____

Name _____ Date _____

 **Assessment for Chapter 5:
Narration: Short Story**
Test 2

In this test, you will be asked to draft an adventure story of three paragraphs in which a 13-year-old and an animal survive a life-threatening disaster together. Plan to include some dialogue.

Prewriting

1. List three important details about the main character in your story.
   _____
   _____
   _____
   _____

2. List two details about the animal.
   _____
   _____

3. What is the problem—or conflict—in your story? Describe it in one or two sentences.
   _____
   _____
   _____
   _____

4. Who might be the audience for your story?
   _____

Drafting

5. Plan what will happen in your story by filling in the plot diagram below.

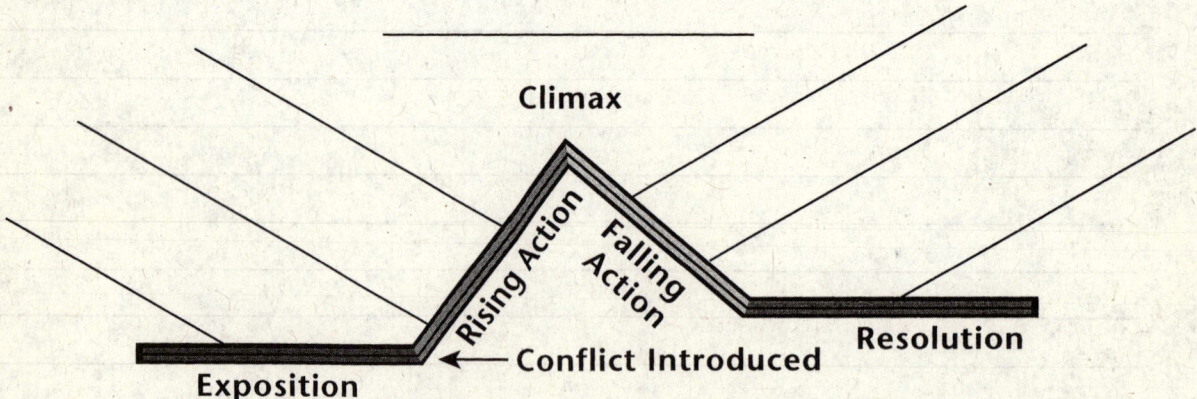

6. On a separate sheet of paper, use your notes and information from the plot diagram to draft your short story. Be sure to *show* rather than *tell* what happens.

Name _____

Revising

7. Read your draft. Draw a star at one point where you could show more about the character or the action. On the lines below, write an additional sentence that you could insert at the point you have marked with a star.
   _____
   _____
   _____

8. Add or subtract words to combine the sentence below into one sentence. Write it on the line.

   Eve walked into the zoo. At the zoo, she saw a balloon man. She bought a balloon.
   _____

9. Find two short sentences in your draft that could be combined into a longer sentence. Underline them. On the lines below, write a sentence that combines the two short sentences.
   _____
   _____

10. Circle two of the colorless verbs below. On the lines, write examples of more vivid verbs.

    Because the cage door was open, I thought that the tiger had left. I went to tell a guard.
    _____
    _____
    _____
    _____

11. Circle three verbs in your story. Below, write two that are the most colorless. Beside them, write two vivid verbs that could replace the colorless ones.

    Colorless Verbs   Vivid Verbs
    _____   _____
    _____   _____

Editing and Proofreading

12. Proofread this passage for errors in punctuation of dialogue. Find the four errors and correct them using proofreading marks.

    "Come, Duke"! Vanessa yelled to the dog. "Good boy" she said, patting his head when he came bounding out of the woods. What would I do without you"?

    Now, review your draft for any errors in dialogue punctuation. Write corrections on the lines below. If your dialogue does not contain punctuation errors, write *none*.
    _____
    _____
    _____
    _____

Name _____

13. Evaluate your draft based on the criteria in the rubric below. List any changes that you may need to make in your story.

	Score 4	Score 3	Score 2	Score 1
Audience and Purpose	Contains an engaging introduction; successfully entertains or presents a theme	Contains a somewhat engaging introduction; entertains or presents a theme	Contains an introduction; attempts to entertain or to present a theme	Begins abruptly or confusingly; leaves purpose unclear
Organization	Creates an interesting, clear narrative; told from a consistent point of view	Presents a clear sequence of events; told from a specific point of view	Presents a mostly clear sequence of events; contains inconsistent points of view	Presents events without logical order; lacks a consistent point of view
Elaboration	Provides insight into character; develops plot; contains dialogue	Contains details and dialogue that develop character and plot	Contains details that develop plot; contains some dialogue	Contains few or no details to develop characters or plot
Use of Language	Uses word choice and tone to reveal story's theme; contains no errors in grammar, punctuation, or spelling	Uses interesting and fresh word choices; contains few errors in grammar, punctuation, and spelling	Uses some clichés and trite expressions; contains some errors in grammar, punctuation, and spelling	Uses uninspired word choices; has many errors in grammar, punctuation, and spelling

_____
_____
_____
_____
_____

Publishing and Presenting

14. Name a type of magazine that might be interested in publishing your short story. _____
_____
_____

15. How has writing a short story changed how you will read stories from now on?
_____
_____
_____
_____
_____
_____
_____
_____
_____
_____
_____
_____

Name _____ Date _____

Assessment for Chapter 5: Narration: Short Story
Test 3

In this test, you will be asked to draft a fantasy story of three or four paragraphs that takes place in the future on a distant planet. Make sure your story includes a conflict and a resolution. Use rich details and lively dialogue. If necessary, use a separate sheet of paper to complete your responses.

Prewriting

1. Begin by freewriting for 2–3 minutes on the lines below. When you have finished, circle the words or phrases that are the most interesting ideas for a story.

   _____
   _____
   _____
   _____
   _____

2. List three important details about the main character in your story.

   _____
   _____
   _____

3. List three details about the setting in which your story will occur.

   _____
   _____
   _____

4. What is the problem—or conflict—in your story? Describe it in one or two sentences.

   _____
   _____
   _____
   _____

Drafting

5. Plan what will happen in your story by filling in the plot diagram below.

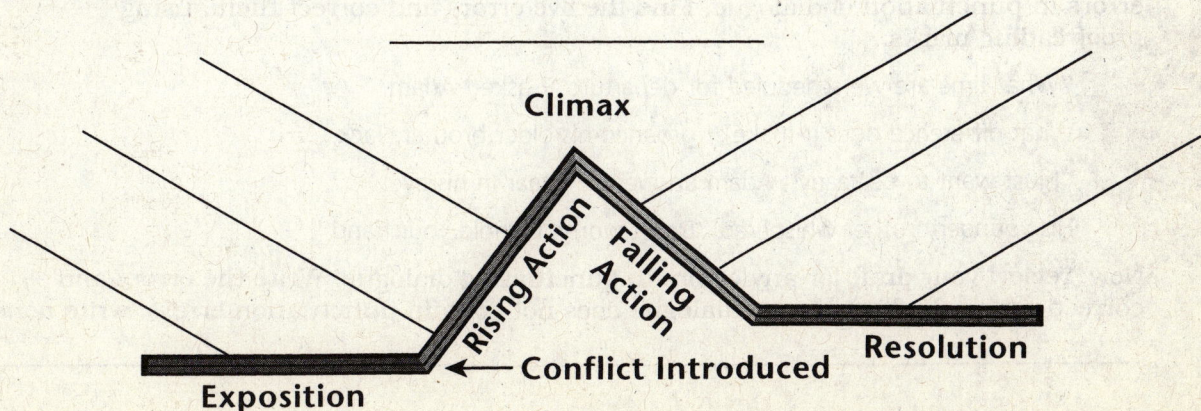

© Prentice-Hall, Inc.

Chapter 5: Narration: Short Story • 27

Name _____

6. On a separate sheet of paper, use your notes and information from the plot diagram to draft your short story. Be sure to *show* rather than *tell* what happens.

Revising

7. Read your draft. Draw a star at one point where you could show more about the character or the action. On the lines below, write an additional sentence that you could insert at the point you have marked with a star.
   _____
   _____

8. Add or subtract words to combine the sentences below into one sentence. Write it on the line.

   Anna picked up the blue paper. She picked up the green yo-yo. She picked up the small yellow rubber duck.
   _____

9. Find two short sentences in your draft that could be combined into a longer sentence. Underline them. On the lines below, write a sentence that combines the two short sentences.
   _____
   _____

10. Circle three of the colorless verbs below. On the line, write vivid verbs that could replace the colorless ones.

    I looked through a telescope and saw the moon. The moon had features that looked like rivers. I could also see some craters.
    _____

11. Circle four verbs in your story. Below, write three that are the most colorless. Beside them, write three more vivid verbs that could replace the colorless ones.

Colorless Verbs	Vivid Verbs
_____	_____
_____	_____
_____	_____

Editing and Proofreading

12. Imagine that you are a peer reviewer for a classmate's story. Proofread this passage for errors in punctuation of dialogue. Find the five errors and correct them, using proofreading marks.

    "What time are we scheduled for departure"? asked Adam.

    What difference does it make?" groaned his older brother, Jack.

    "I just want to be ready" Adam answered, a tear in his eye.

    His younger brother whispered "Don't worry. I'll hold your hand".

    Now, review your draft for any errors in punctuating dialogue. Write the errors and corrections on the line. If your dialogue does not contain punctuation errors, write *none*.
    _____

Name _____

13. Evaluate your draft based on the criteria in the rubric below. List any changes that you may need to make in your story.

	Score 4	Score 3	Score 2	Score 1
Audience and Purpose	Contains an engaging introduction; successfully entertains or presents a theme	Contains a somewhat engaging introduction; entertains or presents a theme	Contains an introduction; attempts to entertain or to present a theme	Begins abruptly or confusingly; leaves purpose unclear
Organization	Creates an interesting, clear narrative; told from a consistent point of view	Presents a clear sequence of events; told from a specific point of view	Presents a mostly clear sequence of events; contains inconsistent points of view	Presents events without logical order; lacks a consistent point of view
Elaboration	Provides insight into character; develops plot; contains dialogue	Contains details and dialogue that develop character and plot	Contains details that develop plot; contains some dialogue	Contains few or no details to develop characters or plot
Use of Language	Uses word choice and tone to reveal story's theme; contains no errors in grammar, punctuation, or spelling	Uses interesting and fresh word choices; contains few errors in grammar, punctuation, and spelling	Uses some clichés and trite expressions; contains some errors in grammar, punctuation, and spelling	Uses uninspired word choices; has many errors in grammar, punctuation, and spelling

_____
_____
_____
_____
_____
_____
_____

Publishing and Proofreading

14. How would you prepare for an oral presentation of your short story?
_____
_____
_____

15. Write some thoughts about how the experience of writing a short story has given you some new insights.
_____
_____
_____
_____
_____
_____
_____
_____
_____

Name _____ Date _____

Assessment for Chapter 6: Description
Test 1

In this test, you will be asked to draft a three-paragraph description of a location that is meaningful to you. Your goal is to show your readers why the place is so special. If necessary, use a separate sheet of paper to complete your responses.

Prewriting

1. List three places that are possible subjects for your description. Circle the one that you will write about.
   _____
   _____
   _____

2. Fill in the personal-experience timeline with important memories from each year of your life. Choose one to be your description topic.

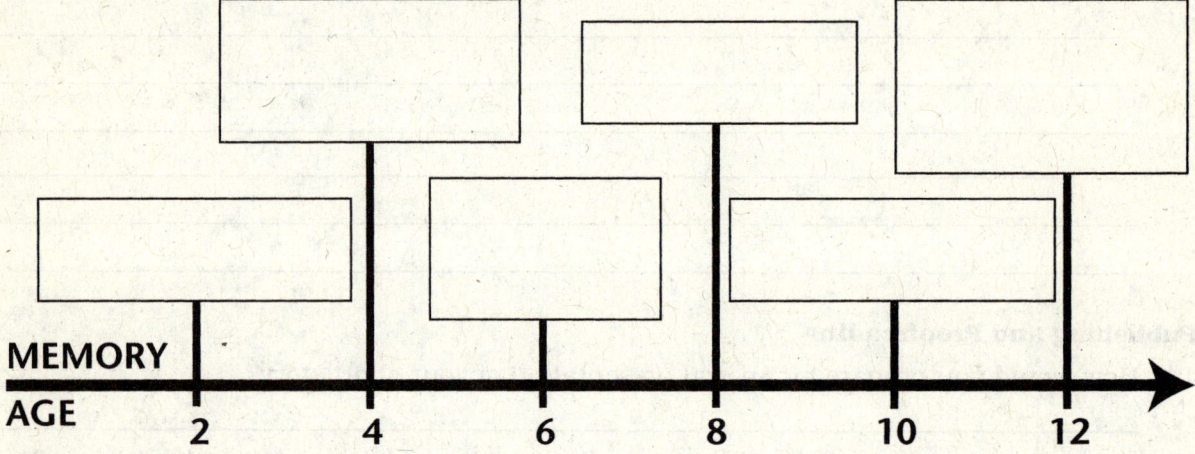

3. On the lines below, list sensory details about your subject that you can include in your draft.
   SIGHTS _____
   SMELLS _____
   TASTES _____
   TOUCH _____
   SOUNDS _____

Drafting

4. Describe the main impression, including the mood, that the details will give. The main impression that my description will give is _____
   _____
   _____
   _____
   _____

5. On a separate sheet of paper, use information from your notes to draft your description.

Name _____

Revising

6. Read the sentence below. Add a sentence with additional details that will strengthen the impression of the house.

    The house we lived in was huge.
    _____
    _____

7. Find the sentence in your draft that gives the reader the main impression of your description. Write it below, and add another sentence with details that strengthen your main impression.

    _____
    _____
    _____
    _____

8. Imagine that you are working with a classmate who has written the following sentence in a draft. Correct it, using proofreading marks.

    The attic was usually warm and musty there were lots of cobwebs in the corners.

9. Now, look through your draft for run-on sentences. If you see one, underline it and correct it. Write the old and new versions of the sentences below. If there are no run-on sentences, write *none*.

    _____
    _____
    _____

10. Circle two empty words or phrases in your draft. Write them below. Then, write two precise words that could replace those in your draft.

    Empty Words   Precise Words
    _____   _____
    _____   _____

Editing and Proofreading

11. Imagine that you are reviewing a classmate's description. Here is part of the draft. Find three errors in using commas with adjectives, and correct them, using proofreading marks.

    The musty warm attic was full of cobwebs. One box held our elementary, school papers.

    Another held our most precious, holiday decorations. The attic was truly a treasure chest.

12. Now, review your draft for any similar comma errors. Write the errors and corrections on the lines. If your draft does not contain similar comma errors, write *none*.

    _____
    _____
    _____
    _____
    _____

Name _____

13. Evaluate your draft based on the criteria in the rubric below. List any changes that you may need to make in your essay.

	Score 4	Score 3	Score 2	Score 1
Audience and Purpose	Creates a memorable main impression through effective use of details	Creates a main impression through use of details	Contains extraneous details that detract from main impression	Contains details that are unfocused and create no main impression
Organization	Is organized consistently, logically, and effectively	Is organized consistently	Is organized, but not consistently	Is disorganized and confusing
Elaboration	Uses figurative language effectively, creating interesting comparisons	Uses some figurative language effectively	Contains mostly overused figurative language	Contains no figurative language
Use of Language	Contains rich sensory language that appeals to the five senses; contains no errors in grammar, punctuation, or spelling	Contains some rich sensory language; contains few errors in grammar, punctuation, and spelling	Contains some rich sensory language, but it appeals to only one or two of the senses; contains some errors in grammar, punctuation, and spelling	Contains only flat language; contains many errors in grammar, punctuation, and spelling

_____
_____
_____
_____
_____
_____
_____
_____

Publishing and Presenting

14. Which images would you use—photographs or illustrations—to add to your written description?
_____
_____
_____

15. Which revision strategy did you find most helpful?
_____
_____
_____
_____
_____
_____
_____
_____

Name _____   Date _____

Assessment for Chapter 6: Description
Test 2

In this test, you will be asked to write a three-paragraph descriptive essay. Write an observation of an interesting event that occurred in your school, neighborhood, or community. Use specific descriptive details to make that event come to life for your readers. If necessary, use a separate sheet of paper to complete your responses.

Prewriting

1. List two possible events that you could write about. Circle the one that will be the topic of your description.
   _____
   _____

2. Instead of trying to write about the whole event, zoom in on one part of it. In the space below, explain the focus of your description.
   _____
   _____

3. Fill in the sentences below.
   I can describe my subject as _____.
   I can associate my subject with _____.
   I can apply my subject to _____.

Drafting

4. Explain the main impression of the event—the feeling or mood that your details will show.
   The main impression of the event will be _____
   _____.

5. On a separate sheet of paper, use your notes to draft your description.

Revising

6. Read the sentence below. Write another sentence with additional details that will strengthen the impression of an empty school.
   The school was completely empty.
   _____

7. Find the sentence in your draft that gives the reader the main impression of your description. Write it below, and add another sentence with details that strengthen your main-impression sentence.
   _____
   _____
   _____

8. Imagine that you are working with a classmate who has written this sentence in a draft. Correct it, using proofreading marks.

   The juggler tossed four flaming torches into the air then he threw in a fifth and a sixth I couldn't believe my eyes.

© Prentice-Hall, Inc.

Name _____

9. Now, look through your draft for run-on sentences. If you see one, underline it and correct it. Write the old and new versions of the sentences below. If there are no run-on sentences in your draft, write *none* in the space below.
   _____
   _____

10. Circle three empty words in your draft. Write them below. Then, write three precise words that could replace the three in your draft.

   Empty Words   Precise Words
   _____   _____
   _____   _____
   _____   _____

Editing and Proofreading

11. Imagine that you are peer reviewing a classmate's description. Here is part of one of the drafts. Find three errors in using commas with adjectives, and correct them using proofreading marks.

    The light from the torches illuminated the many, upturned faces of the crowd. Everyone was silent as the fiery, lit torches flew higher and higher in the cold, night air.

12. Now, review your draft for any similar comma errors. Write the errors and corrections on the line. If your draft does not contain similar comma errors, write *none*.
    _____
    _____

13. Evaluate your draft based on the criteria in the rubric below. List any changes that you may need to make in your essay.

	Score 4	Score 3	Score 2	Score 1
Audience and Purpose	Creates a memorable main impression through effective use of details	Creates a main impression through use of details	Contains extraneous details that detract from main impression	Contains details that are unfocused and create no main impression
Organization	Is organized consistently, logically, and effectively	Is organized consistently	Is organized, but not consistently	Is disorganized and confusing
Elaboration	Uses figurative language effectively, creating interesting comparisons	Uses some figurative language effectively	Contains mostly overused figurative language	Contains no figurative language
Use of Language	Contains rich sensory language that appeals to the five senses; contains no errors in grammar, punctuation, or spelling	Contains some rich sensory language; contains few errors in grammar, punctuation, and spelling	Contains some rich sensory language, but it appeals to only one or two of the senses; contains some errors in grammar, punctuation, and spelling	Contains only flat language; contains many errors in grammar, punctuation, and spelling

_____
_____
_____
_____

Name _____

Publishing and Presenting

14. Name a school or community publication that would be an appropriate place to publish your descriptive essay.
   _____
   _____
   _____
   _____

15. What did you learn as you revised your essay?
   _____
   _____
   _____
   _____
   _____
   _____
   _____
   _____
   _____
   _____
   _____
   _____

Name _____   Date _____

 **Assessment for Chapter 6:
Description**
Test 3

In this test, you will be asked to write an essay of three or four paragraphs. Write a vignette that captures a single moment in your life, based on an experience you have had during school, in a club, or at an extracurricular activity. If necessary, use a separate sheet of paper to complete your responses.

Prewriting

1. Fill in the personal-experience timeline with some of the most important moments or events you experienced at each age.

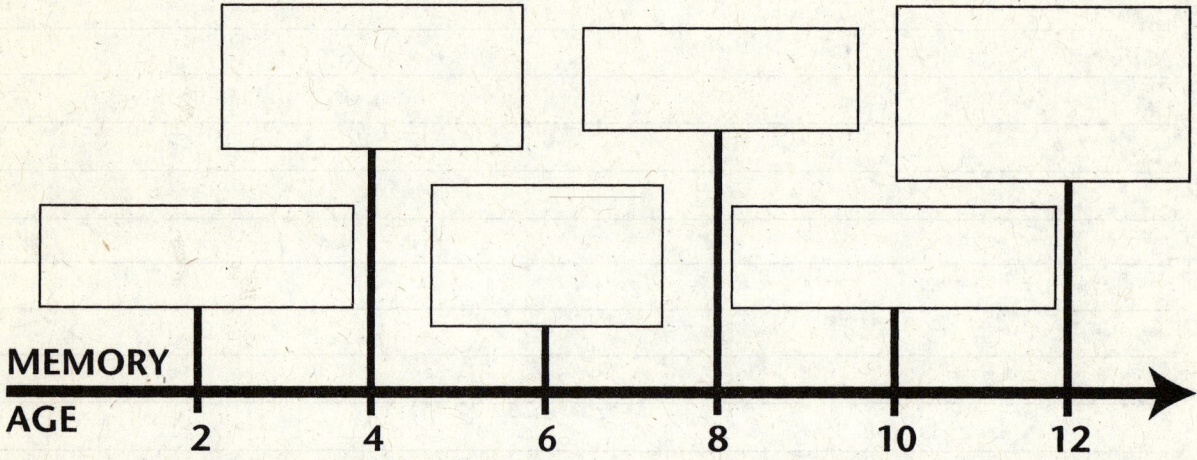

2. Choose one event from your timeline. "Zoom in" to a single moment in time. Describe the moment in one sentence below.

   I will write about _____
   _____.

3. Follow these steps to "cube" your subject.

   Describe it. _____
   _____

   Associate it. _____
   _____

   Apply it. _____
   _____

   Analyze it by breaking it into parts. _____
   _____
   _____

   Compare or contrast it. _____
   _____

   Argue for or against it. (If this instruction does not apply, write "does not apply.")
   _____
   _____

Name _____

Drafting

4. What will be the main impression—the feeling or mood—that your details will give?

   The main impression of my vignette will be _____
   _____.

5. On a separate sheet of paper, use your notes and information from the chart above to draft your vignette.

Revising

6. Imagine that you are working with a classmate who has written this sentence in a draft. Correct it, using proofreading marks.

   To get there you must walk past the large oak tree over the grassy knoll and along the gravel path.

7. Now look through your draft for run-on sentences. If you see one, underline it and correct it. Write the old and new versions of the sentences below. If there are no run-on sentences, write *none*.
   _____
   _____

8. Circle four empty words in your draft. Write them below. Then, write four precise words that will replace the four words in your draft.

   Empty Words   Precise Words
   _____   _____
   _____   _____
   _____   _____
   _____   _____

9. Imagine that you have just had a peer read your work, and you are waiting to hear his or her reaction. Do you expect that he or she will like the beginning, middle, or end of your essay best? Explain your answer.
   _____
   _____
   _____

10. Explain whether you think a peer might say that a particular paragraph in your essay lacks information. How can you fix this problem?
    _____
    _____
    _____

Editing and Proofreading

11. Imagine that you are reviewing a classmate's vignette. Here is part of one of the drafts. Find three errors in using commas with adjectives, and correct them using proofreading marks.

    My legs and arms ached from digging in the dry stony soil. I could hear distant rumbling thunder heralding a quick much-needed shower.

© Prentice-Hall, Inc.

Name _____

12. Now, review your draft for any comma errors. Write the errors and corrections on the lines. If your draft does not contain similar comma errors, write *none*.
   _____
   _____

13. Evaluate your draft based on the criteria in the rubric below. List any changes that you may need to make in your essay.

	Score 4	Score 3	Score 2	Score 1
Audience and Purpose	Creates a memorable main impression through effective use of details	Creates a main impression through use of details	Contains extraneous details that detract from main impression	Contains details that are unfocused and create no main impression
Organization	Is organized consistently, logically, and effectively	Is organized consistently	Is organized, but not consistently	Is disorganized and confusing
Elaboration	Uses figurative language effectively, creating interesting comparisons	Uses some figurative language effectively	Contains mostly overused figurative language	Contains no figurative language
Use of Language	Contains rich sensory language that appeals to the five senses; contains no errors in grammar, punctuation, or spelling	Contains some rich sensory language; contains few errors in grammar, punctuation, and spelling	Contains some rich sensory language, but it appeals to only one or two of the senses; contains some errors in grammar, punctuation, and spelling	Contains only flat language; contains many errors in grammar, punctuation, and spelling

_____
_____
_____
_____
_____
_____
_____

Publishing and Presenting

14. What sound effects might accompany an oral presentation of your vignette?
   _____
   _____
   _____

15. What new insights did you gain about your subject from writing this essay?
   _____
   _____
   _____
   _____
   _____
   _____
   _____

Name _____ Date _____

Assessment for Chapter 7: Persuasion: Persuasive Essay
Test 1

In this test, you will be asked to write a three-paragraph essay in the form of a letter to a family member to persuade him or her to make a change in a household routine. For example, you might argue for a change in the daily meal schedule. If necessary, use a separate sheet of paper to complete your responses.

Prewriting

1. First, choose a topic and complete the sentence below.

   I will try to persuade _____ to change _____.

2. Make a T-chart for your topic. Write your topic at the top. Then, write two details that support your position and two that could be used to argue against your position.

   My Topic: _____

Pro	Con

Drafting

3. Write a thesis statement for your letter on the lines below.
   _____
   _____

4. Fill in the outline below to create a rhythm for your argument.
   I. Introduction

      Thesis statement: _____
   II. First Argument
      _____

   III. Acknowledgment of the Opposition
      _____

   IV. Strongest Argument
      _____

   V. Conclusion
      Summary: _____

5. On a separate sheet of paper, use your notes and information from the chart and outline to draft your persuasive letter.

Revising

6. Review your draft. Find the main point of your letter and underline it. Write it below.
   _____

© Prentice-Hall, Inc.

Chapter 7: Persuasion: Persuasive Essay • 39

Name _____

7. Write a sentence that supports your main point.
   _____

8. Now, rewrite the sentence so that it provides stronger support for your main point.
   _____

9. Read your draft. Find two short, related sentences that can be combined into one sentence. Underline them. Using proofreading marks to add or delete words, combine the two sentences. Write the new sentence below.

10. Read your draft again. Circle two vague, general words, such as *good, bad, right, wrong,* or *nice*. Write them below. Then, write two precise words that can replace them.

    Vague Words   Precise Words
    _____   _____
    _____   _____

Editing and Proofreading

11. Imagine that you are a peer reviewer for a classmate. Here is part of his draft. It contains two errors in end punctuation and two errors in spelling. Find the errors and correct them, using proofreading marks.

    Having my own room would give me more privacey Would I keep it clean and neat. I certinly would!

12. Now, review your draft for punctuation and spelling errors. Write the errors and corrections on the lines. If your draft contains no punctuation or spelling errors, write *none*.
    _____
    _____

13. Evaluate your draft based on the criteria in the rubric below. List any changes that you may need to make in your letter.

	Score 4	Score 3	Score 2	Score 1
Audience and Purpose	Provides arguments, illustrations, and words that forcefully appeal to the audience and effectively serve the persuasive purpose	Provides arguments, illustrations, and words that appeal to the audience and serve the persuasive purpose	Provides some support that appeals to the audience and serves the persuasive purpose	Shows little attention to the audience or persuasive purpose
Organization	Uses a clear, consistent organizational strategy	Uses a clear organizational strategy with occasional inconsistencies	Uses an inconsistent organizational strategy	Shows a lack of organizational strategy; writing is confusing
Elaboration	Provides specific, well-elaborated support for the writer's position	Provides some elaborated support for the writer's position	Provides some support, but with little elaboration	Lacks support
Use of Language	Uses transitions to connect ideas smoothly; shows few mechanical errors	Uses some transitions; shows few mechanical errors	Uses few transitions; shows some mechanical errors	Shows little connection between ideas; shows many mechanical errors

_____
_____
_____

Name _____

Publishing and Presenting

14. What would you change if you were to present your argument orally to the person addressed in your letter?
    _____
    _____
    _____
    _____
    _____

15. Write one insight you gained from the experience of writing the letter.
    _____
    _____
    _____
    _____
    _____
    _____
    _____
    _____
    _____
    _____

Name _____ Date _____

Assessment for Chapter 7: Persuasion: Persuasive Essay
Test 2

In this test, you will be asked to draft a three-paragraph essay. Imagine that your local recycling center now lets citizens recycle paper and glass. Someone has proposed that it be expanded to include cardboard, metal, and plastics. Write an editorial for your local newspaper in which you either support or disagree with the proposal to expand the recyclables. If necessary, use a separate sheet of paper to complete your responses.

Prewriting

1. Make a T-chart for your topic. Write your topic statement at the top, and write two details that support your position (pros) and two that could be used to argue against your position (cons).

My Topic: _____

Pro	Con

2. Choose two of the kinds of support below. Write an example of each kind of support as it relates to your opinion.

   Logical arguments   Statistics
   Expert opinions   Personal observations
   Charged language   Striking images

   _____
   _____
   _____
   _____

Drafting

3. Write a thesis statement for your editorial on the lines below.
   _____
   _____

4. Fill in the outline below to create a rhythm for your argument.
   I. Introduction
      Thesis statement: _____
   II. First Argument
      _____
   III. Acknowledging the Opposition
      _____
   IV. Strongest Argument
      _____
   V. Conclusion
      Summary: _____

Name _____

5. On a separate sheet of paper, use your notes and information from the chart and outline to draft your editorial.

Revising

6. Review your draft. Find the main point of your editorial and underline it. Write it below.
   _____
   _____
   _____

7. Write a sentence that supports your main point.
   _____
   _____
   _____

8. Now, rewrite the sentence so that it provides stronger support for your main point.
   _____
   _____
   _____

9. Read your draft. Find two sentences that are related and can be combined into one sentence. Underline them. Use proofreading marks to add or delete words to combine the two sentences. Write the new sentence below.
   _____

10. Read your draft again. Circle three vague, general words, such as *good, bad, right, wrong,* or *nice*. Write them below. Then, think of three precise words or phrases that can replace them.

    Vague Words   Precise Words
    _____   _____
    _____   _____
    _____   _____

Editing and Proofreading

11. Imagine that you are a peer reviewer for a classmate. Here is part of his draft. It contains three errors in end punctuation and three errors in spelling. Find them, and correct them using proofreading marks.

    My family uses ten to twelve metal cans per week If every family in town recycled this amount, we could recycle about 20,000 pounds of metal each month, Just imagin that much metal cloging up a landfill?

12. Now, review your draft for any punctuation and spelling errors. Write the errors and corrections on the lines. If your draft contains no errors, write *none*.
    _____
    _____
    _____
    _____
    _____

Name _____

13. Evaluate your draft based on the criteria in the rubric below. List any changes that you may need to make in your editorial.

	Score 4	Score 3	Score 2	Score 1
Audience and Purpose	Provides arguments, illustrations, and words that forcefully appeal to the audience and effectively serve the persuasive purpose	Provides arguments, illustrations, and words that appeal to the audience and serve the persuasive purpose	Provides some support that appeals to the audience and serves the persuasive purpose	Shows little attention to the audience or persuasive purpose
Organization	Uses a clear, consistent organizational strategy	Uses a clear organizational strategy with occasional inconsistencies	Uses an inconsistent organizational strategy	Shows a lack of organizational strategy; writing is confusing
Elaboration	Provides specific, well-elaborated support for the writer's position	Provides some elaborated support for the writer's position	Provides some support, but with little elaboration	Lacks support
Use of Language	Uses transitions to connect ideas smoothly; shows few mechanical errors	Uses some transitions; shows few mechanical errors	Uses few transitions; shows some mechanical errors	Shows little connection between ideas; shows many mechanical errors

_____
_____
_____
_____
_____
_____
_____

Publishing and Presenting

14. Imagine that you are mailing your editorial to your local newspaper, hoping that it will be published. In a short cover note—two or three sentences—to the newspaper editor, explain the content of your editorial and why it should be published.

_____
_____
_____
_____
_____
_____
_____

15. What was the most difficult part of writing the editorial?

_____
_____
_____
_____
_____

Name _____ Date _____

Assessment for Chapter 7:
Persuasion: Persuasive Essay
Test 3

In this test, you will be asked to write an essay of three or four paragraphs. Imagine that you are writing the script for a public service announcement in which you persuade young people to wear bicycle helmets. If necessary, use a separate sheet of paper to complete your responses.

Prewriting

1. Make a T-chart for your topic. Write your topic at the top, and write at least two details that support your position and two that could be used to argue against your position.

My Topic: _____

Pro	Con

2. Choose three of the kinds of support listed below. Write either:

   1) a possible example of each kind of support as it relates to your opinion

   or

   2) a suggestion for where to find each kind of support as it applies to your opinion.

   Logical arguments   Statistics
   Expert opinions   Personal observations
   Charged language   Striking images

   _____
   _____
   _____
   _____
   _____
   _____
   _____
   _____

Drafting

3. Write a thesis statement for your public service announcement on the lines below.

   _____
   _____
   _____
   _____
   _____

© Prentice-Hall, Inc.

Name _____

4. Fill in the outline below to create a rhythm for your argument.
   I. Introduction
      A. _____
      B. _____
   II. First Set of Arguments
      A. _____
      B. _____
   III. Acknowledging the Opposition
      A. _____
      B. _____
   IV. Strongest Argument
      A. _____
      B. _____
   V. Conclusion
      A. _____
      B. _____

5. On a separate sheet of paper, use your notes and information from the chart and outline to draft your public service announcement.

Revising

6. Review your draft. Find the main point of your public service announcement and underline it. Write it below.
   _____
   _____

7. Write a sentence that supports your main point.
   _____
   _____

8. Now, rewrite the sentence so that it provides stronger support for your main point.
   _____
   _____

9. Read your draft. Find two short, related sentences that can be combined into one sentence. Underline them. Use proofreading marks to add or delete words to combine the two sentences. Write the new sentence below.
   _____
   _____
   _____

10. Find a sentence in your draft that could be written more precisely and persuasively. Rewrite it, and write the old and new versions of the sentence below.
    _____
    _____
    _____
    _____
    _____

Name _____

Editing and Proofreading

11. Imagine that you are a peer reviewer for a classmate. Here is part of her draft. It contains three errors in end punctuation and three errors in spelling. Find the errors and correct them, using proofreading marks.

    Are knee, wrist, and elbow pads expensive. Compard to the cost of an emergency room visit, these protective pads are a bargin If you can't afford them, the Central Inline Skate Club provides low-cost knee, wrist, and elbow pads at their anual Spring Skatefest It's a small price to pay for safety.

12. Now, review your draft for punctuation and spelling errors. Write the errors and corrections on the lines. If your draft contains no errors, write *none*.
    _____
    _____

13. Evaluate your draft based on the criteria in the rubric below. List any changes that you may need to make in your announcement.

	Score 4	Score 3	Score 2	Score 1
Audience and Purpose	Provides arguments, illustrations, and words that forcefully appeal to the audience and effectively serve the persuasive purpose	Provides arguments, illustrations, and words that appeal to the audience and serve the persuasive purpose	Provides some support that appeals to the audience and serves the persuasive purpose	Shows little attention to the audience or persuasive purpose
Organization	Uses a clear, consistent organizational strategy	Uses a clear organizational strategy with occasional inconsistencies	Uses an inconsistent organizational strategy	Shows a lack of organizational strategy; writing is confusing
Elaboration	Provides specific, well-elaborated support for the writer's position	Provides some elaborated support for the writer's position	Provides some support, but with little elaboration	Lacks support
Use of Language	Uses transitions to connect ideas smoothly; shows few mechanical errors	Uses some transitions; shows few mechanical errors	Uses few transitions; shows some mechanical errors	Shows little connection between ideas; shows many mechanical errors

_____
_____
_____
_____

Publishing and Presenting

14. If you were planning to post your public-service announcement for discussion on the Internet, what kind of discussion group would be an appropriate forum?
    _____
    _____

15. Describe one aspect of writing this announcement that was difficult for you.
    _____
    _____
    _____
    _____
    _____

Name _____ Date _____

 **Assessment for Chapter 8: Exposition: Comparison-and-Contrast Essay**
Test 1

In this test, you will be asked to write a three-paragraph essay. Choose one of the following pairs, and consider how the subjects are alike or different: (1) reading a book and taking a vacation, (2) a flower garden and a fireworks display, or (3) two pets—a cat and a dog, a bird and a hamster, or another pair of your choice. Write your topic on the line. If necessary, use a separate sheet of paper to complete your responses.

_____

Prewriting

1. Make a BUT chart for the two subjects you have chosen. On the left, write at least two ways in which the subjects are similar. On the right, write at least two ways in which they are different.

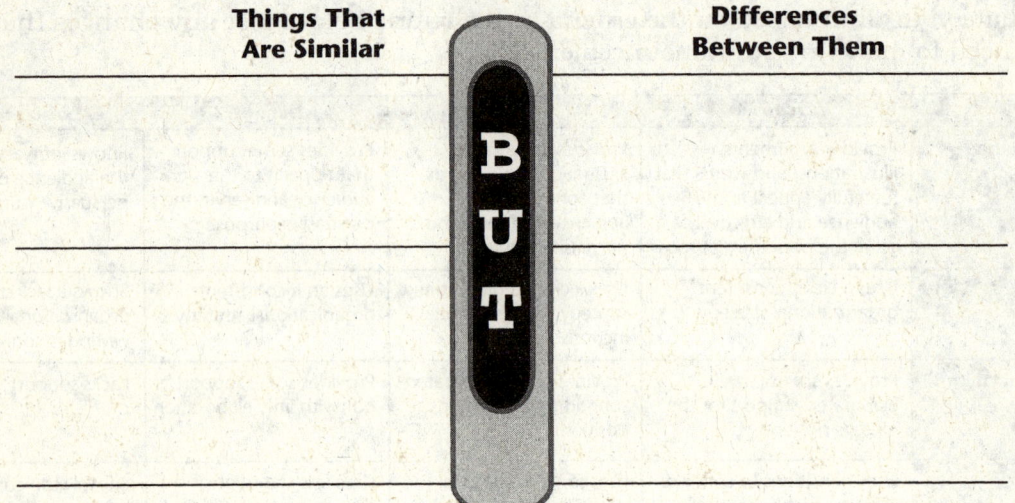

2. Analyze the purpose of your essay by completing this sentence:

   In my essay, I will show _____
   _____.

Drafting

3. On the line below, write a sentence that states the main idea of your essay.
   _____

4. Extend your main idea by restating it in a new sentence.
   _____
   _____

5. On a separate sheet of paper, use your notes and information from the graphic organizer to draft your comparison-and-contrast essay.

Name _____

Revising

6. Reread your draft. Write your lead sentence on the line below.
   _____

   Now, rewrite your lead to make it more interesting to your readers by using a strong image to support it.
   _____
   _____

7. Write your concluding sentence on the line below.
   _____

   Now, rewrite your concluding sentence to leave the reader with a more vivid image or something to think about.
   _____
   _____

8. Find a topic sentence in one of your paragraphs and write it below.
   _____

   Restate the main idea of the topic sentence, using different words. Consider adding this sentence to the paragraph to elaborate on the main idea.
   _____
   _____

9. Read the two sentences below.

   An almanac is a good source of up-to-date information. The Internet is a good source of up-to-date information, too.

   On the line below, combine these sentences into one sentence with a compound subject.
   _____

10. In your draft, find two short, related sentences that you can combine into one sentence with a compound subject. Write the new sentence below.
    _____
    _____

Editing and Proofreading

11. Here is part of a student's comparison-and-contrast essay. It contains errors in pronoun-antecedent agreement and spelling. Correct the errors, using proofreading marks.

    When a person reads books, they travel in their mind. A book is like an airline tickit to places you've never been befor.

12. Now, review your draft for errors in pronoun-antecedent agreement and spelling. Write the errors and corrections on the lines. If your draft does not contain these kinds of errors, write *none*.
    _____
    _____

© Prentice-Hall, Inc.   Chapter 8: Exposition: Comparison-and-Contrast Essay • 49

Name _____

13. Evaluate your draft based on the criteria in the rubric below. List any changes that you may need to make to improve your essay.

	Score 4	Score 3	Score 2	Score 1
Audience and Purpose	Clearly attracts audience interest in the comparison and contrast	Adequately attracts audience interest in the comparison and contrast	Provides a reason for the comparison and contrast	Does not provide a reason for a comparison and contrast
Organization	Clearly presents information in a consistent organization best suited to the topic	Presents information using an organization suited to the topic	Chooses an organization not suited to comparison and contrast	Shows a lack of organizational strategy
Elaboration	Elaborates ideas with facts, details, or examples; links all information to comparison and contrast	Elaborates most ideas with facts, details, or examples; links most information to comparison and contrast	Does not elaborate all ideas; does not link some details to comparison and contrast	Does not provide facts or examples to support a comparison and contrast
Use of Language	Demonstrates excellent sentence and vocabulary variety; includes very few mechanical errors	Demonstrates adequate sentence and vocabulary variety; includes few mechanical errors	Demonstrates repetitive use of sentence structure and vocabulary; includes many mechanical errors	Demonstrates poor use of language; generates confusion; includes many mechanical errors

_____
_____
_____
_____
_____
_____
_____

Publishing and Presenting

14. If you were to read your essay to the class, what visual aids might you use to support it?
_____
_____
_____

15. Describe how you improved your essay as you revised it.
_____
_____
_____
_____
_____
_____
_____
_____
_____

Name _____   Date _____

 **Assessment for Chapter 8: Exposition: Comparison-and-Contrast Essay**
Test 2

In this test, you will be asked to write a three-paragraph essay. Choose two movies or television shows that you have seen: two adventure stories, two mysteries, or two family dramas. Write an essay that compares and contrasts the two. Write your topic on the line. If necessary, use a separate sheet of paper to complete your responses.

_____

Prewriting

1. Use the Venn diagram below to fill in details about the two shows you've chosen. Write at least two points in each part of the diagram.

VENN DIAGRAM

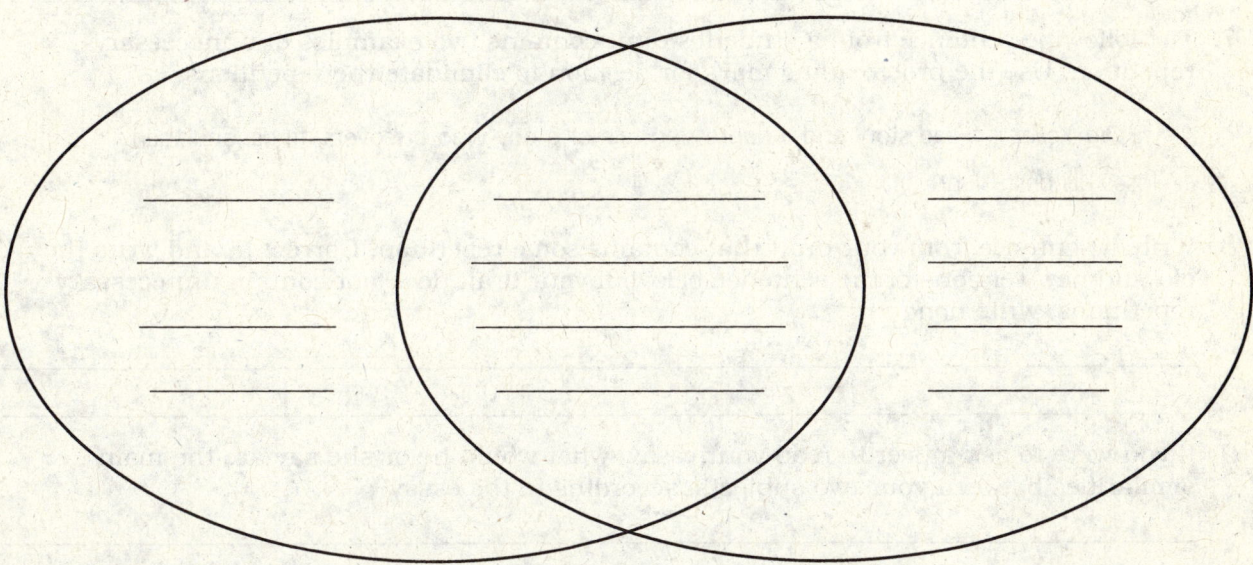

2. Analyze the purpose of your essay by completing this sentence:

   In my essay, I plan to _____
   _____.

Drafting

3. Circle the method you plan to use for your essay, and write the topic on the line below.

   Block Method   Point-by-Point Method
   TOPIC: _____ vs. _____

   Now, fill in the outline, using the method you chose.

   A. _____
      1. _____
      2. _____
   B. _____
      1. _____
      2. _____

Name _____

4. On a separate sheet of paper, use your notes and information from the graphic organizer to draft your comparison-and-contrast essay.

Revising

5. Reread your draft. Mark each of your sentences as a *T* (topic sentence), an *R* (restatement of the main idea in the topic sentence), or an *I* (illustration of the main idea).
   On the lines, write a topic sentence, a restatement, and an illustration from your draft.
   _____
   _____
   _____

6. Underline in your draft two short, related sentences that could be combined. In the space below, combine the sentences by using a compound subject if possible.
   _____
   _____

7. The following sentence from a student's draft contains two examples of unnecessary repetition. Use the proofreading mark for deletion to eliminate the repetitions.

   Old Yeller is a sad story and a depressing tale of a boy who discovers, finds, and then loses his best friend.

8. Write a sentence from your draft that contains some repetition. Correct it, and write the old and new versions of the sentence below. If your draft does not contain unnecessary repetitions, write *none*.
   _____
   _____

9. If you were to ask a peer to read your essay, what would he or she say are the main similarities between your two subjects, according to the essay?
   _____
   _____

10. What would your peer say are the main differences between your two subjects, according to your essay?
    _____
    _____

Editing and Proofreading

11. Here is part of a student's comparison-and-contrast essay. It contains errors in pronoun-antecedent agreement and spelling. Correct the errors, using proofreading marks.

    I read *Where the Red Fern Grows* and *Summer of the Monkeys* in the same summer. It was an exciteing book that I couldn't put down. Wilson Rawls is a wonderfull writer.

12. Now, review your draft for pronoun-antecedent and spelling errors. Write the errors and corrections on the lines below. If your draft does not contain these kinds of errors, write *none*.
    _____
    _____

Name _____

13. Evaluate your draft based on the criteria in the rubric below. List any changes that you may need to make to improve your essay.

	Score 4	Score 3	Score 2	Score 1
Audience and Purpose	Clearly attracts audience interest in the comparison and contrast	Adequately attracts audience interest in the comparison and contrast	Provides a reason for the comparison and contrast	Does not provide a reason for a comparison and contrast
Organization	Clearly presents information in a consistent organization best suited to the topic	Presents information using an organization suited to the topic	Chooses an organization not suited to comparison and contrast	Shows a lack of organizational strategy
Elaboration	Elaborates ideas with facts, details, or examples; links all information to comparison and contrast	Elaborates most ideas with facts, details, or examples; links most information to comparison and contrast	Does not elaborate all ideas; does not link some details to comparison and contrast	Does not provide facts or examples to support a comparison and contrast
Use of Language	Demonstrates excellent sentence and vocabulary variety; includes very few mechanical errors	Demonstrates adequate sentence and vocabulary variety; includes few mechanical errors	Demonstrates repetitive use of sentence structure and vocabulary; includes many mechanical errors	Demonstrates poor use of language; generates confusion; includes many mechanical errors

_____
_____
_____
_____
_____
_____
_____
_____

Publishing and Presenting

14. In what type of publication might you publish this essay?
_____
_____
_____

15. Did writing this essay change how you thought about either or both topics?
_____
_____
_____
_____
_____
_____
_____
_____
_____
_____

Name _____ Date _____

Assessment for Chapter 8: Exposition: Comparison-and-Contrast Essay
Test 3

In this test, you will be asked to write an essay of three or four paragraphs. Choose two famous people—two athletes, performers, writers, or politicians—and write an essay that compares and contrasts their personalities and/or achievements. If necessary, use a separate sheet of paper to complete your responses.

Prewriting

1. Use the Venn diagram below to fill in details about the two people you've chosen. Write at least three details in each section of the diagram.

VENN DIAGRAM

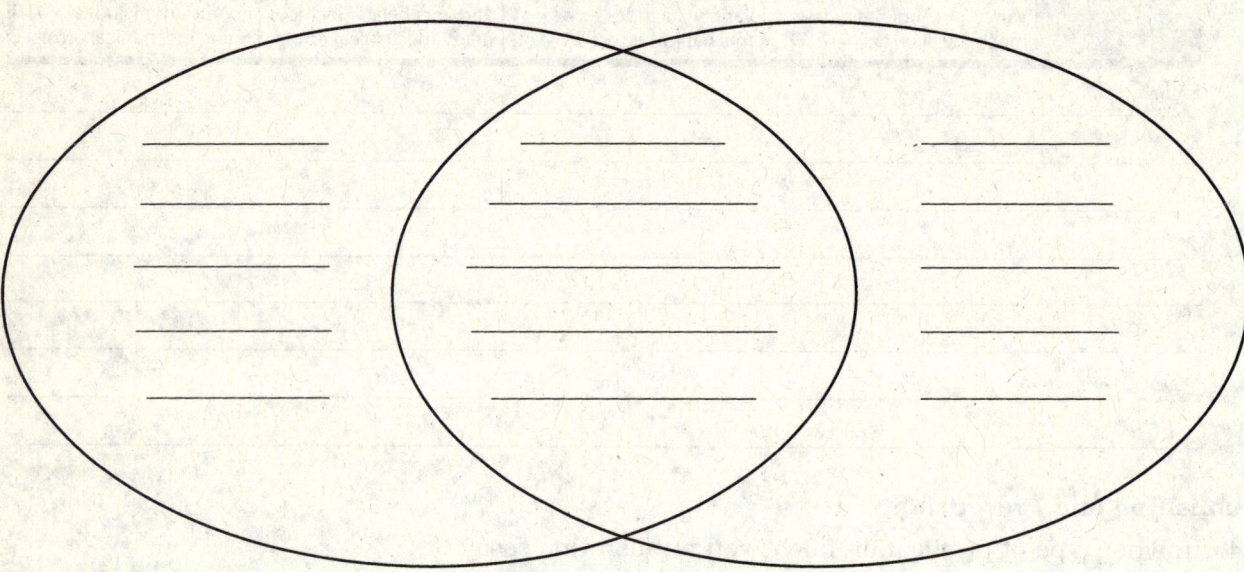

2. On the lines below, explain the purpose of your essay.
   _____
   _____

Drafting

3. Circle the method you plan to use to organize your essay, and write the topic on the line below.

   Block Method   Point-by-Point Method

   TOPIC: _____ vs. _____

   Now, fill in the outline using the method you chose.

   A. _____
      1. _____
      2. _____
   B. _____
      1. _____
      2. _____

4. On a separate sheet of paper, use your notes and information from the graphic organizer to draft your comparison-and-contrast essay.

Name _____

5. Reread your draft. Mark each of your sentences as a *T* (topic sentence), an *R* (restatement of the main idea in the topic sentence), or an *I* (illustration of the main idea). If you find a group of *I*'s, make sure there is a *T* they support. If you find a *T* by itself, add at least one *I* sentence.
   On the lines, list a topic sentence, a restatement, and an illustration from your draft.
   _____
   _____
   _____
   _____

6. Underline two sentences in your draft that express a similarity between two things. In the space below, combine your sentences, using a compound subject if possible.
   _____
   _____
   _____
   _____

7. The following sentence from a student's draft contains unnecessary repetition. Using proofreading marks, delete the repetition, and replace it with an appropriate pronoun.

   Adults often cannot tell one popular music group from another. Adults think most of
   the bands sound alike.

8. Write a sentence from your draft that contains some repetition. Correct it, and write the old and new versions of the sentence below.
   _____
   _____
   _____

9. If you were to ask your peers to read your essay, what would they say are the main similarities between your two subjects, according to the essay?
   _____
   _____
   _____
   _____

10. What would your peers say are the main differences between your two subjects, according to your essay?
    _____
    _____
    _____
    _____

Editing and Proofreading

11. Here is part of a student's comparison-and-contrast essay. It contains errors in pronoun-antecedent agreement and spelling. Correct the errors by using proofreading marks.

    Some popular female singers have terific voices and increadible ranges. She can capture
    the attention of an audiance and not let go.

© Prentice-Hall, Inc.   Chapter 8: Exposition: Comparison-and-Contrast Essay • 55

Name _____

12. Now, review your draft for errors in pronoun-antecedent agreement and spelling. Write the errors and corrections on the lines. If your draft does not contain these kinds of errors, write *none*.

_____
_____

13. Evaluate your draft based on the criteria in the rubric below. List any changes that you may need to make to improve your essay.

	Score 4	Score 3	Score 2	Score 1
Audience and Purpose	Clearly attracts audience interest in the comparison and contrast	Adequately attracts audience interest in the comparison and contrast	Provides a reason for the comparison and contrast	Does not provide a reason for a comparison and contrast
Organization	Clearly presents information in a consistent organization best suited to the topic	Presents information using an organization suited to the topic	Chooses an organization not suited to comparison and contrast	Shows a lack of organizational strategy
Elaboration	Elaborates ideas with facts, details, or examples; links all information to comparison and contrast	Elaborates most ideas with facts, details, or examples; links most information to comparison and contrast	Does not elaborate all ideas; does not link some details to comparison and contrast	Does not provide facts or examples to support a comparison and contrast
Use of Language	Demonstrates excellent sentence and vocabulary variety; includes very few mechanical errors	Demonstrates adequate sentence and vocabulary variety; includes few mechanical errors	Demonstrates repetitive use of sentence structure and vocabulary; includes many mechanical errors	Demonstrates poor use of language; generates confusion; includes many mechanical errors

_____
_____
_____
_____
_____
_____
_____

Publishing and Presenting

14. Explain how your essay might be useful to other people, and describe an appropriate place to publish it.

_____
_____
_____
_____

15. Describe the most important improvement you made to this essay during the revision process.

_____
_____
_____
_____
_____

Name _____   Date _____

Assessment for Chapter 9:
Exposition: Cause-and-Effect Essay
Test 1

In this test, you will be asked to draft a three-paragraph essay. Imagine that there is a garden outside your school that began with one student's idea. Imagine the steps that made the garden become a reality, including the cause-and-effect relationship between each step. Write a newspaper report about how the garden came to be. If necessary, use a separate sheet of paper to complete your responses.

Prewriting

1. Identify the purpose of your essay by answering the following questions:
   What type of language is appropriate for this essay—formal, informal, or a combination?
   _____
   _____
   What do you hope to accomplish by writing this essay—are you informing your readers, or do you want them to take some sort of action?
   _____
   _____

2. Who is the audience for your essay?
   _____

Drafting

3. Your topic consists of a series of causes and effects. Therefore, you can organize it in chronological order. Fill in the flowchart below to show how one step leads to another, which, in turn, causes the next step.

```
                              ┌──────────────┐
                              │   EFFECT     │
                              └──────┬───────┘
                                     ▼
                              ┌──────────────┐
                              │   EFFECT     │
                              └──────┬───────┘
                                     ▼
┌──────────────┐              ┌──────────────┐
│   CAUSE      │              │   EFFECT     │
└──────────────┘              └──────┬───────┘
                                     ▼
                              ┌──────────────┐
                              │   EFFECT     │
                              └──────┬───────┘
                                     ▼
                              ┌──────────────┐
                              │   EFFECT     │
                              └──────────────┘
```

Name _____

4. Write a sentence that provides more detailed elaboration for the cause-and-effect sentence below.

    The blooming flowers produced a wall of color.

    _____
    _____
    _____

5. On a separate sheet of paper, use your notes and information from the graphic organizer to draft your cause-and-effect essay.

Revising

6. Read the passage below. On the lines, number the sentences in the order in which the steps should occur.

    (1) If you want to paint wood, you have to sand it first. (2) Now the wood is clean and ready for your first coat of paint. (3) Use a brush or hand vacuum to clean the sandpaper dust off the wood. (4) Take a medium-grade piece of sandpaper and rub it steadily over the wood.

    _____   _____   _____   _____

7. Go back to your draft and number the steps in the order in which they should occur. If any steps are out of order, rearrange them so they reflect the order accurately. Write your first two steps on the lines below.

    _____
    _____
    _____
    _____

8. Add one of these transitions—*because* or *as a result*—to a sentence in your draft to show a cause-and-effect connection. Write the old and new versions of the sentence below.

    _____
    _____
    _____
    _____

9. Circle the verbs in your draft, and note whether the tense is consistent. Correct any unnecessary changes in tense, and write the original and the corrected verbs on the lines. If your draft does not contain unnecessary tense changes, write *none*.

    _____
    _____

10. Find two verbs in your draft that could be more precise. Write them below. Then, write two precise verbs that would be good replacements.

    General Verbs   Precise Verbs

    1. _____   1. _____

    2. _____   2. _____

Name _____

Editing and Proofreading

11. Imagine that you are a peer reviewer for another writer. Here is part of her draft. Find errors involving the use of prepositions and spelling. Correct them by using proofreading marks.

    In March, Mrs. Martin's class ordered seeds. Because the seeds arrived so soon, the class planted them indoors, up on a high ledge. In Aprel, they moved them into under the ground, because the weather reports said their would be no more frost.

12. Now, review your draft for preposition and spelling errors. Write the errors and corrections below. If your draft does not contain these kinds of errors, write *none*.
    _____
    _____

13. Evaluate your draft based on the criteria in the rubric below. List any changes that you may need to make to improve your essay.

	Score 4	Score 3	Score 2	Score 1
Audience and Purpose	Consistently targets an audience through word choice and details; clearly identifies purpose in introduction	Targets an audience through most word choice and details; identifies purpose in introduction	Misses a target audience by including a wide range of word choice and details; presents no clear purpose	Addresses no specific audience or purpose
Organization	Presents a clear, consistent organizational strategy to show cause and effect	Presents a clear organizational strategy with occasional inconsistencies to show cause and effect	Presents an inconsistent organizational strategy; creates illogical presentation of causes and effects	Demonstrates a lack of organizational strategy; creates a confusing presentation
Elaboration	Successfully links causes with effects; fully elaborates connections among ideas	Links causes with effects; elaborates connections among most ideas	Links some causes with some effects; elaborates connections among some ideas	Develops and elaborates no links between causes and effects
Use of Language	Chooses clear transitions to convey ideas; presents very few mechanical errors	Chooses transitions to convey ideas; presents few mechanical errors	Misses some opportunities for transitions to convey ideas; presents many mechanical errors	Demonstrates poor use of language; presents many mechanical errors

_____
_____
_____
_____

Publishing and Presenting

14. Describe how a diagram of your topic might help you present your information.
    _____
    _____
    _____
    _____

15. Which writing strategy did you find most helpful in writing your cause-and-effect essay? Why?
    _____
    _____
    _____

Name _____ Date _____

Assessment for Chapter 9:
Exposition: Cause-and-Effect Essay
Test 2

In this test, you will be asked to draft a three-paragraph essay. Imagine that one of your teachers has just been elected mayor. Write a newspaper account of the events that led to his or her election. Think of the events that would lead to such an election as you write a cause-and-effect essay. If necessary, use a separate sheet of paper to complete your responses.

Prewriting

1. Identify the purpose of your essay by answering the following questions:
   What type of language is appropriate for this essay—formal, informal, or a combination of both?
   _____
   _____
   What do you hope to accomplish by writing this newspaper account—are you informing your audience, or do you want them to take some sort of action?
   _____
   _____
   _____

2. Who is the audience for your newspaper account?
   _____

Drafting

3. Your topic consists of a series of causes and effects. Therefore, you can organize it in chronological order. Fill in the flowchart below to show how one step leads to another, which, in turn, causes the next step.

```
                                    ┌─────────────┐
                                    │   EFFECT    │
                                    └──────┬──────┘
                                           ▼
                                    ┌─────────────┐
                                    │   EFFECT    │
                                    └──────┬──────┘
                                           ▼
┌─────────────┐                     ┌─────────────┐
│   CAUSE     │                     │   EFFECT    │
└─────────────┘                     └──────┬──────┘
                                           ▼
                                    ┌─────────────┐
                                    │   EFFECT    │
                                    └──────┬──────┘
                                           ▼
                                    ┌─────────────┐
                                    │   EFFECT    │
                                    └─────────────┘
```

60 • Chapter 9: Exposition: Cause-and-Effect Essay © Prentice-Hall, Inc.

Name _____

4. For each of the cause-and-effect sentences below, write a sentence that provides more detailed elaboration.
   - One of the campaign promises caused a great swelling of support.
   _____
   _____
   _____

   - Nice weather produced a good voter turnout.
   _____
   _____
   _____

5. On a separate sheet of paper, use your notes and information from the graphic organizer to draft your cause-and-effect essay.

Revising

6. Go back to your draft and number the steps in the order in which they should occur. If any steps are out of order, rearrange them so they reflect the order accurately. Write your first two steps on the lines below.
   _____
   _____

7. Look at the first sentence of one of the paragraphs in your essay. Does it clearly state the main idea? Rewrite the first sentence here, with a "tug" that will draw your reader's attention.
   _____
   _____

8. Add two of the following transitions to sentences in your draft: *because, as a result, consequently,* or *therefore*. Write the new version of the sentences below.
   _____
   _____

9. Which is the dominant tense in your report? Circle one.

   Past   Present

   On the line below, write any verbs that are not in the dominant tense of your draft. Then, revise them so that they are.
   _____
   _____
   _____

10. Find three verbs in your draft that could be more precise. Write them below. Then, write three more precise verbs that would be good replacements.

    General Verbs   Precise Verbs
    1. _____   1. _____
    2. _____   2. _____
    3. _____   3. _____

Name _____

Editing and Proofreading

11. Imagine that you are a peer reviewer for another writer. Here is part of his draft. Find two errors involving prepositions and two errors in spelling. Correct all four, using proofreading marks.

    Mr. Chin became the mayor! His promises to end taxes and bild new schools caused the vote to go off of the charts. His name will appear up in the headlines. Because he won, however, the school has to hire a new histery teacher next year.

12. Now, review your draft for any preposition and spelling errors. Write the errors and corrections below. If your draft does not contain these kinds of errors, write *none*.

    _____
    _____

13. Evaluate your draft based on the criteria in the rubric below. List any changes that you may need to make to improve your essay.

	Score 4	Score 3	Score 2	Score 1
Audience and Purpose	Consistently targets an audience through word choice and details; clearly identifies purpose in introduction	Targets an audience through most word choice and details; identifies purpose in introduction	Misses a target audience by including a wide range of word choice and details; presents no clear purpose	Addresses no specific audience or purpose
Organization	Presents a clear, consistent organizational strategy to show cause and effect	Presents a clear organizational strategy with occasional inconsistencies to show cause and effect	Presents an inconsistent organizational strategy; creates illogical presentation of causes and effects	Demonstrates a lack of organizational strategy; creates a confusing presentation
Elaboration	Successfully links causes with effects; fully elaborates connections among ideas	Links causes with effects; elaborates connections among most ideas	Links some causes with some effects; elaborates connections among some ideas	Develops and elaborates no links between causes and effects
Use of Language	Chooses clear transitions to convey ideas; presents very few mechanical errors	Chooses transitions to convey ideas; presents few mechanical errors	Misses some opportunities for transitions to convey ideas; presents many mechanical errors	Demonstrates poor use of language; presents many mechanical errors

_____
_____
_____
_____
_____
_____

Publishing and Presenting

14. If your essay were published in the local newspaper, what kind of illustration would be a helpful addition?

    _____
    _____

15. What was the most interesting thing you discovered while writing this essay?

    _____
    _____
    _____

Name _____   Date _____

Assessment for Chapter 9:
Exposition: Cause-and-Effect Essay
Test 3

In this test, you will be asked to write an essay of three or four paragraphs. Imagine that you have been told the following information: "Elementary schools now include keyboarding among their standard courses." Write an essay for your school newspaper that explores the causes and the effects of this change. If necessary, use a separate sheet of paper to complete your responses.

Prewriting

1. Who is the audience for your essay?
   _____

2. Make a T-chart to gather details about your topic.

   Topic: _____

What causes _____ ?	What are the effects of _____ ?
1.	1.
2.	2.

Drafting

3. Now that you've explored your topic, write an introductory sentence for your essay that summarizes the main point.
   _____
   _____

4. For the two cause-and-effect connections listed below, write a sentence that provides more detailed elaboration.
   • Additions to the curriculum cause more teacher training.
   _____
   _____

   • An increase in computer use causes more computer breakdowns.
   _____
   _____

5. On a separate sheet of paper, use your notes and information from the graphic organizer to draft your cause-and-effect essay.

Name _____

Revising

6. Go back to your draft and find the "tug" sentence in each paragraph. Underline the "tug" sentences and write them below.
   _____
   _____
   _____
   _____

   If one or two paragraphs have no "tug" sentences, supply them below, and indicate where they should go in your draft.

   1. _____
      _____

   2. _____
      _____

7. Add two of the following transitions to sentences in your draft: *because, as a result, consequently,* or *therefore*. Write the new versions of the sentences below.
   _____
   _____
   _____
   _____
   _____

8. Which is the dominant tense in your essay? Circle one.

   　　　　　　　Past　　　　　Present

9. Now, write three verbs from your essay that are in this tense.
   _____ _____ _____ _____

10. Find three verbs in your draft that could be more precise. Write them below. Then, write three more precise verbs that would be good replacements.

    General Verbs   Precise Verbs
    1. _____   1. _____
    2. _____   2. _____
    3. _____   3. _____

Editing and Proofreading

11. You are a peer reviewer for another writer. Here is part of her draft. Find two errors involving prepositions and three errors in spelling. Correct all five, using proofreading marks.

    　　It's impossible to teach keyboarding without a separite keyboard on each student. This means 20–25 keyboards for an average elemintary school. This expence would be the first to come from the budget with many schools.

12. Now, review your draft for any preposition or spelling errors. Write the errors and corrections below. If your draft does not contain these kinds of errors, write *none*. _____
    _____
    _____

64 • Chapter 9: Exposition: Cause-and-Effect Essay　　　　　© Prentice-Hall, Inc.

Name _____

13. Evaluate your draft based on the criteria in the rubric below. List any changes that you may need to make to improve your essay.

	Score 4	Score 3	Score 2	Score 1
Audience and Purpose	Consistently targets an audience through word choice and details; clearly identifies purpose in introduction	Targets an audience through most word choice and details; identifies purpose in introduction	Misses a target audience by including a wide range of word choice and details; presents no clear purpose	Addresses no specific audience or purpose
Organization	Presents a clear, consistent organizational strategy to show cause and effect	Presents a clear organizational strategy with occasional inconsistencies to show cause and effect	Presents an inconsistent organizational strategy; creates illogical presentation of causes and effects	Demonstrates a lack of organizational strategy; creates a confusing presentation
Elaboration	Successfully links causes with effects; fully elaborates connections among ideas	Links causes with effects; elaborates connections among most ideas	Links some causes with some effects; elaborates connections among some ideas	Develops and elaborates no links between causes and effects
Use of Language	Chooses clear transitions to convey ideas; presents very few mechanical errors	Chooses transitions to convey ideas; presents few mechanical errors	Misses some opportunities for transitions to convey ideas; presents many mechanical errors	Demonstrates poor use of language; presents many mechanical errors

_____
_____
_____
_____
_____
_____
_____

Publishing and Presenting

14. If your final essay were published in the local newspaper, what kind of chart might be a helpful addition?
_____
_____
_____

15. Which writing strategy did you find most useful in writing this essay? Why?
_____
_____
_____
_____
_____
_____
_____
_____
_____
_____

Name _____ Date _____

 **Assessment for Chapter 10:
Exposition: How-to Essay**
Test 1

In this test, you will be asked to write a three-paragraph essay. If necessary, use a separate sheet of paper to complete your responses. Choose one of the following "how-to" topics:
- How to make your favorite breakfast
- How to ride a bike
- How to play chess or checkers

Prewriting

1. Explain the purpose of your essay.
   _____

2. How much do you think your audience knows about your topic? Explain your answer.
   _____
   _____

3. Make a list of five steps for your topic. Then, itemize one of the steps by drawing an arrow to the box on the right and generating specific details for that step.

Drafting

4. Write one of the steps you listed in the previous question.

   "Explode the moment" by adding details to the step.
   _____
   _____
   _____

5. On a separate sheet of paper, use your notes and information from the graphic organizer to draft your how-to essay.

Name _____

Revising

6. Reread the first paragraph of your draft, and rewrite your lead sentence so that it grabs the reader's attention. Write the new version of the sentence below.
   _____
   _____

7. Reread your draft. At appropriate places, add two of these connecting words that indicate steps: *first, next, finally, and, furthermore, for instance, because, consequently, but, however, on the other hand, rather.* Write the new sentences below.
   _____
   _____
   _____

8. Read the passage below, and then circle the first word of each sentence. On the lines, list other words or phrases that could be used to vary the beginnings of four of the sentences.

   For a treasure hunt, you need a map. You have to draw a clear map. Then, circle where the treasure will be found. Then, pass out copies to your friends. Then, have them all start at the same time. For extra fun, have them find the treasure in the dark.
   _____
   _____
   _____
   _____
   _____

9. List the first word in the first six sentences of your draft. Change at least one of these words to create more variety in your sentence beginnings.
   1. _____ 3. _____ 5. _____
   2. _____ 4. _____ 6. _____
   Revised sentence: _____

10. Find at least one word that you have repeated several times in your draft. On the lines below, write two other words that are good substitutions for the repeated word.
    Repeated word: _____
    Good substitutions: _____   _____

Editing and Proofreading

11. Imagine that you are proofreading a how-to essay for a friend. Here is part of her draft. In it, find four errors involving commas to separate items in a series and two errors in spelling. Use proofreading marks to correct the errors.

    Take two fresh eggs and brake them into a bowl. Stir them well and add 1/2 cup of greated cheddar cheese a pinch of salt and pepper to taste. While they are cooking, you can toast the rye bread slice the strawberries and make the hot chocolate.

© Prentice-Hall, Inc.   Chapter 10: Exposition: How-to Essay • 67

Name _____

12. Now, review your draft for errors in spelling and in using commas to separate items in a series. Write the errors and corrections on the line. If your draft does not contain these kinds of errors, write *none*.

    _____

13. Evaluate your draft based on the criteria in the rubric below. List any changes that you may need to make to improve your essay.

	Score 4	Score 3	Score 2	Score 1
Audience and Purpose	Clearly focuses on procedures leading to a well-defined end	Focuses on procedures leading to a well-defined end	Includes procedures related to an end, but presents some vaguely	Includes only vague descriptions of procedures and results
Organization	Gives instructions in logical order; subdivides complex actions into steps	Gives instructions in logical order; subdivides some complex actions into steps	For the most part, gives instructions in logical order	Gives instructions in a scattered, disorganized manner
Elaboration	Provides appropriate amount of detail; gives needed explanations	Provides appropriate amount of detail; gives some explanations	Provides some detail; gives few explanations	Provides few details; gives few or no explanations
Use of Language	Shows overall clarity and fluency; uses transitions effectively; contains few mechanical errors	Shows some sentence variety; uses some transitions; includes few mechanical errors	Uses awkward or overly simple sentence structures; contains many mechanical errors	Contains incomplete thoughts and confusing mechanical errors

_____
_____
_____
_____
_____
_____
_____
_____

Publishing and Presenting

14. Describe a demonstration you might give, based on your essay.

    _____
    _____
    _____
    _____
    _____

15. How did explaining this topic affect your understanding of the activity?

    _____
    _____
    _____
    _____
    _____

Name _____   Date _____

 **Assessment for Chapter 10:
Exposition: How-to Essay**
Test 2

In this test, you will be asked to write a three-paragraph essay. Choose one of the following "how-to" topics:
- How to improve your vocabulary
- How to improve your singing voice
- How to improve your computer literacy

Prewriting

1. Explain the purpose of your essay.
   _____

2. How much do you expect your audience to know about your topic? Explain your answer.
   _____
   _____

3. Make a list of five steps for your topic. Then, itemize two of the steps by drawing arrows to the boxes on the right and generating specific details for both steps.

Drafting

4. Think of a step you left out of your original list. Write it on the self-sticking note below. Then, draw an asterisk on the list in the previous question, in the place where the note belongs chronologically.

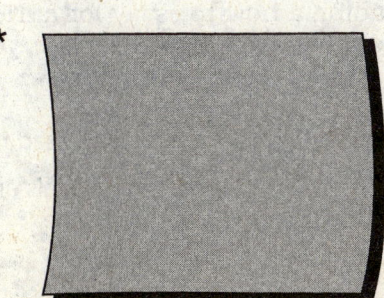

© Prentice-Hall, Inc.   Chapter 10: Exposition: How-to Essay • 69

Name _____

5. For the step you added in the previous question, "explode the moment" by writing additional details that provide elaboration for that step.
   _____
   _____
   _____
   _____

6. On a separate sheet of paper, use your notes and information from the graphic organizers to write a draft for your how-to essay.

Revising

7. Reread the first paragraph of your draft, and rewrite your lead sentence so that it grabs the reader's attention. Write the new version of the sentence below.
   _____
   _____
   _____

8. Reread your draft. At appropriate places, add at least two of these connecting words that indicate steps, stacks, chains, and balances: *first, next, finally, furthermore, for instance, because, consequently, but, however, on the other hand, rather*. Write the revised sentences on the lines.
   _____
   _____
   _____
   _____
   _____
   _____

9. List the first word in the first six sentences of your draft. On your draft, circle any that are repeated. Change at least one of them to create more variety in your sentence beginnings.

   1. _____   3. _____   5. _____
   2. _____   4. _____   6. _____

10. Find at least one word that you have repeated several times in your draft and write it below. Then, write two other words that are good substitutions for the repeated word.

    Repeated word: _____

    Good substitutions: _____   _____

Editing and Proofreading

11. Imagine that you are proofreading a how-to essay for a friend. Here is part of her draft. In it, find five errors involving commas to separate items in a series and two errors in spelling. Use proofreading marks to correct the errors.

    The best way to improve your vocabulary is simply to read read and read some more.

    Read mistery novels computer magazines newspaper articals and video game directions.

    Read anything you can get your hands on.

70 • Chapter 10: Exposition: How-to Essay   © Prentice-Hall, Inc.

Name _____

12. Now, review your draft for similar errors. Write the errors and corrections on the lines below. If your draft does not contain errors in spelling or in using commas to separate items in a series, write *none*.
   _____
   _____

13. Evaluate your draft based on the criteria in the rubric below. List any changes that you may need to make to improve your essay.

	Score 4	Score 3	Score 2	Score 1
Audience and Purpose	Clearly focuses on procedures leading to a well-defined end	Focuses on procedures leading to a well-defined end	Includes procedures related to an end, but presents some vaguely	Includes only vague descriptions of procedures and results
Organization	Gives instructions in logical order; subdivides complex actions into steps	Gives instructions in logical order; subdivides some complex actions into steps	For the most part, gives instructions in logical order	Gives instructions in a scattered, disorganized manner
Elaboration	Provides appropriate amount of detail; gives needed explanations	Provides appropriate amount of detail; gives some explanations	Provides some detail; gives few explanations	Provides few details; gives few or no explanations
Use of Language	Shows overall clarity and fluency; uses transitions effectively; contains few mechanical errors	Shows some sentence variety; uses some transitions; includes few mechanical errors	Uses awkward or overly simple sentence structures; contains many mechanical errors	Contains incomplete thoughts and confusing mechanical errors

_____
_____
_____
_____
_____
_____
_____

Publishing and Presenting

14. Describe a poster you might make to illustrate the steps in your how-to essay.
   _____
   _____
   _____
   _____
   _____

15. Imagine that you are a person reading this essay for the first time. Do you think any of the steps should be explained more clearly? Why?
   _____
   _____
   _____
   _____
   _____

Name _____ Date _____

 **Assessment for Chapter 10:
Exposition: How-to Essay**
Test 3

In this test, you will be asked to write an essay of three or four paragraphs. Choose one of the following "how-to" topics.
- How to eat healthier foods
- How to organize your computer files
- How to succeed in an interview

Prewriting

1. Describe the purpose of this essay.
   _____
   _____
   _____

2. How much do you expect your audience to know about your topic?
   _____
   _____
   _____

   What skills might your audience already have that relate to your topic?
   _____
   _____
   _____

3. Make a preliminary list of five steps for your topic. Then, itemize two of the steps by drawing arrows to the boxes on the right and generating specific details for both steps.

72 • Chapter 10: Exposition: How-to Essay   © Prentice-Hall, Inc.

Name _____

Drafting

4. Think of a step you left out of your original list. Write it on the self-sticking note below. Then, draw an asterisk on the list in the previous question, in the place where the note belongs chronologically.

5. For the step you added in the previous question, "explode the moment" by writing additional details that provide elaboration for that step.
   _____
   _____

6. On a separate sheet of paper, use your notes and information from the graphic organizers to draft your how-to essay.

Revising

7. Reread the first paragraph of your draft, and rewrite your lead sentence so that it grabs the reader's attention. Write the new version of the sentence below.
   _____
   _____

8. Reread your draft. At appropriate places, add at least three of these connecting words that indicate steps, stacks, chains, and balances: *first, next, finally, and, furthermore, for instance, because, consequently, but, however, on the other hand,* and *rather*. Write the new sentences on the lines.
   _____
   _____
   _____
   _____

9. List the first word in the first nine sentences of your draft. On your draft, circle any that are repeated. Change at least one of them to create more variety in your sentence beginnings.

   1. _____ 4. _____ 7. _____
   2. _____ 5. _____ 8. _____
   3. _____ 6. _____ 9. _____

10. Find at least two words that you have repeated several times in your draft and write them below. Then, below each one, write two other words that are good substitutions.

    Repeated words: _____   _____

    Good substitutions: _____   _____

                           _____   _____

Name _____

Editing and Proofreading

11. Imagine that you are proofreading a how-to essay for a friend. Here is part of her draft. In it, find errors in spelling and in using commas to separate items in a series. Use proofreading marks to correct the errors.

    On your desktop, keep the file folders and applications that you are currently working on. Don't let them pile up. Limit yourself to eight or ten. Organise everything else by category. For example: letters to family finished work miscelaneous documents or college applicasion materials.

12. Now, review your draft for any errors in spelling or in using commas to separate items in a series. Write the errors and corrections on the line. If your draft does not contain these kinds of errors, write *none*.

    _____

13. Evaluate your draft based on the criteria in the rubric below. List any changes that you may need to make to improve your essay.

	Score 4	Score 3	Score 2	Score 1
Audience and Purpose	Clearly focuses on procedures leading to a well-defined end	Focuses on procedures leading to a well-defined end	Includes procedures related to an end, but presents some vaguely	Includes only vague descriptions of procedures and results
Organization	Gives instructions in logical order; subdivides complex actions into steps	Gives instructions in logical order; subdivides some complex actions into steps	For the most part, gives instructions in logical order	Gives instructions in a scattered, disorganized manner
Elaboration	Provides appropriate amount of detail; gives needed explanations	Provides appropriate amount of detail; gives some explanations	Provides some detail; gives few explanations	Provides few details; gives few or no explanations
Use of Language	Shows overall clarity and fluency; uses transitions effectively; contains few mechanical errors	Shows some sentence variety; uses some transitions; includes few mechanical errors	Uses awkward or overly simple sentence structures; contains many mechanical errors	Contains incomplete thoughts and confusing mechanical errors

_____
_____
_____
_____

Publishing and Presenting

14. Describe how you would present a demonstration based on your essay.
    _____
    _____
    _____

15. Name two ways in which explaining this topic has affected your understanding of the activity.
    _____
    _____
    _____

Name _____ Date _____

 # Assessment for Chapter 11: Research Report
Test 1

For this test, you'll use the work of Kevin, a student like you, who is writing a research paper about basketball great Michael Jordan. If necessary, use a separate sheet of paper to complete your responses.

Prewriting

Kevin used a variety of sources. Here are some note cards he made:

Note Card #1

"Michael plays more exciting basketball than anyone else. He can jump higher than anyone. He can slam the dunk shot and make fans scream."

Sports Stars, p. 8

Note Card #2

In January 2000, Jordan purchased 10% of the Washington Wizards for about $25 million and became director of the team.

Sports Illustrated, p. 52

Note Card #3

Fortune magazine estimates that Jordan has been worth $5.2 billion to a certain sneaker and sports apparel company and another $408 million to other companies whose products he endorses.

www.cbs.sportsline.com/

Note Card #4

SOURCE CARD

Sports Stars: Michael Jordan

Chicago: Childrens Press

1. Which note card contains a direct quotation? How can you tell?
   _____
   _____

2. What information did Kevin forget to include on Note Card #4?
   _____
   _____

3. What is the source for Note Card #3?
   _____

© Prentice-Hall, Inc.   Chapter 11: Research Report • 75

Name _____

Drafting

4. Kevin is developing his thesis statement. He has written four possibilities. Circle the one you think is best, and then, on the lines below, explain your choice.

   Michael Jordan was born on February 17, 1963.

   Michael Jordan has achieved greatness in many ways.

   If I could be anyone else, I would be Michael Jordan.

   Michael Jordan is charming, open, and sincere.

   _____
   _____

5. Kevin must now group his note cards by category. Circle the method of organization that will better suit his topic and explain your answer on the lines below.
   Chronological order   Ordering by type
   _____
   _____

   Here are the main sections of Kevin's outline. Use this list and the note cards on the previous page to answer questions 6–8 below.
   I. Introduction
   II. Basketball Star
   III. Businessman
   IV. Team Owner
   V. Role Model
   VI. Conclusion

6. Which section does Note Card #1 support? _____

7. Which section does Note Card #2 support? _____

8. Which section does Note Card #3 support? _____

Revising

Here is part of Kevin's draft. Use it to answer questions 9–11 below.

> It is clear to everyone that Michael Jordan is the "unofficial coach of the Wizards" (McCallum 53). His next challenge is to turn the team's record around.
> Jordan supports a lot of charities, such as the "Say No to Drugs Program," children's hospitals, the United Negro College Fund, and the Ronald McDonald House.

9. Kevin realizes that the paragraph that begins "Jordan supports" needs to be more clearly connected to the one above it. Add a sentence or phrase—using *next*, *as a result*, or *in addition*—that will act as a transition. Write the new sentence below.
   _____
   _____

10. A peer reviewer tells Kevin that he needs to vary the length of his sentences. How could he do this in one of the paragraphs above?
    _____
    _____

11. If a peer reviewer were to read the above paragraphs, what would he or she say is the main idea in each one?
    _____
    _____

Name _____

Editing and Proofreading

Here are two entries from Kevin's list of works cited. Use them to answer questions 12 and 13.

McCallum, Jack. "I Own You." Sports Illustrated, February 14, 2000.

Herbert, Mike. *Sports Stars: Michael Jordan*. Chicago: Childrens Press, 1987.

12. Which of these entries should appear first on Kevin's final list?
    _____
    _____
    _____

13. One of the entries contains a mistake in the way a title is written. Correct it on the line below.
    _____
    _____
    _____

Publishing and Presenting

14. Name an illustration that Kevin could include if his research report were to appear on a Web site.
    _____
    _____
    _____

15. Which revising strategy would you recommend to another student? Why?
    _____
    _____
    _____
    _____
    _____
    _____

Name _____ Date _____

 **Assessment for Chapter 11: Research Report**
Test 2

For this test, you'll use the work of Sarah, a student like you who is writing a research paper on the life of Eleanor Roosevelt, the wife of President Franklin Roosevelt. If necessary, use a separate sheet of paper to complete your responses.

Prewriting

Sarah used a variety of sources. Here are some note cards she made:

Note Card #1

"Eleanor Roosevelt was the most active and influential first lady in American history. After her husband lost the ability to walk, she traveled all over the world for him."

"Eleanor, My Heroine," p. 39

Note Card #2

Married Franklin on March 17, 1905. Six children: Anna, James, Franklin, Jr. (died in infancy), Elliot, Franklin, Jr., and John.

Lives of Famous Women, p. 102

Note Card #3

Became a powerful voice on behalf of youth and civil rights: conducted press conferences, her own radio program, and wrote a daily newspaper column.

www.gi.grolier.com/president/aae/first

Note Card #4

SOURCE CARD

Lives of Famous Women by Kelly Martin

Chicago: Acme Press

1. Which note card contains a direct quotation? How can you tell?
   _____
   _____

2. What information did Sarah forget to include on Note Card #4?
   _____
   _____

3. What is the source for Note Card #3?
   _____

Name _____

Drafting

4. Sarah is developing her thesis statement. She has written four possibilities. Circle the one you think is best, and then, on the lines below, explain your choice.

   Eleanor Roosevelt was born in 1884.

   Throughout her life, Eleanor Roosevelt was a leader and pioneer.

   Most people don't know a lot about Eleanor Roosevelt.

   I am going to write about Eleanor Roosevelt.

   _____
   _____

5. Sarah must now group her note cards by category. Circle the method of organization that will better suit her topic and explain your answer on the lines below.

   Chronological order   Ordering by type

   _____
   _____

Here are the main sections of Sarah's outline. Use this list and the note cards on the previous page to answer questions 6–8 below.
   I. Introduction
   II. Early Years
   III. Marriage and Children
   IV. World Travel as First Lady
   V. The United Nations
   VI. Writer and Speaker
   VII. Conclusion

6. Which section does Note Card #1 support? _____

7. Which section does Note Card #2 support? _____

8. Which section does Note Card #3 support? _____

Revising

Here is the end of Sarah's introductory paragraph. Use it to answer questions 9–11 below.

   Most people know Eleanor Roosevelt only as a president's wife, but she was a lot more. She held high office on her own and spoke out for the rights of children and minorities. "A tireless worker for social causes" (Martin 103), Roosevelt's life was admired and respected.

9. Using the detail below, write a first sentence for Sarah's second paragraph that is clearly connected to the paragraph above. Circle the word or phrase that acts as the "glue." Detail: Born October 11, 1884, in New York City to wealthy parents

   _____
   _____

10. A peer reviewer tells Sarah that she needs to vary her sentence length more. How could she do this in the paragraph above? Write one revision on the lines.

    _____
    _____

11. If a peer reviewer were to read the above paragraph, what would he or she say is the main idea?

    _____

Name _____

Editing and Proofreading

Here are three entries from Sarah's list of works cited. Use them to answer questions 12 and 13.

    Roosevelt, Eleanor. *This I Remember*. Westport, CT: Greenwood Publishing Group, 1970.

    Skarmeas, Nancy J. Eleanor Roosevelt: A Photobiography. New York: Ideals Publications, 1997.

    Miller, Aaron. Eleanor, My Heroine. *Hero Magazine*, August 1998, pp. 35–38.

12. Write the authors' names in the order in which they would appear on Sarah's final list of citations.
    _____
    _____
    _____

13. Two of the entries contain mistakes in their titles. Correct them on the lines below.
    _____
    _____

Publishing and Presenting

14. Imagine that Sarah's research report will be part of a "Wall of Fame." Subjects of other reports will be on the wall, described as "famous inventor" or "famous speaker." How should Sarah label Eleanor Roosevelt? Why?
    _____
    _____
    _____
    _____
    _____

15. Which revising strategy would you recommend to another student? Why?
    _____
    _____
    _____
    _____
    _____

Name _____   Date _____

 # Assessment for Chapter 11: Research Report
Test 3

For this test, you'll use the work of Erin, a student like you, who is writing a research paper about the Battle of Gettysburg.

Prewriting

Erin used a variety of sources. Here are some note cards she made:

Note Card #1

"The Battle of Gettysburg was fought because the Confederate army needed shoes. At least that was the way the story was told."

To Hold, p. 13

Note Card #2

After Gettysburg, the odds were against the South. After this battle, it was downhill all the way. Poet Stephen Vincent Benét remarked that all roads lead to surrender.

Battle of Gettysburg

Note Card #3

Battle began July 1, 1863, at 5:30 A.M. At first, Confederates were overcome. Later in the day, Federals retreated through Gettysburg to Cemetery Hill. In first day, 9,000 Federal troops killed; and about 6,500 Confederates killed.

www.civilwarhome.com/gettyscampaign.htm

Note Card #4

SOURCE CARD

To Hold this Ground

by Susan Provost Beller

New York, 1995

1. Which note card contains a direct quotation? How can you tell?
   _____
   _____

2. Which information did Erin forget to include on Note Card #2?
   _____
   _____
   _____

3. Why is Note Card #4 incomplete?
   _____
   _____
   _____

Name _____

Drafting

4. Erin is developing her thesis statement. She has written four possibilities. Circle the one you think is best, and then, on the lines below, explain your choice.

   The Battle of Gettysburg was fought in 1863.

   The Battle of Gettysburg was the turning point of the Civil War.

   I wish I could have actually witnessed the Battle of Gettysburg.

   General Lee's army was tough, hard, and used to victory.

   _____
   _____

5. Erin must now group her note cards by category. Circle the method of organization that will better suit her topic and explain your answer on the lines below.

   Chronological order   Ordering by type

   _____
   _____

   Here are the main sections of Erin's outline. Use this list and the note cards on the previous page to answer questions 6–8 below.
   I. Introduction
   II. Reasons for the Battle
   III. Days 1 and 2
   IV. Day 3
   V. The Aftermath
   VI. The Turning Point of the War
   VII. Conclusion

6. Which section does Note Card #1 support? _____

7. Which section does Note Card #2 support? _____

8. Which section does Note Card #3 support? _____

Revising

The following excerpt from Erin's draft is the end of section V and the beginning of section VI. Use it to answer questions 9–11 below.

   General John Imoden was in charge of the wagon train of Confederate wounded. It took him four hours to ride from the head to the end of it. He said later that the ride taught him more about war than all of his other experiences put together.
   When General Lee offered to resign, Jefferson Davis refused his resignation, and Lee continued to command the Southern armies for two more years of fighting.

9. Erin realizes that the paragraph that begins "When General Lee offered" needs "glue" to connect it to the one above it. Write a sentence, or add a phrase, that will act as a transition. Write the new or revised sentence below.

   _____
   _____

10. A peer reviewer tells Erin that she needs to vary her sentence length more. How could she do this in the passage above? Write one revision on the lines.

   _____
   _____

82 • Chapter 11: Research Report

Name _____

11. If a peer reviewer were to read the excerpt from Erin's draft, what would he or she say is the main idea of each paragraph? _____
_____
_____
_____

Editing and Proofreading

Here are three entries for Erin's list of works cited. Use them to answer questions 12 and 13.

    McPherson, James. *Gettysburg: The Paintings of Mort Künstler*. Atlanta: Turner Publishing, 1993.

    Catton, Bruce. The Battle of Gettysburg. New York: American Heritage Publishing Co., 1963.

    Beller, Susan Provost. "To Hold this Ground." New York: McElderry Books, 1995.

12. Write the authors' names in the order in which they should appear on Erin's final list.
_____
_____
_____

13. Two of the entries contain mistakes in the way their titles are written. Correct them on the lines below.
_____
_____
_____
_____

Publishing and Presenting

14. If you were to create a Web site about this topic, what kinds of images might you include for one of the pages on the Web site?
_____
_____
_____

15. Give an example of information that others will learn from reading Erin's research report.
_____
_____
_____
_____
_____
_____
_____

Name _____ Date _____

 **Assessment for Chapter 12: Response to Literature**
Test 1

In this test, you will be asked to draft a three-paragraph letter to Naomi Long Madgett, letting her know what you find enjoyable in her poem "Life." If necessary, use a separate sheet of paper to complete your responses.

Life
By *Naomi Long Madgett*

Life is but a toy that swings on a bright gold chain
Ticking for a little while
To amuse a fascinated infant,
Until the keeper, a very old man,
Becomes tired of the game
And lets the watch run down.

Prewriting

1. Use a pentad to select an aspect of the poem on which to focus your writing.

    Actor: Who does the action? _____
    Acts: What is done? _____
    Scene: When or where is it done? _____
    Agency: How is it done? _____
    Purpose: Why is it done? _____

2. Madgett compares life to "a toy that swings on a bright gold chain." What happens to that image as the poem continues?

    _____
    _____
    _____

3. Does the imagery in the poem remind you of something you have experienced in your life? Write a sentence about an experience or association that you connect with the poem.

    _____

Name _____

4. Circle 3–5 words that you think are important to the poem. Use them to write a one-sentence summary of the poem, in your own words.

_____
_____
_____

Drafting

5. Describe your response to the poem.

   I like/do not like (circle one) this poem because _____
   _____.

6. Elaborate on your response to the poem by choosing two details that support it. Write them on the lines below.

   _____
   _____

7. On a separate sheet of paper, use your notes and information from the graphic organizer to write a draft of your letter to the poet.

Revising

8. Review your draft. Circle your strongest point—the one that is most interesting or that summarizes the other ideas. Write it on the lines below. Then, make sure it is at a memorable place in your essay, such as the end.

   _____
   _____

9. Find a place in your draft where you can add a detail using one of these connecting words or phrases that explain *why* you reached a particular conclusion about the poem. Write your new sentence below, and circle the connecting word.

as a result of	since
because	so that
despite	due to

   _____
   _____

10. Find two general words in your draft (such as *good* or *bad*). Write them below. Then, write two precise words that could replace them.

    General words: _____   _____

    Precise words: _____   _____

Editing and Proofreading

11. Imagine you are proofreading another student's response to a different poem. Here is part of her draft. Use proofreading marks to correct three errors in punctuation of quotations and two errors in spelling.

    When Merriam rites that her thumbprint is 'My universe key,' she means that her individuality unlocks the meening of her life. This is what makes it so valuable. In fact, she calls it ''a treasure.

Name _____

12. Now, review your draft for errors in spelling and punctuation of quotations. Write the errors and corrections on the line. If your draft does not contain these kinds of errors, write *none*.
   _____
   _____

13. Evaluate your draft based on the criteria in the rubric below. List any changes that you may need to make to improve your letter.

	Score 4	Score 3	Score 2	Score 1
Audience and Purpose	Presents sufficient background on the work(s); presents the writer's reactions forcefully	Presents background on the work(s); presents the writer's reactions clearly	Presents some background on the work(s); presents the writer's reactions at points	Presents little or no background on the work(s); presents few of the writer's reactions
Organization	Presents points in logical order, smoothly connecting them to the overall focus	Presents points in logical order and connects many to the overall focus	Organizes points poorly in places; connects some points to an overall focus	Presents information in a scattered, disorganized manner
Elaboration	Supports reactions and evaluations with elaborated reasons and well-chosen examples	Supports reactions and evaluations with specific reasons and examples	Supports some reactions and evaluations with reasons and examples	Offers little support for reactions and evaluations
Use of Language	Shows overall clarity and fluency; uses precise, evaluative words; makes few mechanical errors	Shows good sentence variety; uses some precise evaluative terms; makes some mechanical errors	Uses awkward or overly simple sentence structures and vague evaluative terms; makes many mechanical errors	Presents incomplete thoughts; makes mechanical errors that create confusion

_____
_____
_____
_____
_____
_____
_____
_____

Publishing and Presenting

14. How could you obtain the author's address if you wanted to mail your letter?
   _____
   _____
   _____

15. How did writing about this poem help you to understand it better?
   _____
   _____
   _____
   _____
   _____
   _____
   _____

Name _____ Date _____

Assessment for Chapter 12: Response to Literature
Test 2

In this test, you will be asked to write a three-paragraph essay in response to the following poem. Your essay should show how or why you find the poem enjoyable or meaningful. If necessary, use a separate sheet of paper to complete your responses.

"The Hippopotamus"
By *Ogden Nash*

Behold the hippopotamus!
We laugh at how he looks to us,
And yet in moment dark and grim
I wonder how we look to him.

Peace, peace, thou hippopotamus!
We really look all right to us,
As you no doubt delight the eye
Of other hippopotami.

Prewriting

1. Use a pentad to select an aspect of the poem on which to focus your writing.

   (Pentad diagram with points labeled: Actor, Acts, Scene, Agency, Purpose)

   Actor: Who does the action? _____
   Acts: What is done? _____
   Scene: When or where is it done? _____
   Agency: How is it done? _____
   Purpose: Why is it done? _____

2. Explain who your readers will be and why you chose this audience.
   _____
   _____

3. What kinds of poetic devices does the poet use? Give at least one example.
   _____
   _____

© Prentice-Hall, Inc.   Chapter 12: Response to Literature • 87

Name _____

4. What is the theme of this poem? Write a single sentence that expresses what the poem is trying to convey.
   _____
   _____

Drafting

5. Do you like this poem? Why, or why not? Support your answer with at least two details from the poem.
   _____
   _____
   _____
   _____

6. Show that you know how to use a quotation in your writing by writing a sentence about the hippopotamus that uses a direct quotation.
   _____
   _____
   _____

7. On a separate sheet of paper, use your notes and information from the graphic organizer to write a draft for your essay.

Revising

8. Review your draft. Circle your strongest point—the one that is most interesting or that summarizes the other ideas. Write it on the lines below. Then, make sure it is at a memorable place in your essay, such as the end.
   _____
   _____
   _____
   _____

9. Find a place in your draft where you can add a detail using one of these connecting words or phrases that explain *why* you reached a particular conclusion. Write your new sentence below, and circle the connecting word.

as a result of	since
because	so that
despite	due to

   _____
   _____
   _____

10. Find two general words in your draft (such as *good* or *bads*). Write them below. Then, write two precise words that could replace them.

    General: _____   _____
    Precise: _____   _____

88 • Chapter 12: Response to Literature

Name _____

Editing and Proofreading

11. Imagine that you are proofreading another student's response to a different animal poem. Here is part of his draft. Use proofreading marks to correct three errors in punctuation of quotations and three errors in spelling.

    When Emerson writes, "Bun replied, "You are doubtless very big," " he shows a tiny squirrel talking to a big mountain. The rest of the poem is the squirrel's speech. It points out sevral differences between the two and ends with the deliteful truth, "Neither can you crack a nut.

12. Now, review your draft for errors in punctuation of quotations and spelling. Write the errors and corrections on the lines below. If your draft does not contain these kinds of errors, write *none*.

    _____
    _____

13. Evaluate your draft based on the criteria in the rubric below. List any changes that you may need to make to improve your essay.

	Score 4	Score 3	Score 2	Score 1
Audience and Purpose	Presents sufficient background on the work(s); presents the writer's reactions forcefully	Presents background on the work(s); presents the writer's reactions clearly	Presents some background on the work(s); presents the writer's reactions at points	Presents little or no background on the work(s); presents few of the writer's reactions
Organization	Presents points in logical order, smoothly connecting them to the overall focus	Presents points in logical order and connects many to the overall focus	Organizes points poorly in places; connects some points to an overall focus	Presents information in a scattered, disorganized manner
Elaboration	Supports reactions and evaluations with elaborated reasons and well-chosen examples	Supports reactions and evaluations with specific reasons and examples	Supports some reactions and evaluations with reasons and examples	Offers little support for reactions and evaluations
Use of Language	Shows overall clarity and fluency; uses precise, evaluative words; makes few mechanical errors	Shows good sentence variety; uses some precise evaluative terms; makes some mechanical errors	Uses awkward or overly simple sentence structures and vague evaluative terms; makes many mechanical errors	Presents incomplete thoughts; makes mechanical errors that create confusion

_____
_____
_____
_____

Publishing and Presenting

14. If you were to post your essay on a library bulletin board, what kind of eye-catching picture would you use to attract attention to it?

    _____

15. How did writing about this poem help you appreciate its humor?

    _____
    _____
    _____
    _____

Name _____ Date _____

Assessment for Chapter 12: Response to Literature
Test 3

In this test, you will be asked to draft an essay of three or four paragraphs. Compare and contrast these two poems, highlighting the meaning of the poems and their specific features. If necessary, use a separate sheet of paper to complete your responses.

Stopping by Woods on a Snowy Evening
By *Robert Frost*

Whose woods are these I think I know,
His house is in the village though;
He will not see me stopping here
To watch his woods fill up with snow.

My little horse must think it queer
To stop without a farmhouse near
Between the woods and frozen lake
The darkest evening of the year.

He gives his harness bells a shake
To ask if there is some mistake.
The only other sound's the sweep
Of easy wind and downy flake.

The woods are lovely, dark, and deep,
But I have promises to keep,
And miles to go before I sleep,
And miles to go before I sleep.

Winter
By *Nikki Giovanni*

Frogs burrow the mud
snails bury themselves
and I air my quilt
preparing for the cold

Dogs grow more hair
mothers make oatmeal
and little boys and girls
take Father John's Medicine

Bears store fat
chipmunks gather nuts
and I collect books
for the coming winter

Prewriting

1. Complete the hexagon to gather details about your response to each poem.

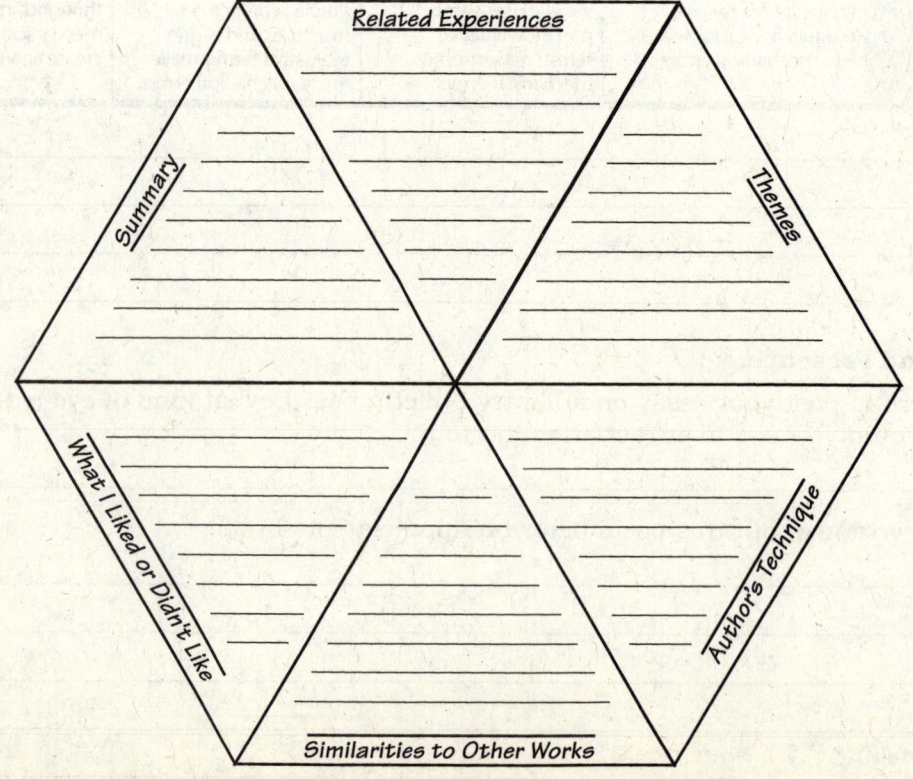

90 • Chapter 12: Response to Literature © Prentice-Hall, Inc.

Name _____

Drafting

2. Think about the speakers in the two poems. How are they alike? How are they different?

   • Similarities: _____
   _____

   • Differences: _____
   _____

3. On a separate sheet of paper, use your notes and information from the graphic organizer to draft your comparison-and-contrast essay. Include at least one direct quotation from each poem in your draft.

Revising

4. Review your draft. Circle your strongest point—the one that is most interesting or that summarizes the other ideas. Write it on the lines below. Then, make sure it is at a memorable place in your essay, such as the end.
   _____
   _____

5. Find a place in your draft where you can add a detail using one of these connecting words or phrases that explain *why* something happened or *why* you came to a particular conclusion. Write your new sentence below and circle the connecting word.

as a result of	since
because	so that
despite	due to

   _____
   _____

6. Find three general words in your draft (such as *good* or *bad*). Write them below. Then, write three precise words that could replace them.

   General: _____ _____ _____

   Precise: _____ _____ _____

Editing and Proofreading

7. Imagine that you are proofreading another student's comparison of two different poems. Here is part of his draft. Use proofreading marks to correct errors in spelling and punctuation of quotations.

   It seems that flowers are common images in Bashō's haiku. In one line, he writes about 'sweet plum blossoms,' and in another he writes that "fragrant blossoms remane. Blossoms seems to mean beuty and beginings.

   Now, review your draft for errors in spelling and punctuation of quotations. Write the errors and corrections on the lines. If your draft does not contain these kinds of errors, write *none*.
   _____
   _____

Name _____

8. Evaluate your draft based on the criteria in the rubric below. List any changes that you may need to make to improve your essay.

	Score 4	Score 3	Score 2	Score 1
Audience and Purpose	Presents sufficient background on the work(s); presents the writer's reactions forcefully	Presents background on the work(s); presents the writer's reactions clearly	Presents some background on the work(s); presents the writer's reactions at points	Presents little or no background on the work(s); presents few of the writer's reactions
Organization	Presents points in logical order, smoothly connecting them to the overall focus	Presents points in logical order and connects many to the overall focus	Organizes points poorly in places; connects some points to an overall focus	Presents information in a scattered, disorganized manner
Elaboration	Supports reactions and evaluations with elaborated reasons and well-chosen examples	Supports reactions and evaluations with specific reasons and examples	Supports some reactions and evaluations with reasons and examples	Offers little support for reactions and evaluations
Use of Language	Shows overall clarity and fluency; uses precise, evaluative words; makes few mechanical errors	Shows good sentence variety; uses some precise evaluative terms; makes some mechanical errors	Uses awkward or overly simple sentence structures and vague evaluative terms; makes many mechanical errors	Presents incomplete thoughts; makes mechanical errors that create confusion

_____
_____
_____
_____
_____
_____
_____

Publishing and Presenting

9. What kind of magazine or newspaper might publish your essay?
_____
_____
_____

10. How did comparing and contrasting these poems help you to better understand them?
_____
_____
_____
_____
_____
_____
_____
_____
_____
_____
_____

Name _____   Date _____

 # Assessment for Chapter 13: Writing for Assessment
Test 1

In this test, you will be asked to draft a three-paragraph essay. If necessary, use a separate sheet of paper to complete your responses. On a math test, your teacher asks you to show that you understand a mathematical process by writing about it. Here is your writing prompt:

> Explain the process of long division. Use the problem 379 divided by 7 to show that you understand the steps.

Prewriting

1. What type of writing does the prompt require? Circle the correct answer.
   a. persuasive writing
   b. comparison-and-contrast writing
   c. response to literature
   d. cause-and-effect writing

2. Find the key words in the prompt above. Write them below. Then, explain the purpose of this essay.
   _____
   _____
   _____

3. How should you begin the writing process for the prompt above? Circle the letter of the correct answer.
   a. Take a position to defend the presentation of the math problem.
   b. Think of something to compare and contrast with your topic.
   c. Focus on writing clear and complete sentences about the math problem.
   d. Solve the math problem, and list the steps as you do so.

4. Use the space below to begin the writing process based on your answer to the previous question.
   _____
   _____
   _____
   _____
   _____

Drafting

5. Make a sequence of steps to plan your organization. You may add more steps if necessary.
   First, _____
   Then, _____
   Next, _____
   Next, _____
   Next, _____
   Finally, _____

6. On a separate sheet of paper, use your notes to draft your essay.

© Prentice-Hall, Inc.

Name _____

Revising

7. Evaluate your introductory sentence to make sure that it clearly states what your essay explains. If not, write a new introductory sentence below. If it does, revise the sentence to capture the reader's interest more effectively.
   _____
   _____
   _____

8. Does your concluding sentence restate what you have explained? If not, write a new concluding sentence below. If it does, revise the sentence to present a final thought about your subject.
   _____
   _____
   _____

9. Circle three transition words in your draft—such as *then, next, after,* or *finally*—that show the connections between steps. If they are missing, insert them and circle them. On the lines, write the new sentences you have created.
   _____
   _____
   _____
   _____
   _____

10. Find two words in your draft that could be more precise. Write them below. Then, write two replacement words—words that "show, don't tell"—that would improve your writing.

    <u>General Words</u>   <u>More Precise Words</u>
    _____   _____
    _____   _____

Editing and Proofreading

11. Find the sentence fragment and correct it on the line below.

    The number 9. Bring it down by the side. Then, divide 29 by 7.
    _____
    _____

12. Now, review your draft for sentence fragments. Write corrections on the lines. If your draft does not contain fragments, write *none*.
    _____
    _____
    _____
    _____
    _____

Name _____

13. Evaluate your draft based on the criteria in the rubric below. List any changes that you may need to make to improve your essay.

	Score 4	Score 3	Score 2	Score 1
Audience and Purpose	Uses word choices and supporting details appropriate to the specified audience; clearly addresses writing prompt	Mostly uses word choices and supporting details appropriate to the specified audience; adequately addresses prompt	Uses some inappropriate word choices and details; addresses writing prompt	Uses inappropriate word choices and details; does not address writing prompt
Organization	Presents a clear, consistent organizational strategy	Presents a clear organizational strategy with few inconsistencies	Presents an inconsistent organizational strategy	Shows a lack of organizational strategy
Elaboration	Adequately supports the thesis; elaborates on each idea; links all details to the thesis	Supports the thesis; elaborates on most ideas; links most information to the thesis	Partially supports the thesis; does not elaborate on some ideas	Provides no thesis; does not elaborate on ideas
Use of Language	Uses excellent sentence variety and vocabulary; includes very few mechanical errors	Uses adequate sentence variety and vocabulary; includes few mechanical errors	Uses repetitive sentence structure and vocabulary; includes some mechanical errors	Demonstrates poor use of language; includes many mechanical errors

_____
_____
_____
_____
_____
_____
_____

Publishing and Presenting

14. For you, what is the hardest part of taking tests that ask for written answers?
_____
_____
_____

15. Which writing strategy from this chapter did you find most useful for writing for assessment? Why?
_____
_____
_____
_____
_____
_____
_____
_____
_____
_____

Name _____ Date _____

 # Assessment for Chapter 13:
Writing for Assessment
Test 2

In this test, you will be asked to draft a three-paragraph essay. If necessary, use a separate sheet of paper to complete your responses. On a test in physical education, your teacher asks you to show that you understand the rules of a game by writing about it. Here is your writing prompt:

> Explain the rules of basketball. (Note: If you don't know how to play basketball, you may choose another team sport or a different activity that you enjoy.)

Prewriting

1. What type of writing does this prompt require? Circle the correct answer.
   a. persuasive writing
   b. comparison-and-contrast writing
   c. response to literature
   d. how-to essay

2. Find the key words in the prompt above. Write them on the line. Then, explain the purpose of the essay.
   _____
   _____

3. How should you begin the writing process for the prompt above? Circle the letter of the correct answer.
   a. Take a position to defend.
   b. Think of something to compare and contrast with your topic.
   c. Focus on writing clear and complete sentences.
   d. List details that belong in your writing.

4. Use the space below to begin the writing process based on your answer to the previous question.
   _____
   _____
   _____
   _____
   _____
   _____

Drafting

5. Make a quick outline to plan your organization. You may add more numbers if necessary.
   1. _____
   2. _____
   3. _____
   4. _____
   5. _____

6. On a separate sheet of paper, use your notes to draft your essay.

Name _____

Revising

7. Does your introductory sentence clearly state what your draft explains? If not, write a new introductory sentence below. If it does, revise the sentence to capture your reader's interest more effectively.

   _____
   _____
   _____

8. Does your concluding sentence restate what you have explained? If not, write a new concluding sentence below. If it does, revise the sentence to present a final thought about your subject.

   _____
   _____
   _____

9. Circle three transition words in your draft—such as *next, for this reason*, or *before*—that show the connections between sentences. If they are missing, insert them and circle them. On the lines, write the new sentences that you have created.

   _____
   _____
   _____
   _____
   _____

10. Find three words in your draft that could be more precise or vivid. Write them below. Then, write three replacement words—words that "show, don't tell"—that would improve your writing.

    General Words   More Precise Words

    _____   _____
    _____   _____
    _____   _____

Editing and Proofreading

11. Find the sentence fragment, and correct it on the lines below.

    Soccer is an action-packed sport. Two teams of eleven players each. The teams line up in three lines on a field, facing each other. One player on each side defends the goal.

    _____
    _____

12. Now, review your draft for sentence fragments. Write corrections on the lines. If your draft does not contain fragments, write *none*.

    _____
    _____
    _____

Name _____

13. Evaluate your draft based on the criteria in the rubric below. List any changes that you may need to make to improve your essay.

	Score 4	Score 3	Score 2	Score 1
Audience and Purpose	Uses word choices and supporting details appropriate to the specified audience; clearly addresses writing prompt	Mostly uses word choices and supporting details appropriate to the specified audience; adequately addresses prompt	Uses some inappropriate word choices and details; addresses writing prompt	Uses inappropriate word choices and details; does not address writing prompt
Organization	Presents a clear, consistent organizational strategy	Presents a clear organizational strategy with few inconsistencies	Presents an inconsistent organizational strategy	Shows a lack of organizational strategy
Elaboration	Adequately supports the thesis; elaborates on each idea; links all details to the thesis	Supports the thesis; elaborates on most ideas; links most information to the thesis	Partially supports the thesis; does not elaborate on some ideas	Provides no thesis; does not elaborate on ideas
Use of Language	Uses excellent sentence variety and vocabulary; includes very few mechanical errors	Uses adequate sentence variety and vocabulary; includes few mechanical errors	Uses repetitive sentence structure and vocabulary; includes some mechanical errors	Demonstrates poor use of language; includes many mechanical errors

_____
_____
_____
_____
_____
_____
_____

Publishing and Presenting

14. For you, what is the hardest part of taking tests that ask for written answers?
_____
_____
_____

15. Which writing strategy from this chapter did you find most useful for writing for assessment? Why?
_____
_____
_____
_____
_____
_____
_____
_____
_____

Name _____ Date _____

Assessment for Chapter 13: Writing for Assessment
Test 3

In this test, you will be asked to draft an essay of three or four paragraphs. If necessary, use a separate sheet of paper to complete your responses. On a test in science, your teacher asks you to show that you understand a life cycle by writing about it. Here is your writing prompt:

> Explain how a caterpillar turns into a butterfly.

Prewriting

1. What type of writing does this prompt require? Circle the correct answer.
   a. persuasive writing
   b. comparison-and-contrast writing
   c. response to literature
   d. cause-and-effect writing

2. Find the key words in the prompt above. Write them on the line. Then, explain the purpose of the essay.
   _____

3. How should you approach the writing process for the prompt above? Circle the letter of the correct answer.
   a. Take a position to defend.
   b. Think of something to compare and contrast with your topic.
   c. Focus on writing clear and complete sentences.
   d. List the details that belong in your writing.

4. Use the space below to begin the writing process based on your answer to the previous question.
   _____
   _____
   _____
   _____
   _____
   _____
   _____

Drafting

5. Plan the organization of your essay by writing the steps in a logical sequence. You may add more steps if necessary.

   First, _____
   Then, _____
   Next, _____
   Next, _____
   Next, _____
   Finally, _____

6. On a separate sheet of paper, use your notes to draft your essay.

© Prentice-Hall, Inc.   Chapter 13: Writing for Assessment • 99

Name _____

Revising

7. Does your introductory sentence clearly state what your draft explains? If not, write a new introductory sentence below. If it does, revise the sentence to capture your reader's attention more effectively.

   _____
   _____
   _____

8. For each paragraph in your essay, list the main idea and one detail that supports it.

   _____
   _____
   _____
   _____

9. Circle three transition words in your draft that show the connections between sentences. If the transition words are missing, insert them and circle them. On the lines, write the new sentences you have created.

   _____
   _____
   _____
   _____
   _____
   _____

10. Find three words in your draft that could be more precise or vivid. Write them below. Then, write three replacement words—words that "show, don't tell"—that would improve your writing.

    General Words   More Precise Words

    _____   _____
    _____   _____
    _____   _____

Editing and Proofreading

11. Find the sentence fragment and correct it on the line below.

        A butterfly begins as an egg. After the larvae grow big enough. They break out of their shells. This can take a few days or a few weeks.

    _____
    _____

12. Now, review your draft for sentence fragments. Write corrections on the lines. If your draft does not contain fragments, write *none*.

    _____
    _____
    _____
    _____
    _____

Name _____

13. Evaluate your draft based on the criteria in the rubric below. List any changes that you may need to make to improve your essay.

	Score 4	Score 3	Score 2	Score 1
Audience and Purpose	Uses word choices and supporting details appropriate to the specified audience; clearly addresses writing prompt	Mostly uses word choices and supporting details appropriate to the specified audience; adequately addresses prompt	Uses some inappropriate word choices and details; addresses writing prompt	Uses inappropriate word choices and details; does not address writing prompt
Organization	Presents a clear, consistent organizational strategy	Presents a clear organizational strategy with few inconsistencies	Presents an inconsistent organizational strategy	Shows a lack of organizational strategy
Elaboration	Adequately supports the thesis; elaborates on each idea; links all details to the thesis	Supports the thesis; elaborates on most ideas; links most information to the thesis	Partially supports the thesis; does not elaborate on some ideas	Provides no thesis; does not elaborate on ideas
Use of Language	Uses excellent sentence variety and vocabulary; includes very few mechanical errors	Uses adequate sentence variety and vocabulary; includes few mechanical errors	Uses repetitive sentence structure and vocabulary; includes some mechanical errors	Demonstrates poor use of language; includes many mechanical errors

_____
_____
_____
_____
_____
_____
_____

Publishing and Presenting

14. Which writing strategy from this chapter did you find most useful for writing for assessment? Why?
_____
_____
_____

15. Which strategy might you apply when writing other types of essays? Why?
_____
_____
_____
_____
_____
_____
_____
_____
_____

Part 2:
Grammar, Usage, and Mechanics

Name _____ Date _____

Grammar, Usage, and Mechanics: Cumulative Diagnostic Test

Part 1: Identifying Parts of Speech
On the line after each sentence, identify the part of speech of the underlined word. Choose from these parts of speech: *noun, pronoun, verb, adjective, adverb, preposition, conjunction,* or *interjection.*

1. Frogs <u>are</u> tiny animals. _____
2. Varieties of frogs come in many sizes <u>and</u> colors. _____
3. Perhaps the smallest of all frogs <u>lives</u> in Brazil. _____
4. This small frog has a body length <u>of</u> less than four tenths of an inch, not counting its legs. _____
5. This largest of all frogs has a body length of <u>almost</u> twelve inches. _____
6. The West African goliath frog is the name of the largest known <u>type</u> of frog. _____
7. Many frogs have <u>smooth</u>, moist skin. _____
8. <u>Who</u> has seen the rough skins of frogs in less humid environments? _____
9. Some small tree frogs have thin, <u>transparent</u> skin on their undersides. _____
10. <u>Wow</u>! I can see the heart and other organs through the skin of this frog. _____

Part 2: Identifying Parts of Sentences
On the line after each sentence, identify the underlined section as one of the following: *sentence, fragment, complete subject, complete predicate, direct object, indirect object, predicate noun,* or *predicate adjective.*

11. Leaping is the <u>way</u> most frogs move. _____
12. <u>Long and powerful back legs.</u> _____
13. A frog's movement <u>begins in a crouch.</u> _____
14. From the crouch, the frog straightens its rear <u>legs</u>. _____
15. <u>It</u> is then propelled through the air. _____
16. <u>Many tree frogs</u> have adhesive disks on the ends of their fingers and toes. _____
17. Tree frogs <u>can leap from branch to branch or from leaf to leaf.</u> _____
18. That frog's leap seemed very <u>bold</u>. _____
19. <u>Certain species of frogs burrow into the ground.</u> _____
20. "Please show <u>me</u> all your tree frogs," said Kimberly to the salesperson. _____

© Prentice-Hall, Inc.

Name _____

Part 3: Identifying Phrases and Clauses
On the line after each sentence, identify the underlined section as one of the following: *prepositional phrase used as an adjective, prepositional phrase used as an adverb, appositive, appositive phrase, participle, participial phrase, infinitive, independent clause, adjective clause,* or *adverb clause.*

21. <u>Moving forward by a series of short hops</u>, that frog crossed the path. _____

22. That hopping frog, <u>Michael's favorite pet</u>, has relatively short back legs. _____

23. Although many frogs are plain in color, <u>some species have brilliant markings</u>. _____

24. The frogs <u>that are at the pet store</u> are fairly expensive. _____

25. <u>Colored</u> frogs are rarely just one color. _____

26. Michael's pet frog, <u>Hoppy</u>, is bright blue and yellow. _____

27. The markings of a frog may seem bold <u>when the frog is seen outside its natural habitat</u>. _____

28. Frogs' markings can hide the frog <u>in its environment</u>. _____

29. Poisonous frogs are brightly colored as a warning <u>to predators</u>. _____

30. Frogs are able <u>to inhabit</u> most regions of the world. _____

Part 4: Usage: Effective Sentences
Follow the directions for each item. Write your response on the line provided. If necessary, use a separate sheet of paper to complete your responses.

31. Write whether the following is a *declarative sentence,* an *interrogative sentence,* an *imperative sentence,* or an *exclamatory sentence.*

    Have you ever seen a frog that is twelve inches long?
    _____

32. Combine these two sentences by using a compound subject.

    Jerome is doing a report on poison dart frogs. Monica is doing a report on poison dart frogs.
    _____

33. Combine these two sentences by using a compound verb.

    Frogs croak. Frogs leap.
    _____

34. Combine these sentences by using a compound object.

    Heather bought a bright blue frog. Heather bought a yellow frog.
    _____

35. Combine these sentences by joining the clauses with a comma and a conjunction.

    Frogs in tropical climates may be active all year. Many species breed only in certain seasons.
    _____

Name _____

36. Combine these sentences by using a semicolon.

   Jason bought three poison dart frogs. He keeps them in an aquarium in his room.

   _____

37. Combine these sentences by using a subordinating conjunction to change one of the sentences into a subordinate clause.

   Todd takes good care of his collection of frogs. The frogs are very healthy.

   _____

38. Identify what is missing in this sentence fragment, and then rewrite it as a complete sentence.

   Frogs in their natural surroundings.

   _____

39. Rewrite this sentence to avoid using a misplaced modifier.

   Leaping many times its own body length, Rob was amazed at the frog's ability.

   _____

40. If there are any errors in this sentence, rewrite it correctly. If the sentence is correct as written, write *correct*.

   Janice didn't have no blue frogs in her collection because she couldn't find none.

   _____

Part 5: Using Verbs

Follow the directions for each item. Write your response on the line provided. If necessary, use a separate sheet of paper to complete your responses.

41. Identify the principal part in the underlined verb as *present*, *present participle*, *past*, or *past participle*.

   Tasmania is located about 150 miles south of the state of Victoria in Australia.

   _____

42. Identify the principal part used to form the underlined verb as *present*, *present participle*, *past*, or *past participle*.

   We are planning to visit Tasmania on our Australian tour.

   _____

43. Rewrite this sentence, using the principal part of the verb indicated in parentheses.

   Tasmania is (separate—past participle) from the rest of Australia by a strait.

   _____

44. Rewrite this sentence, using the principal part of the verb indicated in parentheses.

   Have you (speak—past participle) to your Australian friend lately?

   _____

45. Rewrite this sentence, supplying the complete verb in the tense indicated in parentheses.

   Before 1856, people (know—past perfect) Tasmania as Van Diemen's Land.

   _____

46. Rewrite the sentence, supplying the complete verb in the tense indicated in parentheses.

   By the end of our trip, we (visit—future perfect) four of Australia's states.

   _____

Name _____

47. Rewrite this sentence, supplying the complete verb in the tense indicated in parentheses.

   Jake (study—present perfect progressive) the history of Australia.
   _____

48. Rewrite this sentence, supplying the complete verb in the tense indicated in parentheses.

   Suzie (write—past) to her Australian pen pal.
   _____

49. If the sentence has a misused verb, rewrite the sentence correctly. If the sentence does not have a misused verb, write *correct*.

   We tried to join the tour group, but they had already went.
   _____

50. If the sentence has a misused verb, rewrite the sentence correctly. If the sentence does not have a misused verb, write *correct*.

   Have you seen my guidebook on Tasmania?
   _____

Part 6: Using Pronouns
Follow the directions for each item. Write your response on the line provided.

51. Select the correct pronoun from the choices in parentheses. Write it on the line, and then tell its case.

   Mark and (she, her) live in the Australian state of Tasmania, named for explorer Abel Tasman. _____

52. Identify the case of the underlined pronoun as *nominative*, *objective*, or *possessive*.

   Abel Tasman was a Dutch navigator; he was the first European to discover the island off the southern coast of Australia. _____

53. Identify the case of the underlined pronoun as *nominative*, *objective*, or *possessive*.

   Van Diemen, the governor of the East Indies, spoke to Tasman and sent him on a voyage of exploration. _____

54. Write the nominative pronoun, and tell how it is used.

   The island of Tasmania is spectacular to us. It has beautiful mountain, lake, and coastal scenery. _____

55. Write the nominative pronoun, and tell how it is used.

   The explorer of Tasmania in 1642 was he, Abel Tasman. _____

56. Add an appropriate nominative pronoun to the sentence. Then, tell how the pronoun is used.

   _____ are doing a report on the animals of Tasmania. _____

Name _____

57. Add an appropriate nominative pronoun to the sentence. Then, tell how the pronoun is used.

    _____ is doing research about the Tasmanian

    devil. _____

58. Write the objective pronoun, and tell how it is used.

    Dan is reading about the wombats of Tasmania; he had never heard of them

    before. _____

59. Write the objective pronoun, and tell how it is used.

    Sally read me an article about kangaroos. _____

60. Select the correct pronoun from the choices in parentheses. Write it on the line, and then tell its case.

    Tasmania is known for the diversity of (it's, its) natural resources.

    _____

Part 7: Making Words Agree
Follow the directions for each item.

61. Choose the correct verb from the pair in parentheses, and write it on the line.

    Reptiles (is, are) vertebrates, or animals with backbones. _____

62. Choose the correct verb from the pair in parentheses, and write it on the line.

    A reptile (get, gets) oxygen by breathing air. _____

63. Choose the correct verb from the pair in parentheses, and write it on the line.

    Either dry scales or hard plates (cover, covers) reptiles'

    bodies. _____

64. Choose the correct verb from the pair in parentheses, and write it on the line.

    Alligators and turtles (is, are) water reptiles. _____

65. If the subject and verb do not agree in number, rewrite the sentence correctly. If the sentence is correct, write correct.

    Sea snakes, like every other water reptile, has lungs, not gills.

    _____

66. Write the subject in the sentence. Choose the correct verb from the pair in parentheses, and write it next to the subject.

    There (is, are) some snakes that can stay underwater for up to eight

    hours. _____

67. Choose the correct verb from the pair in parentheses and write it on the line.

    Most of the freshwater snakes (come, comes) out of the water often. _____

Name _____

68. Complete this sentence, adding a verb that makes sense. Make sure the verb you use agrees with the subject.

   Some kinds of snakes _____ in the fresh waters of lakes, rivers, and streams.

69. Complete this sentence, filling in the blank with an appropriate pronoun.

   During _____ vacation in Florida, Jane saw an alligator.

70. Choose the correct personal pronoun from the choices given in parentheses, and write it on the line.

   Freshwater snakes go into the water to hide from (its, their) enemies.

   _____

Part 8: Using Modifiers
Follow the directions for each item.

71. Write the comparative and superlative degrees of the following modifier.

   fast _____

72. Write the comparative and superlative degrees of the following modifier.

   sweetly _____

   _____

73. Rewrite this sentence, supplying the form of the modifier indicated in parentheses.

   Alligators are (small—comparative) than crocodiles.

   _____

74. Rewrite this sentence, supplying the form of the modifier indicated in parentheses.

   A crocodile's snout is (pointed—comparative) than an alligator's snout.

   _____

75. Write the degree of the underlined modifier.

   One of the <u>most dangerous</u> snakes in the United States is the cottonmouth.

   _____

76. If the sentence has an error in degree, rewrite it correctly. If the sentence has no errors, write *correct*.

   A cottonmouth is most dangerous than the northern water snake.

   _____

77. The underlined modifier is used incorrectly. Rewrite the sentence, correcting the misused modifier.

   Of all the reptiles, the turtle <u>only</u> has a shell.

   _____

78. The underlined modifier is used incorrectly. Rewrite the sentence, correcting the misused modifier.

   If you are bitten by a cottonmouth, you will undoubtedly react <u>bad</u>.

   _____

Name _____

79. If the sentence has an error in the use of modifiers, rewrite the sentence correctly. If the sentence has no errors, write *correct*.

    Allison just has one turtle in her aquarium.

80. If the sentence has an error in the use of modifiers, rewrite the sentence correctly. If the sentence has no errors, write *correct*.

    The pet shop has fewer snakes than turtles.

Part 9: Using Punctuation Marks
Follow the directions for each item. If necessary, use a separate sheet of paper to complete your responses.

81. Rewrite this sentence, adding a comma where it is needed.

    Fish can breathe underwater but water reptiles must swim to the surface to breathe.

82. Rewrite this sentence, adding commas where they are needed.

    Water reptiles include alligators turtles and certain kinds of snakes.

83. If the sentence requires a comma, rewrite it, adding the comma. If the sentence is correct, write *correct*.

    Most reptiles have long low bodies.

84. Rewrite this sentence, adding or removing commas as appropriate.

    Because a sea turtle, cannot pull its head legs and tail into its shell it cannot protect itself easily.

85. Rewrite this sentence, adding or removing commas as appropriate.

    Listen Carmen while I tell you about crocodiles alligators green turtles and snapping turtles.

86. Rewrite this sentence, adding commas to set off the parenthetical expression.

    The green turtle in my opinion should be protected from its human enemies.

87. Rewrite this sentence, adding commas where necessary.

    I bought my pet turtle on June 18 2001 and my iguana arrived one month later.

88. Rewrite this sentence, adding commas and quotation marks if necessary. If the sentence is correct, write *correct*.

    Snapping turtles said Ed are omnivores, which means they eat plants as well as animals.

Name _____

89. Rewrite this sentence, adding commas and quotation marks if necessary. If the sentence is correct, write *correct*.

   Lydia wondered if it was dangerous to bother a snapping turtle.
   _____

90. Rewrite this sentence, adding hyphens if necessary. If the sentence is correct, write *correct*.

   On his scuba diving trip, Dan saw fifty two green turtles.
   _____

Part 10: Capitalization
On the line after each sentence, rewrite the sentence, adding and deleting capital letters as necessary.

91. have You ever seen a marine iguana?
   _____

92. The marine iguana, i understand, is the only Lizard that lives both in the Sea and on the land.
   _____

93. my friends richard and sandra are helping Me with a report on Lizards.
   _____

94. Marine iguanas are found only on the galápagos islands in the pacific ocean.
   _____

95. Alligators can be found in the southern part of the united states and in china.
   _____

96. In this Cookbook for french food, I found a good recipe for Turtle Soup.
   _____

97. According to the article "Alligators And crocodiles," american Crocodiles are about twelve feet long.
   _____

98. My Dentist, dr. Sam Mallory, has two iguanas at home on fourth street.
   _____

99. Dave asked, "have you ever touched an iguana, mom?"
   _____

100. We read about Reptiles in my Biology class last january.
   _____

Name _____ Date _____

 **Assessment for Chapter 14: Nouns and Pronouns**

Part 1: Identifying Common and Proper Nouns
Identify each noun in the sentences. Tell if each is a *common noun* or a *proper noun*.
1. Mount Fuji is a beautiful volcano in Japan.
   _____

2. The mountain stands in the province of Honshu, a short distance from the Pacific Ocean.
   _____

3. The Japanese admire its almost perfect shape and consider its silhouette the ultimate symbol of beauty.
   _____

4. A volcanic peak, Fuji is covered with snow for a good part of the year.
   _____

5. The lower slopes of the mountain are covered in lush vegetation.
   _____

6. An English traveler named John Morris visited Mount Fuji some time ago.
   _____

7. The Englishman was there just before the start of World War II.
   _____

8. At that time, he said that the peak was best seen from the sea at dawn.
   _____

9. Mr. Morris spoke of "its perfect snow-capped cone."
   _____

10. In the light of early morning, said Morris, Fuji appears suspended in the sky.
    _____

Part 2: Identifying Compound and Collective Nouns
Identify the compound and collective nouns in the sentences. Tell whether each one is *compound* or *collective*.
11. A group of sightseers, accompanied by two guides, approached Mount Fuji.
    _____

12. "I have seen a couple of volcanoes before," said one tourist, "but you could search a lifetime and never see one as beautiful as this."
    _____

13. "Have you ever seen this view at sunrise?" asked one of the guides on the team.
    _____

14. A large crowd of tourists walked through the countryside, admiring the volcano.
    _____

15. Our class found out that Mount Fuji was probably formed after a massive earthquake.
    _____

© Prentice-Hall, Inc.   Chapter 14: Nouns and Pronouns • 113

Name _____

16. Outpourings from several cones helped form Fuji's present shape, the pair of guides said.
_____

17. Jeff's family owns a painting of Mount Fuji originally bought by his great-grandmother.
_____

18. The painting shows the mountain in the background and a herd of cattle in the foreground.
_____

19. A committee of art critics said it was an exceptional landscape.
_____

20. From the top of Mount Fuji, our hiking club admired the sunset.
_____

Part 3: Identifying Pronouns
Write each underlined pronoun on the line. Tell whether the pronoun is *personal*, *demonstrative*, *interrogative*, or *indefinite*. For personal, demonstrative, and indefinite pronouns, indicate whether the pronoun is *singular* or *plural*. For personal pronouns, also indicate whether the pronoun is *first person*, *second person*, or *third person*.

21. <u>Which</u> of these two pictures of Mount Fuji looks better?
_____

22. Mount Fuji is currently dormant; <u>it</u> last erupted in 1707.
_____

23. "If <u>we</u> could go to Japan, would you like to see Mount Fuji?" asked Sam.
_____

24. "Well, wouldn't <u>you</u> put a trip to Mount Fuji at the top of your list?" said Judy to Sam.
_____

25. "<u>Who</u> gave the volcano the name Fuji?" Sam asked.
_____

26. Have you heard about the ancient Ainu tribes of Japan? It was <u>they</u> who named the snow-capped peak.
_____

27. <u>This</u> happened centuries before the Japanese colonized the country about two thousand years ago.
_____

28. <u>These</u> are facts I read about in a history book.
_____

29. Here is <u>something</u> you may not know: five paths lead to the top of Mount Fuji.
_____

30. <u>Anybody</u> who wants to climb the mountain can do so.
_____

Name _____

Part 4: Identifying Pronouns and Antecedents

Identify the pronoun or pronouns in each sentence below. Then, identify each antecedent. You may need to go to previous sentences to find the antecedent.

(31) Sharon pointed to a beautiful picture and said, "This shows Mount Fuji. (32) It was created by the great Japanese painter Katsushika Hokusai. (33) He lived from 1760 to 1849."

(34) "How do you know this information?" asked Spencer. (35) "We went to the same classes, and I don't remember learning this."

(36) "Well," Sharon told him, "I did my most recent term paper on Japanese art. (37) On what subject was yours?"

(38) "Mine was on volcanoes," Spencer told her. (39) "My partner was Harry, and we learned a great deal about Mount Fuji. (40) However, we didn't learn about the art inspired by the beautiful sight."

31. _____
32. _____
33. _____
34. _____
35. _____
36. _____
37. _____
38. _____
39. _____
40. _____

Part 5: Standardized Test Practice

Read the paragraph. Choose the pronoun that correctly completes each sentence. Circle the letter for your answer.

Diane was one of (41) who climbed Mount Fuji last summer. (42) planned well for her trip. She consulted with Brian, who is a travel consultant. (43) described the best bargains he could find for (44). Then Diane spoke to her parents. (45) had made the trip many years ago. "(46) is what you must do," they told her. "(47) must get a good pair of hiking boots. After you do (48), you'll be all set."

Brian handed Diane a pile of travel brochures. "Read (49)," he said. "(50) will tell you all you need to know."

41 A these
    B many
    C whom
    D either

42 F She
    G He
    H It
    J They

Name _____

43 A She
    B Them
    C He
    D Several

44 F me
    G nobody
    H what
    J her

45 A They
    B Them
    C Somebody
    D Those

46 F Which
    G Nothing
    H This
    J These

47 A That
    B He
    C We
    D You

48 F those
    G that
    H something
    J theirs

49 A these
    B it
    C ours
    D anything

50 F She
    G We
    H It
    J They

Name _____   Date _____

 **Assessment for Chapter 15: Verbs**

Part 1
Underline each action verb. Then, identify it as *transitive* or *intransitive*. If it is transitive, write the noun toward which the action is directed.

1. Rugged inland mountains form the center of each major island of Hawaii. _____

2. Valleys in Hawaii lead out to narrow coastal flatlands. _____

3. Coconuts and bananas thrive in abundance on the islands. _____

4. Captain James Cook's first two voyages took him to the South Pacific. _____

5. He entered the ocean for his first voyage in January 1769. _____

6. His second voyage lasted from 1772 to 1775. _____

7. On his second voyage, he covered nearly 65,000 miles in southern waters. _____

8. During these voyages, he never saw the Hawaiian Islands. _____

9. On his third voyage, he traveled from the Society Islands to the west coast of North America. _____

10. On January 18, 1778, during his third voyage, Cook finally encountered the Hawaiian Islands. _____

Part 2
Underline the linking verb in each sentence. Then, draw an arrow connecting the words that are linked by the verb.

11. Kamehameha I was a great ruler in Hawaii.

12. In the 1790s, Honolulu became an important port for visiting ships.

13. Kamehameha had been wise to move his court to Honolulu.

14. Honolulu grew very important as the center of commerce.

15. The city has remained busy to the present day.

16. Kamehameha felt comfortable in Honolulu from 1804 to 1812.

17. By 1812, he had become an elderly man.

18. His home island of Hawaii seemed more suitable to him.

19. After Kamehameha's death in 1819, his son was ready to take over.

20. A few years later, on a visit to England, the son grew quite ill.

© Prentice-Hall, Inc.

Name _____

Part 3
On the line, write the verb phrase from each sentence. Then, underline the main verb and circle the helping verb.

21. Kamehameha's son and his wife had visited England in 1824. _____

22. While there, they must have been exposed to measles. _____

23. They might have survived with better medicine. _____

24. Unfortunately, in those days, nothing could be done for them. _____

25. The deceased ruler was succeeded by his young brother, Kamehameha III. _____

26. Born in 1813, Kamehameha III would have been eleven years old in 1824. _____

27. Despite his age, he did rule from 1824 until his death in 1854. _____

28. American influence in Hawaii would remain important during Kamehameha III's reign. _____

29. The United States could not permit any other nation's intrusion in Hawaii. _____

30. This policy would eventually lead to Hawaii's annexation in 1898. _____

Part 4
Identify the underlined verb as a *linking* verb or an *action* verb. If it is an action verb, identify it as *mental* or *visible* action.

31. The principal Hawaiian Islands <u>are</u> Hawaii, Maui, Oahu, Kauai, Molokai, Lanai, Niihau, and Kahoolawe. _____

32. In 1835, Hawaii's first successful sugar plantation <u>opened</u> at Koloa on the island of Kauai. _____

33. On August 21, 1959, Hawaii <u>became</u> the fiftieth state. _____

34. Most people throughout the United States <u>favored</u> Hawaii's statehood. _____

35. Hawaii <u>is</u> the location of the two most active volcanoes on earth. _____

36. Bird watchers <u>can appreciate</u> the interesting variety of birds in Hawaii. _____

37. A scuba diver <u>might be surprised</u> by the beauty of the fish in Hawaiian waters. _____

38. About six hundred species of fish <u>live</u> in the ocean near Hawaii. _____

39. Islanders <u>planted</u> Hawaii's first pineapples in 1813. _____

40. The Hawaiian word *aloha* <u>can be understood</u> in several ways.

Name _____

Part 5: Standardized Test Practice
Read each passage, and choose the letter of the word or group of words that belongs in each space. Circle the letter of your answer.

> At one time, native Hawaiian plants ____(41)____ of about eighteen hundred species. About ninety-six percent of those ____(42)____ nowhere else in the world. Today, however, most of these native plants ____(43)____. If they survive, native plants ____(44)____ now in remote places that are untouched by progress.

41 A consist
    B consisting
    C consisted
    D will consist

42 F existing
    G will be existing
    H will exist
    J existed

43 A exterminated
    B will be exterminated
    C exterminating
    D have been exterminated

44 F grow
    G growing
    H grew
    J grown

> The Hawaiian islands ____(45)____ extensive rivers and lakes. For this reason, the ocean always ____(46)____ the main source of edible fish for Hawaiians. Scientists ____(47)____ about six hundred species of fish native to Hawaiian waters. They ____(48)____ in size from the tiny humuhumu-nukunuku-a-pua'a to the huge shark. The state ____(49)____ several undersea parks. In these parks, skin divers and scuba divers ____(50)____ many colorful fish up close.

45 A will have lacked
    B will lack
    C lacking
    D lack

46 F has been
    G have been
    H being
    J been

47 A identifying
    B have identified
    C has identified
    D will identify

48 F ranging
    G ranged
    H range
    J could be ranging

49 A has established
    B establishing
    C will establish
    D establish

50 F seen
    G saw
    H seeing
    J can see

© Prentice-Hall, Inc.   Chapter 15: Verbs • 119

Name _____ Date _____

16 Assessment for Chapter 16: Adjectives and Adverbs

Part 1: Recognizing Adjectives and the Words They Modify
Underline the adjective or adjectives (excluding articles) in each sentence. Then, draw an arrow to the word each modifies. If the adjective is a proper or compound adjective, write it and the word *proper* or *compound* on the line.

1. Friendly relationships between dogs and humans go back to cave-dwelling times.
   _____

2. In modern society, most dogs are owned as family pets. _____

3. In the past, the main reason for owning a dog was the special work that the dog did.
   _____

4. In recent times, many breeds were developed specifically to be pets. _____

5. The German shepherd is excellent as a guard dog. _____

6. My good friend has both an Irish setter and a Scottish terrier. _____

7. A sight-impaired person can use some breeds to get around safely.
   _____

8. Many people want a purebred dog. _____

9. A mixed-breed dog is suitable for other people. _____

10. Humane societies and rescue groups often offer free dogs to good homes.
    _____

Part 2: Identifying Pronouns Used as Adjectives
If the underlined word functions as a pronoun, write *pronoun* on the line. If the word functions as an adjective, write *adjective* on the line and write the word it modifies.

11. "I like <u>this</u> dog better than that one," said Sara Jane. _____

12. "Have you already looked at <u>those</u>?" asked Jacob. _____

13. "<u>What</u> kind of dog is that?" asked Sara Jane. _____

14. "<u>That</u> is a Newfoundland," said Jacob, "commonly known as a Newfie." _____

15. Sara did not think a Newfoundland would be happy in <u>her</u> small backyard. _____

120 • Chapter 16: Adjectives and Adverbs © Prentice-Hall, Inc.

Name _____

16. Jacob said that his yard was large enough, for he lived on two acres. _____
17. Sara looked at a Basset hound, wondering about its personality. _____
18. The most important thing is for your dog to fit your personality. _____
19. Which of these three dogs would make the best guard dog? _____
20. Sara would have to train her guard dog to recognize friends. _____

Part 3: Recognizing Adverbs and the Words They Modify
Underline the adverb or adverbs in each of the following sentences. Draw an arrow to the word each adverb modifies.

21. Most puppies are very curious creatures.
22. A more active puppy enthusiastically wags its tail.
23. A less lively puppy behaves more timidly.
24. Feed puppies small servings frequently until the age of about six months.
25. Puppies should grow steadily during that time.
26. Dog-food companies commercially produce three basic kinds of foods—dry, canned, and semi-moist.
27. These foods are mainly produced from wheat, barley, rice, or soy meal.
28. Meat products also are included in the ingredients of dog food.
29. Puppies usually will play vigorously for some time and then nap.
30. Puppies learn certain behaviors easily and instinctively.

Part 4: Distinguishing Between Adjectives and Adverbs
Write whether the underlined word in each sentence functions as an *adjective* or an *adverb*.

31. Do not serve your puppy's breakfast too late. _____
32. For a tired puppy, an early lunch might be followed by a nap. _____
33. Keep your puppy close during walks. _____
34. If you are planning a late dinner, take your puppy for a walk first. _____
35. Your puppy will be happier if you get home early. _____
36. Puppies enjoy close relationships with family members. _____
37. Give your puppy a chance to run fast. _____
38. Take your puppy out for a fast walk. _____
39. Can your puppy jump to this high point on the wall? _____
40. How high can that puppy jump? _____

© Prentice-Hall, Inc.

Chapter 16: Adjectives and Adverbs • 121

Name _____

Part 5: Standardized Test Practice
This is a test on the use of words. It will show how well you can use words according to the standards of correctly written English.
- Look for mistakes in the sentences on this test.
- When you find a mistake, circle the letter of the line containing the mistake.
- Some sentences do not have any mistakes at all. If there is no mistake, circle the letter of the last line.

41 A If a dog makes a mistake,
    B it must be punished
    C immediate and appropriate.
    D (No mistake)

42 J The dog must be able
    K to associate the punishment
    L with the wrong behavior.
    M (No mistake)

43 A Most dogs will accept
    B your authority easy,
    C but some will challenge you.
    D (No mistake)

44 J This is dangerously behavior,
    K and it must be stopped
    L at an early age.
    M (No mistake)

45 A Good training must
    B be sensibly, and commands
    C should be enforceable.
    D (No mistake)

46 J Dogs must be
    K groomed regular
    L from the time they are born.
    M (No mistake)

47 A Starting at about six weeks of age,
    B regular visits to a veterinarian
    C are importantly to a dog's health.
    D (No mistake)

48 J The daily or weekly routine
    K should include brushing
    L of the dog's coat.
    M (No mistake)

49 A After the first round of shots,
    B a dog's annually booster shots
    C include everything except rabies shots.
    D (No mistake)

50 J Rabies shots are usually given
    K every two or three years,
    L depending on the area.
    M (No mistake)

Name _____ Date _____

 **Assessment for Chapter 17: Prepositions**

Part 1: Identifying Prepositional Phrases and the Words They Modify
Underline the prepositional phrase or phrases in each sentence, and circle the preposition in each one. Then, draw an arrow from the prepositional phrase to the word it modifies.

1. Much of Florida is covered by forests.

2. Many tropical trees thrive in southern Florida.

3. Almost half of America's species of trees grow in Florida.

4. Many of Florida's plants were imported into the state.

5. Diane spoke about the soggy environment of the Everglades region.

6. We looked across the swamp and saw thick vegetation.

7. Manatees, or sea cows, swim along the coast of Florida.

8. Dolphins leap near Florida's shores and land sometimes in fishing nets.

9. For the protection of migratory birds, Florida maintains many wildlife refuges.

10. An alligator on a golf course once frightened some people.

Part 2: Identifying and Using Compound Prepositions
Underline the compound preposition in each sentence below. Then, rewrite the sentence using a different compound preposition or a one-word preposition. If necessary, use a separate sheet of paper to complete your responses.

11. In ancient times, people came out of the north and entered Florida.
_____

12. According to some reports, this was about 10,000 years ago.
_____

13. In addition to fishing, some of these early groups began farming.
_____

14. They also survived by means of hunting and gathering.
_____

15. By 1750, these Native Americans suffered on account of many factors.
_____

16. Because of disease and other difficulties, they were virtually destroyed.
_____

17. In place of the dwindling native population, Europeans soon inhabited Florida.
_____

18. Aside from the Spanish settlements, there were also large Italian groups.
_____

© Prentice-Hall, Inc.

Name _____

19. As of 1819, Florida was part of the United States.
_____

20. Older, retired people who want heat instead of cold often come to Florida.
_____

Part 3: Distinguishing Between Prepositions and Adverbs
If the underlined word acts as a preposition, write *preposition* on the line after the sentence. If the underlined word acts as an adverb, write *adverb* on the line.

21. Darlene wants to visit Florida before May 1 this year. _____

    Have you ever before been to Florida? _____

22. Darlene studied a map of Florida and put it down. _____

    Lake Worth is just down the road from Palm Beach. _____

23. In July in Florida, do people stay inside with their air conditioning? _____

    We sat inside the first car of the train to Florida. _____

24. If you look out the window, you can see some flamingos. _____

    Let's go out so that we can see them better. _____

25. The baby flamingo was standing behind its mother. _____

    A large group of flamingos flew off and left a smaller group behind. _____

26. On really hot days in Florida, do many people work outside? _____

    Outside the city, it is a little cooler. _____

27. Michelle saw a beautiful orchid in the Everglades but hasn't seen one like it since. _____

    Since last year, Michelle has been collecting rare orchids. _____

28. I've been near and far, but I haven't had a better vacation. _____

    You probably don't want that alligator near your property line. _____

29. I wouldn't go beyond the edges of that swamp without a guide. _____

    Lee said, "To Florida and beyond!" but I didn't know what she meant. _____

30. We visited St. Augustine and walked around. _____

    Around the town square were many fine old buildings. _____

Part 4: Writing Sentences With Prepositions, Compound Prepositions, and Adverbs
Write ten original sentences that include the following items. Underline the required items in each sentence.

31. prepositional phrase starting with the word *within*
_____

32. the word *up* used as an adverb
_____

33. two prepositional phrases, one starting with *besides* and the other starting with *for*
_____

34. two compound prepositions
_____

124 • Chapter 17: Prepositions

Name _____

35. the word *before* used both as an adverb and as a preposition
_____

36. the word *through* used as a preposition and the word *Florida* used as the object of the preposition
_____

37. two prepositional phrases—one starting with *inside* and the other starting with a compound preposition
_____

38. any compound preposition
_____

39. two prepositional phrases—one starting with *with* and the other starting with *for*
_____

40. the compound preposition *according to*
_____

Part 5: Standardized Test Practice
Read the story. Choose the correct preposition for each sentence. Circle the letter of your answer.

(41) A swamp is an area of land that is permanently saturated _____ water. (42) Sometimes the water _____ a swamp completely covers the land. (43) There are two main types of swamps, and both are dominated _____ trees. (44) Freshwater swamps are usually found inland, and saltwater swamps are usually found in coastal areas that are protected _____ the open ocean.

(45) Cypress and tupelo trees grow _____ many freshwater swamps in the southeastern United States. (46) _____ the branches of these trees, Spanish moss may hang. (47) Tiny plants called duckweed may float _____ the water's surface. (48) The animals that live _____ swamps often include alligators, frogs, and other reptiles and amphibians.

(49) Saltwater swamps form _____ seacoasts. (50) These swamps provide a home to a rich community _____ fish, shellfish, water birds, and other animals.

41 A without
    B during
    C with
    D for

42 F in
    G under
    H behind
    J on account of

43 A under
    B beside
    C for
    D by

Name _____

44 F by
G from
H for
J inside

45 A in
B under
C instead of
D because of

46 F inside
G beyond
H near
J from

47 A on
B after
C behind
D until

48 F on top of
G in
H because of
J opposite

49 A within
B without
C on
D in place of

50 F of
G beyond
H in addition to
J until

Name _____   Date _____

 **Assessment for Chapter 18: Conjunctions and Interjections**

Part 1: Coordinating Conjunctions
Underline the coordinating conjunction in each sentence. Then, circle the words or groups of words that are joined by the conjunction.
1. Long ago, people believed that the ocean floor was smooth and flat.
2. They knew the ocean was deep, but they did not realize it also had mountains.
3. They did not know about the ocean's deep trenches nor its many plains.
4. More recently, scientists wanted a map of the ocean floor, so they used sonar.
5. It was a long process, for each sound wave had to be timed.
6. The scientists would bounce sound off the bottom and wait until its echo returned.
7. The wait might be long or short.
8. A long wait for an echo indicated greater depth, and a short wait indicated less depth.
9. It was a tedious yet exciting process for the scientists.
10. The process is similar to the use of echolocation by bats and whales.

Part 2: Correlative Conjunctions
Underline the correlative conjunctions in each sentence. Then, circle the words or groups of words that are joined by the conjunctions.
11. Ocean currents move both heat from the tropics and cold from the polar regions.
12. This constant movement of cool and warm waters keeps the ocean neither too hot nor too cold.
13. Currents can be either warm or cool, depending on where they originate.
14. People use the ocean not only as a source of food but also as a highway for trade and exploration.
15. The ocean teems with life not only near the shore but also in the deepest trenches.
16. Whether you fish in the deep sea or you stay near the shore, you can catch something.
17. Dave usually fishes for either salmon or tuna.
18. He enjoys fishing whether he catches anything or he comes back empty-handed.
19. When he is fishing, he gets neither bored nor tired.
20. Dave sees a fishing trip as both fun and relaxing.

Part 3: Distinguishing Conjunctions
Underline the conjunction in each sentence. If it is a coordinating conjunction, write *coordinating* on the line after the sentence. If it is a correlative conjunction, write *correlative* on the line.
21. The ocean provides us with a wealth of food and other resources. _____
22. The ocean has many resources, but over the last two hundred years, these resources have been threatened. _____
23. Whales have been hunted not only for their meat but also for their oil. _____
24. In the 1960's and 1970's, catches of both herring and haddock declined. _____

© Prentice-Hall, Inc.   Chapter 18: Conjunctions and Interjections • 127

Name _____

25. Whether from overfishing or from pollution, life in the oceans has been threatened by human activities. _____

26. Perhaps fishermen should not use electronic fish finders, nor should they employ such large trawling nets. _____

27. Either we control pollution in the seas, or we will have serious problems in the future. _____

28. We know the vital importance of the ocean, yet we continue to dump waste into it. _____

29. From the ocean we get not only food but also many minerals, especially common salt. _____

30. The ocean may be vast, but it is also easily damaged. _____

Part 4: Standardized Test Practice
Read the sentences and choose the word or words that belong in the spaces. Mark the letter for your answer.

31 _____! Did you see the size of that whale?
  A Goodness
  B But
  C Tsk
  D Uh

32 Fish live in _____ fresh water _____ salt water.
  F whether . . . or
  G neither . . . nor
  H both . . . and
  J but . . . also

33 Most fish have a head, a body, _____ a tail.
  A or
  B and
  C but
  D yet

34 Fish use their fins _____ to swim _____ to keep their balance.
  F either . . . and
  G neither . . . nor
  H whether . . . or
  J not only . . . but also

35 Some fish give birth to live young, _____ most lay eggs.
  A for
  B so
  C but
  D and

36 _____! That jellyfish stung me!
  F Tsk
  G Hmmmm
  H Ouch
  J Er

Name _____

37 _____ , what do you think we should do about a jellyfish sting?
    A Wow
    B Well
    C But
    D Tsk

38 _____ you can just suffer through the pain, _____ we can take you to the doctor.
    F Either . . . or
    G Whether . . . or
    H Neither . . . nor
    J Both . . . and

39 The jellyfish are very beautiful, _____ you must be careful not to touch them.
    A and
    B or
    C but
    D for

40 _____ ! That sunset over the water is just spectacular!
    F Tsk
    G Hmmm
    H Huh
    J Wow

Name _____ Date _____

 **Assessment for Chapter 19: Basic Sentence Parts**

Part 1: Identifying Complete Subjects and Complete Predicates
Underline the complete subject once and the complete predicate twice. Then, draw a vertical line between the complete subject and the complete predicate.
 1. Sarah Breedlove was born in 1867 on the Burney family plantation in Louisiana.
 2. Sarah married a Mr. McWilliams in 1881.
 3. Mr. McWilliams died six years later.
 4. Sarah and her daughter, A'Lelia, moved to St. Louis, Missouri.
 5. Sarah's job as a washerwoman paid the bills until 1905.
 6. Sarah married Charles J. Walker, a newspaperman, in 1906.
 7. Madame C. J. Walker developed some beauty products.
 8. Her method of straightening curly hair was very popular.
 9. Her agents sold the hair treatments door-to-door.
10. Her company eventually employed 3,000 people.

Part 2: Recognizing Complete Thoughts
Read each group of words. If it is a complete thought, write *sentence*. If it is an incomplete thought, write *fragment*.

11. Saleswomen in long black skirts and white blouses. _____
12. The saleswomen became familiar figures in black communities. _____
13. In time, Walker also established Walker Schools of Beauty Culture. _____
14. Insisted on certain standards of hygiene for her staff. _____
15. Over the years, Madame C. J. Walker became a millionaire through her own efforts. _____
16. Her parents were both ex-slaves. _____
17. Sharecroppers living on the Burney plantation in Delta, Louisiana. _____
18. Actually had only a limited education. _____
19. Madame Walker's system used a hot comb. _____
20. Demonstrated her excellent marketing skills. _____

Part 3: Completing Sentences With Compound Subjects and Compound Verbs
Rewrite the sentences, filling in each blank with another noun or verb that would create a logical compound.

21. Madame C. J. Walker developed and _____ hair-care products.
_____

22. Tonya and _____ are writing a report on Madame C. J. Walker.
_____

23. They will research and _____ in the library today.
_____

Name _____

24. The encyclopedia and _____ will be good sources of information.
_____

25. Tonya will write and _____ the first draft.
_____

26. Her partner will edit and _____ a revised version.
_____

27. _____ and Hector will listen to their presentation.
_____

28. The teacher and _____ will hear the report next week.
_____

29. Madame C. J. Walker owned and _____ her own business.
_____

30. Millions of women sampled and _____ her products.
_____

Part 4: Locating Hard-to-Find Subjects
Write the subject of each sentence. If the subject is understood, write it in parentheses.

31. In which cities did Madame C. J. Walker live? _____
32. Read about Madame C. J. Walker's life. _____
33. Here is some information about Madame C. J. Walker. _____
34. There have been improvements in hair-care products since Madame C. J. Walker's time. _____
35. How many employees did Madame C. J. Walker have? _____
36. What a generous person Madame Walker was! _____
37. Did you know about her large donations to African American charities? _____
38. Among her donations were scholarships to Tuskegee Institute. _____
39. What did people like about her products? _____
40. There were many famous users of Madame Walker's products, including entertainer Josephine Baker. _____

Part 5: Completing Sentences With Complements
Complete each sentence by writing a complement on the line in the sentence. You may add other words as needed to make sense. On the line after the sentence, write whether the complement you added is a *direct object*, a *predicate noun*, or a *predicate adjective*.

41. On my own hair, I use _____. _____
_____

42. My hair is _____. _____
_____

43. At the beauty-supply store, Katherine bought _____.
_____

© Prentice-Hall, Inc.   Chapter 19: Basic Sentence Parts • 131

Name _____

44. Katherine gave the salesperson _____. _____
_____

45. The salesperson showed the customer _____. _____
_____

46. All the salespeople wore _____. _____
_____

47. The customer asked the salesperson _____. _____
_____

48. The salesperson was a _____. _____
_____

49. The customer wanted _____. _____
_____

50. The product seemed very _____. _____
_____

Part 6: Standardized Test Practice
Read each sentence, and choose the word or group of words that best describe the underlined part. Circle the letter of your answer.

51 <u>A'Lelia Walker</u> was the daughter of Madame C. J. Walker.
   A predicate
   B direct object
   C complete subject
   D predicate adjective

52 A'Lelia Walker <u>was associated with the Harlem Renaissance</u>.
   F complete predicate
   G verb
   H sentence
   J compound predicate

53 A'Lelia Walker's original name was <u>Lelia McWilliams</u>.
   A predicate noun
   B direct object
   C indirect object
   D complete predicate

54 A'Lelia Walker attended <u>Knoxville College</u> in Tennessee.
   F predicate noun
   G predicate adjective
   H direct object
   J indirect object

55 Madame C. J. Walker's <u>daughter</u> inherited her mother's business.
   A complete subject
   B subject
   C predicate noun
   D compound subject

Name _____

56 Madame C. J. Walker <u>had made</u> a fortune in the hair-care business.
  F complete predicate
  G verb
  H predicate adjective
  J predicate noun

57 <u>After college, A'Lelia Walker went to work for her mother.</u>
  A complete subject
  B complete predicate
  C fragment
  D sentence

58 A'Lelia inherited <u>the business and the lavish family estate.</u>
  F complete predicate
  G compound subject complement
  H compound subject
  J compound direct object

59 <u>Langston Hughes, Zora Neale Hurston, James Weldon Johnson, Jean Toomer, and other writers</u> were regular guests in A'Lelia's home.
  A compound subject
  B compound direct object
  C compound predicate noun
  D subject complement

60 <u>Entertained writers and artists at her estate and her town house in New York City.</u>
  F sentence
  G complete predicate
  H fragment
  J complete subject

© Prentice-Hall, Inc.   Chapter 19: Basic Sentence Parts • 133

Name _____   Date _____

Assessment for Chapter 20: Phrases and Clauses

Part 1: Identifying Phrases and Verbals
On the line after each sentence, identify the underlined part as a *prepositional phrase used as an adjective, prepositional phrase used as an adverb, participle, participial phrase, infinitive,* or *infinitive phrase.*

1. Yellowstone National Park is one <u>of the largest national parks</u> in the United States. _____

2. Would you like <u>to know more about Yellowstone</u>? _____

3. <u>Located in parts of three states</u>, Yellowstone Park has many interesting geothermal features. _____

4. Old Faithful is one of the most interesting things <u>to see</u>. _____

5. This <u>erupting</u> geyser spouts off every 33 to 120 minutes. _____

6. If you ever get a chance to travel to Yellowstone, make it a point <u>to see Old Faithful</u>. _____

7. The park sits <u>in northwestern Wyoming, southern Montana, and eastern Idaho</u>. _____

8. The park, <u>established by the U.S. Congress on March 1, 1872</u>, is the world's first national park. _____

9. Yellowstone Park also contains the largest mountain lake <u>in North America</u>. _____

10. <u>In the waters</u> of Yellowstone Lake swim several varieties of fishes. _____

Part 2: Identifying Appositives and Appositive Phrases
Underline the appositive or appositive phrase in the following sentences. Then, on the line after each sentence, tell what noun the appositive renames.

11. Yellowstone, the oldest national park in the United States, is quite beautiful. _____

12. Old Faithful, the most famous geyser in Yellowstone, is very impressive. _____

13. Fumaroles, those vapor-emitting holes in the ground, can be seen in Yellowstone. _____

14. In Yellowstone National Park, there is a mountain made of obsidian, the shiny black volcanic glass. _____

15. Another geyser near Old Faithful, the Giantess, erupts every six to eight months. _____

16. Minerva, a multicolored terrace with hot-water cascades, is located at Mammoth Hot Springs. _____

17. The interesting bird the trumpeter swan can be seen in Yellowstone. _____

18. The Grand Canyon of the Yellowstone River, a colorful gorge, is nineteen miles long. _____

19. The John D. Rockefeller Jr. Memorial Parkway, an eighty-mile scenic roadway, runs through Yellowstone. _____

20. Lodgepole pine, a Rocky Mountain pine tree, covers much of Yellowstone Park. _____

Name _____

Part 3: Identifying Adjective and Adverb Clauses
Underline the adjective or adverb clause in each sentence. On the line after the sentence, write whether the clause is an *adjective clause* or *adverb clause* and identify the word it modifies.

21. John Muir, who was born in Scotland in 1838, moved to America at the age of eleven.
_____

22. After he attended college, Muir worked on mechanical inventions. _____
_____

23. In 1867, when an industrial accident almost cost him an eye, he changed his plans.
_____

24. After that, he devoted himself to nature, which became his life's work. _____
_____

25. While keeping a journal, Muir walked from the Midwest to the Gulf of Mexico. _____
_____

26. The journal, which was published in 1916, was called *A Thousand-Mile Walk to the Gulf*.
_____

27. My best friend, Susan, has a copy of that book, which she has read four times. _____
_____

28. In 1868, Muir went to the valley that became so important in his life. _____
_____

29. Whenever I am in Yosemite, I feel grateful to John Muir. _____
_____

30. Because of John Muir's efforts, Yosemite has been protected. _____
_____

Part 4: Identifying Sentence Structures
Identify the sentences in the following paragraph as *simple, compound,* or *complex*. Write your answers below the paragraph, on the lines with the same numbers.

(31) Yosemite, a famous valley in California, is about 150 miles east of San Francisco. (32) It is seven miles long and about a mile wide. (33) The valley walls are made of granite, which has been eroded by the movement of glaciers. (34) The bottom of the valley is level, and it is filled with groves of oak, pine, flowering bushes, and wild gardens. (35) Spectacular waterfalls, such as the Bridal Veil Fall, add to the beauty of the valley. (36) The Bridal Veil Fall, which is 900 feet high, is located in the lower end of the valley. (37) Yosemite Fall, toward the upper end of the valley, cascades from a height of 1,600 feet. (38) The Vernal is famous for its afternoon rainbows, and it is the most popular fall for visitors. (39) As it falls, it seems to change from green to purplish-gray and white. (40) Any trip to Yosemite should include visits to the many beautiful waterfalls, for they are spectacular sights.

31. _____   36. _____
32. _____   37. _____
33. _____   38. _____
34. _____   39. _____
35. _____   40. _____

Name _____

Part 5: Revising to Vary Sentence Structure
Revise the following sentences according to the directions in parentheses. Write your responses on the lines provided.

41. El Capitan is a plain mass of granite 3,300 feet high. It rises from the floor of Yosemite Valley. (Combine to make one complex sentence.)
_____
_____

42. Half Dome, which is the most imposing rock in Yosemite, is 4,740 feet high. (Change to one simple sentence.)
_____

43. Vernal Fall is a favorite with visitors. That is because it is easier to reach than the other waterfalls. (Combine to make one complex sentence.)
_____
_____

44. The tallest pines in Yosemite are more than 200 feet high, and some of the oaks have trunks of eight feet in diameter. (Change to two simple sentences.)
_____
_____

45. No one but Native Americans saw the valley until 1851. By 1856, regular tourist travel had begun. (Combine to make one compound sentence.)
_____
_____

46. Yosemite's first permanent settler moved there in 1860. He built a cabin in the upper end of the valley. (Combine to make one complex sentence.)
_____
_____

47. The first permanent settler planted gardens and orchards. (Change to two simple sentences.)
_____

48. Violets, lilies, and goldenrod grow in Yosemite. Wild roses and azaleas also flourish in the park. (Combine to make one compound sentence.)
_____
_____

49. The climate of Yosemite is surprisingly mild. This mild climate creates excellent growing conditions for the vegetation. (Combine to make one complex sentence.)
_____
_____

50. In its beauty and grandeur, Yosemite has no rivals. However, there are many other valleys of the same type. (Combine to make one compound sentence.)
_____
_____

Name _____

Part 6: Standardized Test Practice
Choose the answer that best identifies the underlined part of each sentence or sentences.
Circle the letter of your answer.

51 Yellowstone, the oldest national park, is known for its lake and rivers.
    A prepositional phrase used as an adjective
    B appositive phrase
    C participial phrase
    D adjective clause

52 Yellowstone Lake has a surface area of 136 square miles.
    F simple sentence
    G complex sentence
    H participial phrase
    J compound sentence

53 Most of Yellowstone Park is covered with trees, and most of these trees are lodgepole pines.
    A complex sentence
    B simple sentence
    C compound sentence
    D adjective clause

54 Yellowstone Park, which has more than 1,000 miles of trails, is a great place to hike.
    F participial phrase
    G appositive phrase
    H prepositional phrase used as an adjective
    J adjective clause

55 Have you ever been to Yellowstone National Park?
    A prepositional phrase used as an adverb
    B infinitive phrase
    C adverb clause
    D adjective clause

56 The best time of year to hike is probably the spring.
    F prepositional phrase used as an adjective
    G participle
    H infinitive
    J appositive

57 If you have never been to Yosemite, you should think about going soon.
    A adjective clause
    B prepositional phrase used as an adjective
    C prepositional phrase used as an adverb
    D adverb clause

© Prentice-Hall, Inc.

Name _____

58 <u>Claire will visit both Yosemite and Yellowstone this summer, which is only three months away</u>.
  F simple sentence
  G complex sentence
  H compound sentence
  J adverb clause

59 The water <u>cascading down the mountain</u> makes a loud roar.
  A participial phrase
  B appositive phrase
  C prepositional phrase used as an adjective
  D adjective clause

60 Is the road <u>to the park</u> open all year?
  F appositive phrase
  G infinitive phrase
  H prepositional phrase used as an adverb
  J prepositional phrase used as an adjective

Name _____ Date _____

Assessment for Chapter 21: Effective Sentences

Part 1: Recognizing Sentence Types
Add the correct end mark to each sentence. Then, on the line after the sentence, identify the sentence as *declarative, interrogative, imperative,* or *exclamatory*.

1. Wild animals have been a part of circuses since about 1831 _____
2. In 1831, the French trainer Henri Martin was performing at the Cirque Olympique in Paris _____
3. Did you know that he performed with lions, boa constrictors, and an elephant _____
4. What a show that must have been _____
5. Not long after that, an American trainer named Isaac A. Van Amburgh followed Martin's lead _____
6. Van Amburgh was supposedly the first man to stick his head into a lion's mouth _____
7. Don't ever do that _____
8. What a dangerous thing to do _____
9. Van Amburgh took his act to England to show to the queen _____
10. Do you know who the queen of England was at that time _____

Part 2: Combining Sentences
Combine each pair of sentences in the way indicated in parentheses. Write the new sentence on the line provided. If necessary, use a separate sheet of paper to complete your responses.

11. In 1838, Queen Victoria saw Van Amburgh's circus act. She enjoyed it. (Use a compound verb.)
    _____

12. She contacted the artist Edwin Landseer. He made her a portrait of the American circus performer. (Use a subordinate clause.)
    _____

13. Many circus performers practice long hours. They give their audiences excellent performances. (Use a compound predicate.)
    _____

14. The performers present the animals as obedient, playful pets. The animals are still wild. (Use a subordinate clause.)
    _____

15. Marsha saw a circus performance last week. Marsha is my best friend. (Use an appositive phrase.)
    _____

16. Elephants are to many people the very symbol of the circus. Elephants have been in circuses since the 1830's. (Use a subordinate clause.)
    _____

17. Elephants are really quite dangerous. Some have been known to turn on their trainers. (Use a semicolon.)
    _____

Name _____

18. The flying trapeze was invented in 1859. A French acrobat invented it. (Use a prepositional phrase.)
_____

19. The French acrobat's name was J. Léotard. His name gave us our word *leotard*. (Use an appositive.)
_____

20. The circus presents people at their best in physical achievement. It presents people at their best in coordination. (Use a compound object of a preposition.)
_____

Part 3: Varying Sentences
On the line after each sentence, rewrite the sentence by following the directions in parentheses.

21. Human circus performers do balancing acts on high wires, and they also do acts with wild animals. (Break into two sentences.)
_____

22. The trapeze artist is skilled and disciplined. She performs a thrilling feat. (Rewrite as a more direct sentence.)
_____

23. The audience, predictably, is almost silent as the artist performs the dangerous act. (Start with an adverb.)
_____

24. For many people, the life of a circus performer would be difficult. (Start with an article and a noun.)
_____

25. Other people would do almost anything to work in a circus. (Start with an infinitive.)
_____

26. Circus performers may work with animal partners. They may work with human partners. (Rewrite as a more direct sentence.)
_____

27. The clown walked into the center ring. (Change the subject-verb order to verb-subject order.)
_____

28. Some clowns wear elegant costumes and paint their faces white, while others wear shabby clothes and use colorful makeup. (Break into two sentences.)
_____

29. On the bicycle rode the black bear. (Change the verb-subject order to subject-verb order.)
_____

30. Some circus animals, surprisingly, are uncaged, even though they can be dangerous. (Start with an adverb.)
_____

Name _____

Part 4: Correcting Sentence Fragments and Run-Ons
If the item below is a fragment, rewrite it as a complete sentence on the line provided. If the item is a run-on, rewrite it as a correct sentence. If the item is correct as is, write *correct*. If necessary, use a separate sheet of paper to complete your responses.

31. Oleg Popov was a great Russian clown.
    _____

32. Wearing a very small amount of makeup.
    _____

33. Became well known not only in the Soviet Union but throughout Europe and also in the United States.
    _____

34. He pretended to copy the acts of the regular circus performers, he would almost succeed.
    _____

35. The circus band, setting the pace.
    _____

36. Over the years, circus music has become an art of its own.
    _____

37. Animals, not always a part of circus acts.
    _____

38. Two-ring circuses began in 1872, three-ring circuses began in 1881.
    _____

39. Some circus tents were big enough to have seven rings.
    _____

40. One big top, covering more than two acres.
    _____

Part 5: Correcting Misplaced Modifiers, Double Negatives, and Usage Problems
If the sentence has a misplaced modifier or a usage problem, rewrite the sentence correctly. If the sentence is correct as is, write *correct*.

41. Depicting exciting times in the Old West, large crowds were drawn to Wild West shows.
    _____

42. A Wild West show usually was held in a large open field surrounded by bleachers.
    _____

43. Annie Oakley gained fame in Wild West shows throughout the United States as "Little Miss Sureshot."
    _____

44. Walking down the midway, the carnival seemed a lot like a circus to me.
    _____

45. A woman told the future wearing fifteen rings and a tall turban.
    _____

46. The reason I won the prize is because I have very good aim.
    _____

© Prentice-Hall, Inc.   Chapter 21: Effective Sentences • 141

Name _____

47. Carrying my prizes, I realized that the car was further away than I had thought.
_____

48. Tony said, "I want to give you a little bit of advise."
_____

49. Tony's words had a negative affect on my mood.
_____

50. He told me not to spend no more money on carnival tickets.
_____

Part 6: Standardized Test Practice
Read the story. Then, answer the questions about it. Circle the letter of your answer.

(51) Walking toward the county fair, the sound of the carnival rides fill the air. (52) I am sort of looking forward to the games of skill. (53) Hope to win a few stuffed animals. (54) Have you ever won a prize at a carnival. (55) I won a few big prizes last year but this year I hope to do even better. (56) My favorite time of year is when the county fair is in town. (57) Accept for the junk food, everything at the fair is wonderful, in my opinion. (58) My sister Alice is usually with me their. Alice likes the fair, two. (59) Alice and I have been looking forward to this evening for weeks, we always have a great time at the fair. (60) We walk the whole length of the fair until we cannot go no further.

51 How is Sentence 51 best written?
  A The sound of the carnival rides fills the air, walking toward the county fair.
  B Walking toward the county fair, I hear the sound of the carnival rides.
  C Walking toward the country fair. The sound of carnival rides fills the air.
  D As it is

52 Choose the best way to write Sentence 52.
  F To the games of skill I am sort of looking forward.
  G I am kind of looking forward to the games of skill.
  H I am rather looking forward to the games of skill.
  J As it is

53 Which is the best way to write Sentence 53?
  A I hope to win a few stuffed animals.
  B Hope to win a few stuffed animals!
  C Hope to win a few stuffed animals?
  D As it is

54 The best way to write Sentence 54 would be—
  F Have you ever won a prize at a carnival!
  G At a carnival, have you ever won a prize.
  H Have you ever won. A prize at a carnival?
  J Have you ever won a prize at a carnival?

55 Choose the best way to write Sentence 55.
  A I won a few big prizes last year, but this year I hope to do even better.
  B I won a few big prizes last year; but this year I hope to do even better.
  C I won a few big prizes last year. But this year I hope to do even better.
  D Last year, I won a few big prizes, I hope to do even better this year.

56 The best way to write Sentence 56 is—
  F My favorite time of year is, when the county fair is in town.
  G My favorite time of year is the week that the county fair is in town.
  H My favorite time of year, the county fair is in town.
  J As it is

142 • Chapter 21: Effective Sentences

Name _____

57 Choose the best way to write Sentence 57.
  A Accept for the junk food. Everything at the fair is wonderful. In my opinion.
  B Except for the junk food. Everything at the fair is wonderful. In my opinion.
  C Accept for the junk food, everything at the fair is wonderful, in my opinion.
  D Except for the junk food, everything at the fair is wonderful, in my opinion.

58 Choose the best way to write Sentence 58.
  F My sister Alice is usually with me their. Alice likes the fair, too.
  G My sister Alice is usually with me there. Alice likes the fair, two.
  H Usually with me there is my sister Alice, who likes the fair, too.
  J As it is

59 The best way to write Sentence 59 is—
  A Alice and I have been looking forward to this evening for weeks. We always have a great time at the fair.
  B Alice and I have been looking forward to this evening for weeks, we always have a great time at the fair!
  C Alice and I have been looking forward to this evening for weeks! We always have a great time at the fair?
  D Alice and I have been looking forward to this evening for weeks, always have a great time at the fair.

60 Which is the best way to write Sentence 60?
  F We walk the whole length of the fair until we cannot go no farther.
  G We walk the whole length of the fair until we cannot go any further.
  H We walk the whole length of the fair until we cannot go any farther.
  J As it is

Name _____ Date _____

 **Assessment for Chapter 22: Using Verbs**

Part 1: Recognizing Principal Parts and Regular or Irregular Verbs
After each sentence, identify the underlined principal part of the verb as *present, present participle, past,* or *past participle*. Also, indicate whether the principal part is regular or irregular.

1. The domestic cat <u>has</u> an interesting history. _____
2. Cats were <u>used</u> as pets in ancient Egypt more than three thousand years ago. _____
3. There <u>are</u> no records of cat domestication before 1500 B.C. _____
4. In Egypt, the cat had been <u>proclaimed</u> a sacred animal much earlier than 1500 B.C. _____
5. The ancient Egyptians probably <u>domesticated</u> cats for a good reason. _____
6. People in ancient Egypt <u>needed</u> cats to control the rodent population. _____
7. Cats have long been <u>known</u> in many cultures. _____
8. That cat is <u>stalking</u> a bird. _____
9. In India, cats have been <u>mentioned</u> in Sanskrit writings more than two thousand years ago. _____
10. The Abyssinian cat <u>resembles</u> pictures and statues of ancient Egyptian cats. _____

Part 2: Supplying the Correct Principal Part
On the line after each sentence, supply the correct principal part of the verb in parentheses. If there is no helping verb in the sentence, do not add one.

11. The average weight of the household cat (vary) from six to ten pounds.
_____

12. The cat is (walk) in an unusual way.
_____

13. Cats (move) the front and back legs on each side at the same time.
_____

14. That cat has (draw) its claws.
_____

15. This cat has (spread) its toes widely.
_____

16. The cat has (make) its foot more than twice its normal width.
_____

17. The cat's paw has been (convert) into a deadly weapon.
_____

18. Yesterday, that cat (scratch) one of the children.
_____

19. This cat has not been (feel) well lately.
_____

144 • Chapter 22: Using Verbs © Prentice-Hall, Inc.

Name _____

20. Have you (take) the cat to the vet yet?
_____

Part 3: Supplying the Correct Basic and Progressive Forms
Rewrite each sentence, supplying the basic or progressive form of the verb indicated in parentheses. If necessary, use a separate sheet of paper to complete your responses.

21. That cat (express—present progressive) its feelings to you.
_____

22. The cat (give—present perfect) you a look of annoyance.
_____

23. That particular vocal sound (indicate—present) that the cat is content.
_____

24. The cat (know—past) that you were getting ready to pet it.
_____

25. The Persian cat (rub—past perfect) its head against the couch.
_____

26. Cats (smell—future) their food before they eat it.
_____

27. Cats' ears (contain—present) thirty muscles, compared to the six in humans.
_____

28. A cat (hear—future perfect) sounds that you never will.
_____

29. Before our last earthquake, the cat (act—past perfect progressive) very oddly.
_____

30. I (wonder—present perfect progressive) why the cat was so nervous.
_____

31. By next week, we (immunize—future perfect) our cats.
_____

32. I (take—future perfect) them for their shots by then.
_____

33. Kittens often (race—future progressive) crazily through the house.
_____

34. Wild behavior in cats (have—present) many causes.
_____

35. Before domestication, cats actively (hunt—past) around dawn and dusk.
_____

36. Our white cat (groom—present perfect) not only herself but our other cat as well.
_____

Name _____

37. The white cat (feel—past perfect progressive) affection for the other cat.
   _____

38. By the time we get home, the cat (sleep—future perfect progressive) for two hours.
   _____

39. I (train—future progressive) the cats to use scratching posts.
   _____

40. The cat (adjust—past progressive) to our new home.
   _____

Part 4: Revising to Correct Misused Verbs
On the line provided, rewrite each sentence, correcting the misused verbs. If no verb in the sentence is misused, write *correct*.

41. Every afternoon, that cat lays on the couch and naps.
   _____

42. It ain't acceptable for the cat to scratch the furniture.
   _____

43. I like to set in the rocker and pet the cat.
   _____

44. The cats have went outside to lie in the sun.
   _____

45. I done some reading about the care and feeding of cats.
   _____

46. I should of chosen a Siamese cat instead of this Persian.
   _____

47. I seen a beautiful Burmese cat at the pet store.
   _____

48. My aunt raises cats and sells them for profit.
   _____

49. That cat has did something very unusual.
   _____

50. The short-haired cat is laying on the windowsill.
   _____

Name _____

Part 5: Standardized Test Practice
This is a test on using verbs. It will show how effectively you use verbs according to the standards of correct English.
- Look for mistakes in the sentences on this test.
- When you find a mistake, circle the letter of the line containing the mistake.
- Some sentences or sentence groups do not have any mistakes at all. If there is no mistake, circle the letter of the last line.

51 A The tongue of the cat had a patch of sharp spines near the tip.
   B The tongue appeared and feeled like a coarse file.
   C The cat used its tongue to groom itself.
   D (*No mistake*)

52 J A cat's purring has been describing as a low, continuous hum.
   K It expresses pleasure or contentment.
   L It is a very relaxing sound.
   M (*No mistake*)

53 A By six o'clock, Fluffy will have been sleeping for hours.
   B Each afternoon, she lays on the closet floor.
   C She rises several hours later.
   D (*No mistake*)

54 J You should of taken the cat to the vet
   K as soon as you noticed that
   L it was behaving strangely.
   M (*No mistake*)

55 A Michelle's cat has always been a house cat.
   B She has never allowed her cat outdoors.
   C It has been protect from a variety of hazards.
   D (*No mistake*)

56 J Outside cats often are hurt in accidents.
   K For example, another cat attacked Mel's cat last week.
   L The cat has been shaken by the incident.
   M (*No mistake*)

57 A Kittens usually need their mothers for two to four months.
   B Have you ever saw any newborn kittens?
   C Ours were lying in a basket pretty helplessly.
   D (*No mistake*)

58 J The diet of our cats ain't so unusual.
   K We have been giving them mainly meat.
   L The doctor also recommended small amounts of vegetables occasionally.
   M (*No mistake*)

59 A I could have did more to make that cat happy.
   B I should have brushed her coat.
   C I might have given her more affection.
   D (*No mistake*)

60 J My cat lies at the foot of my bed.
   K When I rise in the morning, he is still there.
   L I know that he has been awake during the night.
   M (*No mistake*)

Name _____   Date _____

23 Assessment for Chapter 23: Using Pronouns

Part 1: The Three Cases of Personal Pronouns
On each numbered line below the paragraph, write the pronoun from the sentence with the same number, and identify its case as *nominative*, *objective*, or *possessive*.

(1) Did you know that Susan Butcher is the only woman to win the 1,161-mile Iditarod three times in a row? (2) Susan grew up in Boston, but she hated city life. (3) Moving to the Wrangell Mountains of Alaska seemed like a great idea to her. (4) Dog-sled racing had always appealed to her. (5) Another interest of hers was breeding and training huskies. (6) To train the dogs, Susan led them through snowstorms just for practice. (7) During an interview, Susan once said, "In 1985 I was traveling alone at night in the lead of the race and ran into an obviously crazed moose." (8) Susan described how the moose attacked the dogs and killed two of them. (9) Thirteen other dogs were badly injured, and they had to spend two weeks at a veterinary hospital. (10) Theirs was a perilous plight, but in the end the doctors were able to save the injured animals.

1. _____
2. _____
3. _____
4. _____
5. _____
6. _____
7. _____
8. _____
9. _____
10. _____

Part 2: Determining the Use of Personal Pronouns
On the line after each sentence, identify the case of the underlined pronoun as *nominative*, *objective*, or *possessive*. If the pronoun is nominative, tell whether it is used as a *subject of a verb* or as a *predicate nominative*. If the pronoun is objective, tell whether it is used as a *direct object*, an *indirect object*, or an *object of a preposition*.

11. To a person who is dog sledding, or "mushing," wolves are not a threat, for <u>they</u> are simply curious.

    _____

12. Wolves "never cause <u>us</u> any problems," says Susan Butcher.

    _____

13. According to Susan and other mushers, bears in hibernation are not a threat to <u>them</u> either.

    _____

14. Susan said, "The polar bears are much farther north than where <u>we</u> race."

    _____

15. Since the more northern reaches of the Arctic are <u>theirs</u>, the bears rarely venture where the mushers are.

    _____

Name _____

16. In contrast, Susan noted, "The moose sometimes run toward you."
_____

17. Once a moose gave her a very difficult time.
_____

18. The moose attacked Susan's dogs and injured them badly.
_____

19. At the end of that race, the most seriously injured dogs were hers.
_____

20. In contrast, when the winner of the 1988 Iditarod came in, it was she, Susan Butcher.
_____

Part 3: Revise to Eliminate Problems With the Case of Personal Pronouns
On the appropriately numbered lines below the paragraph, rewrite each sentence, correcting any underlined pronoun that needs correcting. If the sentence has no pronoun errors, write *correct*.

(21) John and me have always wanted to talk to Mary Shields. (22) We want to ask her about being the first woman to finish the Iditarod, with all its many dangers. (23) We know that her and Lolly Medley were the only two women in the 1974 Iditarod. (24) They're courage and determination helped them finish the race. (25) The story is inspiring to John and I. (26) Him and I want to ask Mary Shields how she did it. (27) If I were to meet her, I would ask, "How did you train you're dogs?" (28) I wonder if Lolly Medley's answer would be different from hers. (29) Its interesting to talk to winners of such a race, with all it's difficulties. (30) I always wonder how much of the glory is really their's and how much belongs to the dogs.

21. _____
22. _____
23. _____
24. _____
25. _____
26. _____
27. _____
28. _____
29. _____
30. _____

Part 4: Standardized Test Practice
Choose the word or words that correctly complete each sentence. Circle the letter of your choice.

31 Just before _____ turned seventeen, Libby Riddles moved to Alaska.
   A her
   B she
   C hers
   D me

© Prentice-Hall, Inc.

Name _____

32 Nobody really noticed _____ as she started out on the Iditarod in 1985.
  F her
  G she
  H hers
  J her's

33 The first person to get to Safety, the last checkpoint before Nome, was _____.
  A her
  B him
  C yours
  D she

34 It surprised _____ that Libby was five hours ahead of the nearest competitor.
  F we
  G they
  H us
  J her and I

35 _____ all cheered in surprise when she won the race.
  A Them and me
  B We
  C Us
  D Their

36 Victory was _____, and Libby relished the moment.
  F hers
  G her's
  H her
  J she

37 Libby then became partners with Joe Garnie, and _____ bred and trained dogs together.
  A them
  B him and her
  C they
  D their

38 Joe was also a musher, and Libby and _____ took turns racing the dogs in the Iditarod.
  F him
  G his
  H them
  J he

39 In 1984, the third-place award went to _____.
  A him
  B he
  C she
  D his

40 Libby's first place in 1985 and Joe's second place in 1986 really proved that _____ had wonderful dogs.
  F he and her
  G they
  H him and her
  J she and him

Name _____ Date _____

Assessment for Chapter 24: Making Words Agree

Part 1: Identifying Subjects and Checking for Agreement
Choose the correct verb from the pair in parentheses, and write it on the line.

1. Whales and porpoises (is, are) members of the order Cetacea. _____

2. The order Cetacea also (include, includes) dolphins. _____

3. The animals in the order Cetacea (fall, falls) into the category of mammals. _____

4. These particular mammals (do, does) not ordinarily leave their aquatic environment. _____

5. Whales (is divided, are divided) into three suborders. _____

6. One order of these cetaceans (has, have) already become extinct. _____

7. One of the three orders of cetaceans, the baleen whales, (feed, feeds) on tiny sea life. _____

8. Plankton, small crustaceans such as krill, and other tiny sea life (supply, supplies) the dietary needs of baleen whales. _____

9. A dense fringe of blade-shaped, horny plates, called baleen, (hang, hangs) down from the roof of the whale's mouth and acts as a strainer. _____

10. The third order of whales, which has teeth instead of baleen, (swallow, swallows) giant squid, cuttlefish, and fishes of all kinds. _____

Part 2: Supplying Appropriate Verbs
Rewrite each of the following sentences, supplying an appropriate verb in the present tense. If necessary, use a separate sheet of paper to complete your responses.

11. Some whales _____ larger than the largest ancient dinosaurs.
_____

12. That blue whale is 110 feet long, and it _____ more than 150 tons.
_____

13. Baleen whales _____ their food either by swimming with their mouths open or by gulping water.
_____

14. Whales, despite their resemblance to fishes, _____ air and must come to the surface to get it.
_____

15. When washed ashore, whales _____ helpless.
_____

16. It _____ impossible for a whale to move without the support of the water.
_____

17. Whales _____ all the available aquatic habitats, including oceans, seas, estuaries, and rivers.

© Prentice-Hall, Inc.   Chapter 24: Making Words Agree • 151

Name _____

18. Some whales—the ones who are social—_____ in groups called schools, herds, pods, or gams.

19. Two basic types of underwater sound _____ by whales.

20. Whales _____ barks, whistles, screams, and moans to communicate with one another.

Part 3: Checking for Agreement Between Pronouns and Antecedents
Choose the correct answer from the pair given in parentheses and write it on the line.

21. The tour guide told us that (his, their) tour started at eleven o'clock.

22. We were told that whales had been seen in the area, and we hoped to see (it, them).

23. The guide said we would walk out to the bluff; from (it, them), we would look for whales.

24. Jeremy said that (he, they) had seen a whale yesterday.

25. Each person on the tour had (his or her, their) own pair of binoculars.

26. Neither Valerie nor Amy could see the whale through (her, their) binoculars.

27. Twenty people stood on the bluff, trying (his or her, their) best to see the whales.

28. Suddenly a whale surfaced, blowing air through (their, its) blowhole.

29. Each person in the group said it was the highlight of (his or her, their) day.

30. All the members of the tour group thanked (his or her, their) guide for the great tour.

Part 4: Revising a Paragraph to Eliminate Problems in Agreement
Rewrite each sentence in the paragraph, correcting all errors in agreement. You may make any other minor changes that are needed.

31. Researchers in Antarctica launches more than 9,000 balloons each year, hoping that he will learn more.

32. These balloons ranges greatly in size, and its purposes are varied.

152 • Chapter 24: Making Words Agree © Prentice-Hall, Inc.

Name _____

33. Some of them is weather balloons about six feet in diameter.
_____

34. Others stretches to an enormous size.
_____

35. Some of these balloons is big enough to hold three jumbo jets set inside it.
_____

36. The helium inside them expand as the balloons rise.
_____

37. Eventually, the gas burst the balloons.
_____

38. Their plastic skins then drifts slowly back to Earth, landing on the ice or on the oceans.
_____

39. You might think that a scientist who send up a balloon would go out to retrieve them, but often they don't.
_____

40. Any whale that cruise the ocean in that area faces great danger if they happens to eat the plastic.
_____

Part 5: Standardized Test Practice
Read the paragraphs. There are several mistakes that need correcting.

(41) Although most whales live in salt water, some small whales lives in fresh water. (42) The water in which whales swim are colder than their body temperature is. (43) For this reason, whales have special adaptations to keep it warm. (44) Thick layers of fat called blubber help them retain body heat. (45) Another adaptation that helps whales keep warm are the shape of their bodies. (46) Their bodies are so thick that it traps heat.

(47) While on the surface, whales breathe air through blowholes on the tops of their heads. (48) Just before they dive, whales fills its lungs with air and close their blowholes. (49) Many whales is able to stay underwater for an hour. (50) When they come to the top, they blow the old air out of their blowholes in a watery spray.

41 Choose the best way to write Sentence 41. Circle the letter of your answer.
   A Most whales live in salt water, but some small whales lives in fresh water.
   B Although most whales live in salt water, some small whales live in fresh water.
   C Although most whales lives in salt water, some small whales lives in fresh water.
   D Best as it is

42 Which of these shows the best way to write Sentence 42?
   F The water in which whales swim is colder than their body temperature is.
   G The water in which a whale swims is colder than their body temperature is.
   H The water in which whales swim is colder than its body temperature is.
   J Best as it is

43 The best way to write Sentence 43 is
   A For this reason, a whale has special adaptations to keep them warm.
   B For this reason, whales have special adaptations to keep it warm.
   C For this reason, whales have special adaptations to keep them warm.
   D Best as it is

© Prentice-Hall, Inc.

Chapter 24: Making Words Agree • 153

Name _____

44 Choose the best way to write Sentence 44.
  F Thick layers of fat called blubber helps retain the heat.
  G A thick layer of fat called blubber help retain the heat.
  H Blubber, thick layers of fat, help retain the heat.
  J Best as it is

45 Which of these shows the best way to write Sentence 45?
  A Another adaptation that helps whales keep warm is the shape of their bodies.
  B Another adaptation that helps whales keep warm are the shapes of their bodies.
  C Another adaptation that helps a whale keep warm are the shape of its body.
  D Best as it is

46 Choose the best way to write Sentence 46.
  F Its body is so thick that they trap heat.
  G Their bodies are so thick that it traps heat.
  H Their bodies are so thick that they trap heat.
  J Best as it is

47 The best way to write Sentence 47 is
  A While on the surface, a whale breathes air through blowholes on the tops of their heads.
  B While on the surface, whales breathe air through blowholes on the top of its head.
  C While on the surface, a whale breathe air through blowholes on the tops of their heads.
  D Best as it is

48 Choose the best way to write Sentence 48.
  F Just before it dives, a whale fills their lungs with air and closes their blowholes.
  G Just before they dive, whales fill their lungs with air and close their blowholes.
  H Just before they dive, a whale fills its lungs with air and closes its blowhole.
  J Best as it is

49 The best way to write Sentence 49 is
  A Many whales are able to stay underwater for an hour.
  B Many whales are able to stays underwater for an hour.
  C Many whale is able to stay underwater for an hour.
  D Best as it is

50 Which of these shows the best way to write Sentence 50?
  F When it comes to the top, it blows the old air out of their blowholes in a watery spray.
  G When they come to the top, they blow the old air of out of its blowholes in a watery spray.
  H When it comes to the top, they blows the old air out of their blowholes in a watery spray.
  J Best as it is

Name _____ Date _____

 # Assessment for Chapter 25: Using Modifiers

Part 1: Forming Degrees of Modifiers
Complete the chart by writing the missing positive, comparative, and superlative degrees of the modifiers.

Positive Degree	Comparative Degree	Superlative Degree
1. dim		
2.	happier	
3.		soonest
4.	more wonderful	
5. coldly		
6.		most tenderly
7. good		
8.	worse	
9.		most afraid
10. efficient		
11. steadily		
12.	fewer	
13.		most rapidly
14.		loudest
15. icy		
16.	less expensive	
17. interesting		
18.	sharper	
19.		youngest
20.	further	

Part 2: Supplying Modifiers
Complete each sentence with the correct form of the modifier given. Then, identify the form (*positive, comparative, superlative*) you have used and write the other two forms.

21. Of all the dance forms, I like ballet the _____. (good)
    _____

22. I think ballet is _____ than modern dance, for example. (exciting)
    _____

23. To support the ballerina, a male ballet dancer must be very _____.
    (strong) _____

24. When I tried to do ballet, I felt _____ than usual. (clumsy)
    _____

© Prentice-Hall, Inc.   Chapter 25: Using Modifiers • 155

Name _____

25. I am always amazed at how _____ professional ballet dancers are. (graceful) _____

26. That dancer leaped _____ than I have ever seen anyone else leap. (high) _____

27. Last week, I had one of the _____ seats in the entire theater. (good) _____

28. The Russian dancer has the _____ hands I have ever seen. (delicate) _____

29. The dancer on stage now is _____ than the one who just left the stage. (young) _____

30. The costumes in this ballet are _____ than those in Coppelia. (elaborate) _____

Part 3: Revise to Eliminate Errors
Revise the sentences that contain errors in the use of modifiers. Write *correct* if a sentence contains no errors.

31. Have ever you seen a ballet?
_____

32. The one Bob only saw was Swan Lake.
_____

33. From the dancers to the orchestra, everyone performed real good.
_____

34. Swan Lake is one of the famousest of all ballets.
_____

35. Whenever I attend a ballet, I feel well afterward.
_____

36. The last one I saw had the more extraordinary costumes ever!
_____

37. The dancers performed the amazingest steps I have ever seen.
_____

38. That dancer is the gracefulest dancer on the stage today.
_____

39. Ballet dancers must be in excellent physical shape.
_____

40. Tonight's performance was gooder than last night's.
_____

Name _____

Part 4: Standardized Test Practice

Read the passage and choose the word or group of words that belongs in each space. Circle the letter of your answer.

> Ballet is certainly not the (41) dance to be developed. The tango, for example, has been around for (42) years than ballet. The waltz, too, developed (43) than the ballet. Certainly, dances like the jitterbug, the samba, the cha-cha, and the fox trot are (44) than ballet. Ballet, however, is (45) from all these dances. Perhaps the (46) difference is that ballet is meant to be performed on a stage. The other dances, forms of (47) dances, are performed in social settings. (48) ballet performance, you will be enchanted. Some people think it is the (49) art form in the world. Personally, I like ballet (50) than opera, but I like movies best of all.

41 A most recentest
B most recent
C recenter
D more recent

42 F less
G least
H fewer
J fewest

43 A later
B more later
C most later
D late

44 F new
G newest
H more newly
J newer

45 A quitely different
B quite different
C more different
D differenter

46 F big
G biggest
H bigger
J most big

47 A popularest
B more popular
C popularer
D popular

48 F If you go to just one
G If you just go to one
H If just you go to one
J If you go to one just

49 A most high
B higher
C highest
D high

50 F best
G gooder
H better
J more better

Name _____ Date _____

26 Assessment for Chapter 26: Punctuation

Part 1: Revising the Use of End Marks
Write the last word of each sentence on the line below the sentence, followed by the correct end mark for that sentence.

1. Booker T. Washington was born into slavery on a Virginia tobacco farm! _____

2. His mother was the cook on the plantation? _____

3. The small log cabin (fourteen by sixteen feet) where she did her cooking was also where she and her three children lived! _____

4. Imagine living in such a small area. _____

5. How did she find room for cooking. _____

Part 2: Revising the Use of Commas
Revise each sentence, adding and deleting commas where necessary.

6. When the Civil War ended Booker T. Washington, was nine years old.
   _____

7. Newly freed by the Emancipation Proclamation Washington his mother and his brother, moved to West Virginia.
   _____

8. Mrs. Viola Ruffner a New England woman, hired Washington, as a houseboy.
   _____

9. Recognizing Washington's eagerness to learn Mrs. Ruffner encouraged his studies.
   _____

10. Eventually he enrolled in a vocational school and after three years Washington graduated with honors.
    _____

11. Soon after graduation in fact Booker T. Washington, became a teacher, at the same school.
    _____

12. On July 4 1881 Washington opened the school, for which he is famous, Tuskegee Institute.
    _____

13. In November, 1915, while in New York City on business Washington became ill.
    _____

14. He had often said "I was born in the South have lived all my life in the South and expect to die and be buried in the South."
    _____

15. A few hours before he died on November 14 1915 Washington arrived by train in Alabama.
    _____

Name _____

Part 3: Revising the Use of Semicolons and Colons
Rewrite each sentence, deleting or adding semicolons or colons where necessary.

16. Booker T. Washington wrote two volumes of autobiography <u>The Story of My Life and Work</u>; and <u>Up From Slavery</u>.

17. Langston Hughes; called <u>Up From Slavery</u>: "one of America's most revealing books."

18. Washington was given an interesting nickname; the "Wizard of Tuskegee."

19. Washington dined with President Theodore Roosevelt they discussed politics.

20. Education; industriousness; and racial solidarity these were Washington's goals for African Americans.

Part 4: Adding Quotation Marks and Underlining
Rewrite each sentence, supplying and deleting quotation marks and underlining as necessary. If the sentence is written correctly, write *correct*.

21. "Maria asked, Have you ever been to Alabama?"

22. Henry told her that "he had never been there but would like to go."

23. "If you were in Alabama," he asked, "would you visit Tuskegee Institute"?

24. "Absolutely, exclaimed Maria. I wouldn't miss it".

25. Henry asked, "What else would you do in Alabama?"

26. "Well, said Maria, "I'm not sure. What would you suggest."?

27. "We should look in a <u>guidebook</u>", said Henry, "to find out about points of interest.

28. The first "chapter" of Up From Slavery is called <u>A Slave Among Slaves</u>.

29. Booker T. Washington's last book is called <u>The Man Farthest Down</u>.

30. Washington was praised in the <u>magazine</u> the North American Review.

© Prentice-Hall, Inc.   Chapter 26: Punctuation • 159

Name _____

Part 5: Using Hyphens and Apostrophes
Rewrite each sentence, adding and deleting hyphens and apostrophes as necessary. If the sentence is written correctly, write *correct*.

31. Thirty one people started Tuskegee Institute: one teacher and thirty students.
    _____

32. One of Booker T. Washingtons goals was to educate former slaves.
    _____

33. Washington wanted to give student's real world skills.
    _____

34. He wanted to train them for teaching, trades, and farm related work.
    _____

35. At first, Washington did'nt know how he would pay for Tuskegee.
    _____

36. Two Boston womens contribution to Tuskegee was six thousand dollars a year.
    _____

37. Booker T. Washington gave a speech about farm-production in mid June.
    _____

38. The average production of sweet potatoes per acre was forty-nine bushels.
    _____

39. A graduate of Tuskegee grew two-hundred-and-sixty-six bushels per acre.
    _____

40. A self employed farmer could make a good living.
    _____

Part 6: Standardized Test Practice
This is a test on using punctuation. It will show how effectively you use punctuation according to the standards of correct English.

Look for mistakes in the sentences. When you find a mistake, circle the letter of the line containing the mistake. Some sentences or sentence groups do not have any mistakes at all. If there is no mistake, circle the letter of the last line.

41 A Are you sure that
      B Booker T. Washington knew
      C nothing about his ancestry!
      D (*No mistake*)

42 F Wow.
      G It's hard for me
      H to imagine such a thing.
      J (*No mistake*)

43 A Washington said that
      B his owners were'nt
      C especially cruel.
      D (*No mistake*)

44 F When the Civil War ended
      G Booker T. Washington, along with
      H all the other slaves, was set free.
      J (*No mistake*)

Name _____

45 A Booker T. Washington's stepfather sent for
     B his family, so they traveled
     C on foot from Virginia to West Virginia.
     D (No mistake)

46 F The family arrived in
     G Malden, West Virginia after
     H walking for several weeks.
     J (No mistake)

47 A Booker T. Washington's desire
     B to learn to read was very strong; it had been
     C his dream since early childhood.
     D (No mistake)

48 F I know the date
     G of Booker T. Washington's death
     H November 14, 1915.
     J (No mistake)

49 A Washington's well known success
     B as an educator
     C brought honor to Tuskegee Institute.
     D (No mistake)

50 F "Would you care to contribute
     G some money toward Tuskegee's
     H scholarship fund," asked Debbie.
     J (No mistake)

51 A The ninth chapter of the book
     B <u>Up From Slavery</u> is called
     C "Anxious Days and Sleepless Nights".
     D (No mistake)

52 F Throughout Washington's life,
     G his speeches
     H were always well attended.
     J (No mistake)

53 A "Did you know, asked Pat,
     B "that Tuskegee's students actually laid the bricks
     C for thirty-six of the buildings?"
     D (No mistake)

54 F Rex answered, "I'll bet
     G you didn't know that the students
     H also made the bricks them-selves."
     J (No mistake)

55 A It was, to be sure
     B a happy day when
     C the school opened.
     D (No mistake)

Name _____ Date _____

Assessment for Chapter 27: Capitalization

Part 1: Using Capitals for Sentences and the Word *I*
Write any items that require capital letters, adding the missing capitals.
1. one of eight children, Henry Ford was born on the family farm.

2. the farm was located near Dearborn, Michigan.

3. the children were expected to help with the farming chores.

4. not long ago, i visited Dearborn.

5. one of the things i wanted to do was find the Ford family farm.

Part 2: Using Capitals With Proper Nouns and Proper Adjectives
Rewrite the sentences, adding capitals as needed.
6. Henry ford's parents were named william and mary.

7. Ford was born during the civil war.

8. At the time, abraham lincoln was in office.

9. There were only twenty-four states in the union.

10. In the confederacy, there were eleven states.

11. That was a terrible time in american history.

12. The civil war ended, and the united states went back to work.

13. In 1888, ford married a woman named clara bryant.

14. In 1893, they had their only child, edsel bryant ford.

15. Many years later, a car in the ford line would be named the edsel.

16. The edsel was never as popular as other ford cars, such as the mustang.

162 • Chapter 27: Capitalization © Prentice-Hall, Inc.

Name _____

17. Ford thought that more americans should have cars.
_____

18. In october 1908, ford announced the birth of the model t.
_____

19. This car was produced in ford's new plant in highland park, michigan.
_____

20. The american sales of this car far exceeded canadian and british sales.
_____

Part 3: Using Capitals for Titles of People and Things
Rewrite each sentence, adding any missing capitals for titles of people and things. If there are no missing capitals, write *correct*.

21. In 1899, Ford formed the detroit automobile company.
_____

22. My uncle says this company later became the henry ford company.
_____

23. Did you know that uncle dan once collected vintage cars?
_____

24. What kind of car did president eisenhower drive?
_____

25. I heard that my mother's great-grandfather once owned a model a.
_____

26. I remember aunt alice showing me a picture of one of her old cars.
_____

27. She always told me she felt like a queen in that car.
_____

28. The movie bonnie and clyde had some interesting old cars in it.
_____

29. Donald would rather work on old cars than study for his english class.
_____

30. I once wrote a story called "clara and the clunky old car."
_____

Part 4: Standardized Test Practice
Read the sentences and choose the word or words that belong in the spaces. Circle the letter of your answer.

31 Mines in _____ were the source of ore for Ford's early cars.
    A michigan and minnesota
    B Michigan and Minnesota
    C michigan and Minnesota
    D Michigan and minnesota

Name _____

32 Ford would get some supplies from the _____.
    F jungles of Brazil
    G Jungles of Brazil
    H jungles of brazil
    J Jungles of brazil

33 _____, Horace and John, sued Henry Ford for lowering prices and thus reducing stockholders' profits.
    A the Dodge brothers
    B The dodge brothers
    C The Dodge Brothers
    D The Dodge brothers

34 _____ went to an antique auto museum.
    F Sally, june, and i
    G Sally, june, and I
    H Sally, June, and I
    J sally, june, and i

35 During _____, Ford was forced to lower his workers' wages to four dollars a day.
    A the great depression
    B the Great Depression
    C the great Depression
    D The Great Depression

36 _____ collects old cars.
    F My German-speaking uncle
    G My german-speaking Uncle
    H my German-Speaking uncle
    J My German-Speaking Uncle

37 Uncle Jake sent me a picture of one of his cars near _____.
    A The Golden Gate Bridge
    B the golden gate Bridge
    C the Golden Gate Bridge
    D the Golden Gate bridge

38 What kind of car do you suppose _____ prefers?
    F the Mayor of Detroit
    G the mayor of detroit
    H the Mayor of detroit
    J the mayor of Detroit

39 Do you think _____ will come by car or by train?
    A Mayor Brown
    B mayor brown
    C mayor Brown
    D Mayor brown

40 My _____, moved to Detroit last year.
    F dentist, dr. Leon Pritchett
    G dentist, Dr. Leon Pritchett
    H Dentist, Dr. Leon Pritchett
    J Dentist, dr. Leon Pritchett

Name _____ Date _____

Grammar, Usage, and Mechanics: Cumulative Mastery Test

Part 1: Identifying Parts of Speech
On the line after each sentence, identify the part of speech of the underlined word. Choose from these parts of speech: *noun, pronoun, verb, adjective, adverb, preposition, conjunction,* or *interjection.*

1. In the late 1800's, many <u>American</u> cities were crowded. _____
2. New York City <u>grew</u> very fast during the nineteenth century. _____
3. In the 1840's, the number of people in New York rose <u>by</u> more than 60 percent. _____
4. In the 1850's, even more <u>people</u> moved to New York. _____
5. By 1860, the city of <u>New York</u> had more than 800,000 people. _____
6. Twenty years earlier, there had been only about 300,000 people <u>there</u>. _____
7. The population had swelled when Ireland's Great Famine forced <u>many</u> Irish to flee their homeland. _____
8. If they had stayed in Ireland, <u>they</u> would have starved. _____
9. Many German immigrants also came to New York, <u>and</u> there was not enough housing. _____
10. <u>Gee</u>! It must have been terrible. _____

Part 2: Identifying Parts of Sentences
On the line after each item, identify the underlined section as one of the following: *sentence, fragment, complete subject, complete predicate, direct object, indirect object, predicate noun,* or *predicate adjective.*

11. The newcomers to New York City in the 1800's were mostly Irish <u>people</u>. _____
12. <u>Also Germans who had left Germany after the Revolution of 1848.</u> _____
13. All these people <u>had to find low-cost housing for their families</u>. _____
14. <u>A new kind of housing</u> was built. _____
15. <u>It</u> was called the tenement. _____
16. A tenement building housed many <u>families</u>. _____
17. Most of the tenement units <u>were very small and had poor air circulation</u>. _____
18. People were not very <u>comfortable</u> in these buildings. _____
19. <u>The air did not move because there were not enough windows</u>. _____
20. "Please tell <u>me</u> more about the history of the tenement," Katie said. _____

Part 3: Identifying Phrases and Clauses
On the line after each sentence, identify the underlined section as one of the following: *prepositional phrase used as an adjective, prepositional phrase used as an adverb, appositive, appositive phrase, participle, participial phrase, infinitive, infinitive phrase, independent clause, adjective clause,* or *adverb clause.*

21. <u>Hoping for a solution</u>, people held a contest for architects. _____
22. The biggest problem, <u>poor circulation of air</u>, needed to be solved. _____

© Prentice-Hall, Inc. Grammar, Usage, and Mechanics: Cumulative Mastery Test • 165

Name _____

23. Since the buildings needed better air circulation and light, <u>one architect included a narrow shaft between buildings</u>. _____

24. The city built thousands of tenements <u>that followed this design</u>. _____

25. Unfortunately, <u>rotting</u> garbage accumulated in the shafts. _____

26. My great-grandfather, <u>Danny McGuinness</u>, once lived in a New York tenement. _____

27. The air shafts were a fire hazard <u>because they allowed flames to travel more quickly</u>. _____

28. The tenements were not a good solution, and housing <u>for the poor</u> remained dangerous. _____

29. The lack of plumbing, the close quarters, and the dirty conditions encouraged disease <u>to spread</u>. _____

30. <u>Within a few years</u>, the great tenement experiment soon turned into the slums of New York. _____

Part 4: Effective Sentences
Follow the directions for each item. Write the answer on the line provided.

31. Determine whether the following is a *declarative sentence*, an *interrogative sentence*, an *imperative sentence*, or an *exclamatory sentence*.

    Have you ever seen a tenement building?
    _____

32. Combine these two sentences by using a compound subject.

    Irish famine victims came to America in the late 1840's. Many German immigrants came to America then, too.
    _____

33. Combine these two sentences by using a compound verb.

    Most immigrant residences were crowded. Most immigrant residences had poor air circulation.
    _____

34. Combine these sentences by using a compound object.

    The winning design improved air circulation. The winning design improved light.
    _____

35. Combine these sentences by using a semicolon.

    A new kind of housing was built to solve New York's housing problem. It was called the tenement.
    _____

36. Combine these sentences by joining the clauses with a comma and a conjunction.

    The tenements were soon overcrowded. The people inside were not very comfortable.
    _____

Name _____

37. Combine these sentences by using a subordinate clause.

    Sandra's ancestors lived in a New York tenement building. The building has since been torn down.
    _____

38. Rewrite this sentence fragment as a complete sentence. Add details if necessary.

    Wanted to move out of the overcrowded building.
    _____

39. Rewrite this sentence to avoid using a misplaced modifier.

    Hoping to win the contest, the design included an air shaft in the center of several buildings.
    _____

40. If there are any errors in this sentence, rewrite it correctly. If the sentence is correct as written, write *correct*.

    The family didn't have no choice but to except the offer to live in the crowded building.
    _____

Part 5: Using Verbs
Follow the directions for each item. Write the answer on the line after the item.

41. Identify the underlined principal part as *present*, *present participle*, *past*, or *past participle*. Also, indicate whether it is *regular* or *irregular*.

    Originally, basketball players <u>wore</u> one of three styles of uniforms.
    _____

42. Identify the underlined principal part as *present*, *present participle*, *past*, or *past participle*. Also, indicate whether it is *regular* or *irregular*.

    Some of the players were <u>wearing</u> knee-length football trousers.
    _____

43. Rewrite this sentence using the principal part of the verb indicated in parentheses.

    In 1903, officials had (rule—past participle) that all boundary lines on a basketball court must be straight.
    _____

44. Rewrite this sentence using the principal part of the verb indicated in parentheses.

    Before 1903, teams were (draw—present participle) the lines around existing obstructions such as pillars, stairways, or offices.
    _____

45. Rewrite this sentence using the verb and tense indicated in parentheses.

    Max (show—past perfect) us pictures of some old basketball teams.
    _____

46. Rewrite this sentence using the verb and tense indicated in parentheses.

    By the end of the night, our basketball game surely (win—future perfect) the championship.
    _____

Name _____

47. Rewrite this sentence using the verb and tense indicated in parentheses.

    Don (practice—present perfect progressive) some of his basketball moves.
    _____

48. Rewrite this sentence using the verb and tense indicated in parentheses.

    Donna (see—past) the game last night.
    _____

49. If this sentence has a misused verb, rewrite the sentence correctly. If the sentence does not have a misused verb, write *correct*.

    As the game began, we set our bowl of popcorn on the table.
    _____

50. If this sentence has a misused verb, rewrite the sentence correctly. If the sentence does not have a misused verb, write *correct*.

    As Todd watched the game, his dog laid on the floor by the couch.
    _____

Part 6: Using Pronouns
Follow the directions for each sentence. Write the answer on the line.

51. Identify the case of the underlined pronoun as *nominative*, *objective*, or *possessive*.

    John Chapman was born in 1774; he came to be known as Johnny

    Appleseed. _____

52. Identify the case of the underlined pronoun as *nominative*, *objective*, or *possessive*.

    Chapman knew a lot about flowering plants and trees, for his was a lifelong

    interest. _____

53. Identify the case of the underlined pronoun as *nominative*, *objective*, or *possessive*.

    Chapman's interest in apple trees transformed him into an American folk

    character. _____

54. Write the nominative pronoun, and tell how it is used.

    We know that John Chapman was a devoted horticulturist. _____

55. Write the nominative pronoun, and tell how it is used.

    Chapman planted apple seeds throughout the Midwest, and they grew into fine

    orchards. _____

56. Add an appropriate nominative pronoun to the sentence. Then, tell how the pronoun is used.

    _____ am doing a report on Johnny Appleseed. _____

57. Add an appropriate nominative pronoun to the sentence. Then, tell how the pronoun is used.

    Do you know who planted these trees? It was _____, Johnny Appleseed. _____

58. Write the objective pronoun, and tell how it is used.

    Johnny Appleseed met pioneers traveling west, and he gave them seeds and saplings to

    plant once they got there. _____

Name _____

59. Write the objective pronoun, and tell how it is used.

    He wore on his head a tin mush pan, and he used it as a hat and as a cooking pot. _____

60. Select the correct pronoun from the choices in parentheses. Write it on the line, and then tell its case.

    Chapman would often check on an existing orchard to make sure (it's, its) trees were healthy. _____

Part 7: Making Words Agree
Follow the directions for each sentence.

61. Choose the correct verb from the pair in parentheses, and write it on the line.

    John Chapman's playmate from childhood days (was, were) Sam Wilson. _____

62. Choose the correct verb from the pair in parentheses, and write it on the line.

    Sam Wilson (is, are) known as the real-life Uncle Sam. _____

63. Choose the correct verb from the pair in parentheses, and write it on the line.

    The year is 1775, and young Sam Wilson and John Chapman (play, plays) together. _____

64. Choose the correct verb from the pair in parentheses, and write it on the line.

    Chapman or Wilson (join, joins) the army in 1780 and fights in the American Revolution. _____

65. If the subject and verb do not agree in number, rewrite the sentence correctly, keeping the verb in the present tense. If the sentence is correct, write *correct*.

    The Revolution now over, Sam Wilson move to Troy, New York.
    _____

66. Write the subject in the sentence. Then, choose the correct verb from the pair in parentheses, and write it next to the subject.

    There (is, are) an interesting story about the origins of Uncle Sam. _____

67. Choose the correct verb from the pair in parentheses, and write it on the line.

    Because of Sam Wilson's good reputation, people in Troy (begin, begins) calling him Uncle Sam. _____

68. Complete the sentence, adding a verb that makes sense. Make sure the verb you use is in the present tense and agrees with the subject.

    During the War of 1812, Sam Wilson _____ a government contract to supply meat for American troops.

69. Complete the sentence, filling in the blank with an appropriate pronoun.

    Once the government meat contract is _____, Sam's employees stamp the meat packages with a large "U.S." for United States.

© Prentice-Hall, Inc.   GRAMMAR, USAGE, AND MECHANICS: Cumulative Mastery Test • 169

Name _____

70. Choose the correct personal pronoun from the choices given in parentheses, and write it on the line.

    A worker jokingly explains the initials, saying (it, they) originated with his employer's nickname, Uncle Sam. _____

Part 8: Using Modifiers
Follow the directions for each sentence.

71. Write the comparative and superlative degrees of the following modifier.

    patriotically _____

72. Write the comparative and superlative degrees of the following modifier.

    unclear _____

    _____

73. Rewrite this sentence using the form of the modifier indicated in parentheses.

    Today's drawings of Uncle Sam are (colorful—comparative) than the early sketches in black and white.

    _____

74. Rewrite this sentence, supplying the form of the modifier indicated in parentheses.

    The (good—superlative) images of Uncle Sam today are in red, white, and blue.

    _____

75. Write the degree of the underlined word.

    The <u>most famous</u> painting of Uncle Sam appeared on World War I posters. _____

76. If the sentence has an error in degree, rewrite it correctly. If the sentence has no errors, write *correct*.

    After the flag, the image of Uncle Sam is probably the more familiar of all American symbols.

    _____

77. The underlined modifier is used incorrectly. Rewrite the sentence, correcting the misused modifier.

    At the antique show, I <u>only</u> want to buy an original World War I poster of Uncle Sam.

    _____

78. The underlined modifier is used incorrectly. Rewrite the sentence, correcting the misused modifier.

    After I found the antique poster, I felt really <u>well</u>.

    _____

79. If the sentence has an error in the use of modifiers, rewrite the sentence correctly. If the sentence has no errors, write *correct*.

    I just need one more poster to complete my collection.

    _____

80. If the sentence has an error in the use of modifiers, rewrite the sentence correctly. If the sentence has no errors, write *correct*.

    It took less time to find the poster than it took to get the poster framed.

    _____

Name _____

Part 9: Using Punctuation Marks
Follow the directions for each sentence.

81. A comma has been left out of this sentence. On the line, write the word before the comma, the comma, and the word following the comma.

    You would probably not recognize the first Uncle Sam illustrations for the figure was quite different in 1820. _____

82. Rewrite the sentence, adding commas where they are needed.

    The first Uncle Sam illustrations did not show the figure as tall thin and hollow-cheeked.
    _____

83. If the sentence requires a comma, rewrite it, adding the comma. If the sentence is correct, write *correct*.

    The first Uncle Sam figure wore a solid black top hat.
    _____

84. Revise the sentence, adding or removing commas as appropriate.

    During Andrew Jackson's presidency the bright red pants were added, to the figure of Uncle Sam.
    _____

85. Revise this sentence, adding or removing commas as appropriate.

    Look Jane at this interesting old poster of Uncle Sam.
    _____

86. Rewrite this sentence, adding commas to set off the parenthetical expression.

    This poster I believe will go up in value within the next five years.
    _____

87. Rewrite this sentence, adding commas where necessary.

    Frances found this poster on April 24 2001 and she paid only fifty dollars for it.
    _____

88. Rewrite this sentence, adding commas and quotation marks as needed. If the sentence is correct as is, write *correct*.

    It starts with every one of us giving a little more said Sam Wilson instead of only taking and getting all the time.
    _____
    _____

89. Rewrite the sentence, adding commas and quotation marks as needed. If the sentence is correct as is, write *correct*.

    Carl wondered if John F. Kennedy got an idea for one of his speeches from Sam Wilson.
    _____

90. Rewrite this sentence, adding hyphens as necessary. If the sentence is correct as is, write *correct*.

    Sam Wilson, owner of a meat packing company, died in 1854 at the age of eighty eight.
    _____

Name _____

Part 10: Capitalization
Rewrite each sentence, adding and deleting capital letters as necessary.

91. Many people think That there was no real-life uncle Sam.

92. In fact, i used to think that the figure was just a Myth.

93. a Historian named thomas gerson discovered an old Newspaper dated may 12, 1830.

94. The article talked about pheodorus bailey, a postmaster in new york city.

95. It said that mr. bailey went to sam wilson's meat-packing plant in october of 1812.

96. Mr. bailey confirms that one of the Workers said that *U.S.* meant "Uncle Sam."

97. Samuel wilson is buried at oakwood cemetery in troy, new york.

98. My favorite Cousin, dr. Alice May, visited that Cemetery last Year.

99. Sylvia asked, "do you like my new Poster, dad?"

100. I did a presentation on Historical posters for my History class last Month.

Part 3: Academic and Workplace Skills

Name _____ Date _____

 # Assessment for Chapter 28: Speaking, Listening, Viewing, and Representing

1. Give an example of a step you could take to prepare for a class discussion. Explain why this step is important.
   _____
   _____

2. What are two things you can do to give clear and accurate directions? Write them below.
   _____
   _____

3. How would you introduce your brother to your teacher? Write the introduction on the lines below.
   _____
   _____
   _____

4. Write the letter of the definition next to the type of speech it describes.
   _____ explanatory   a. a speech that amuses the audience
   _____ persuasive   b. a speech used to get the audience to agree with the speaker
   _____ entertaining   c. a speech that explains an idea or an event

5. Which kind of speech would you give if you were campaigning for class president?
   _____

6. Which kind of speech would you give if you were describing the history of your city?
   _____

Use the following information to help you answer questions 7–8.

   Imagine that your city wants to sell some land near your school. The land is currently the site of a community garden. You oppose the plan. Prepare a short persuasive speech that you will deliver at the next meeting of the city council.

7. What is the purpose of your speech?
   _____

8. Who will be the audience for your speech?
   _____

9. On the lines below, write an outline for your speech. The outline should include two main points. Under each main point, list two details.
   _____
   _____
   _____
   _____
   _____
   _____

© Prentice-Hall, Inc.   Chapter 28: Speaking, Listening, Viewing, and Representing • 175

Name _____

10. Write a sample note card you could use while delivering your speech.

```
┌─────────────────────────────────────────────────┐
│                                                 │
│                                                 │
│                                                 │
│                                                 │
│                                                 │
│                                                 │
│                                                 │
│                                                 │
└─────────────────────────────────────────────────┘
```

11. Circle the letter of a strategy you should remember when delivering a speech. On the line, explain your answer.
    a. Speak as quickly as you can, so that you can get all the information across.
    b. Use as much time as you need to get your point across to the audience.
    c. Read directly from your note cards so that you don't forget to say anything.
    d. Be aware of nonverbal language while you deliver your speech.
    _____

12. Circle the letter of a rule you should follow to build your listening skills. On the line, explain your answer.
    a. Look around the room and let your mind absorb the speaker's words.
    b. Keep paper and a pencil ready for note taking.
    c. Focus on the speaker's style and gestures to help you to understand his or her message.
    d. Open the classroom windows to let fresh air and nature sounds into the room.
    _____

13. Why is it helpful to identify a speaker's main idea and major details?
    _____
    _____
    _____

14. Give an example of a feature on a map, graph, or photograph that would tell you the kind of information you should expect to learn.
    _____
    _____
    _____

15. Why is it important to determine your purpose for studying a map, graph, or photograph?
    _____
    _____
    _____

Name _____

Study the map below, and use it to answer questions 16–17.

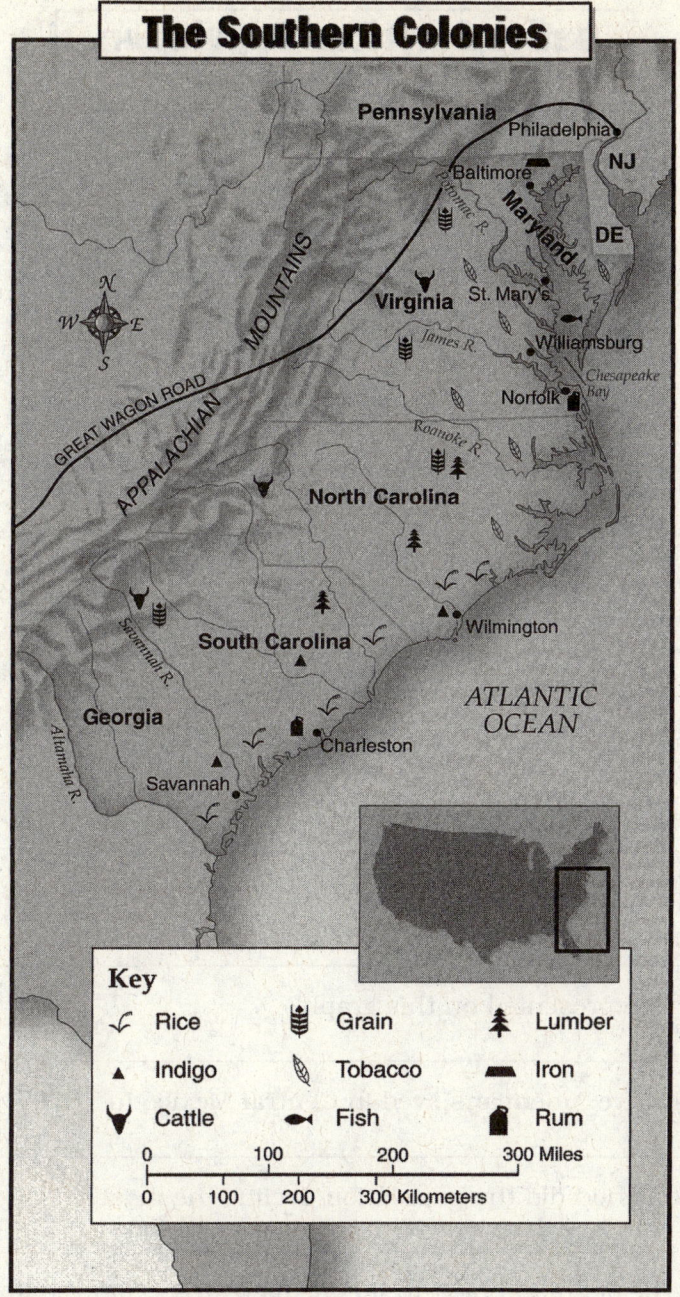

16. What is the purpose of this map?
_____

17. What products were produced in North Carolina?
_____

Name _____

Study the graph below, and use it to answer questions 18–21.

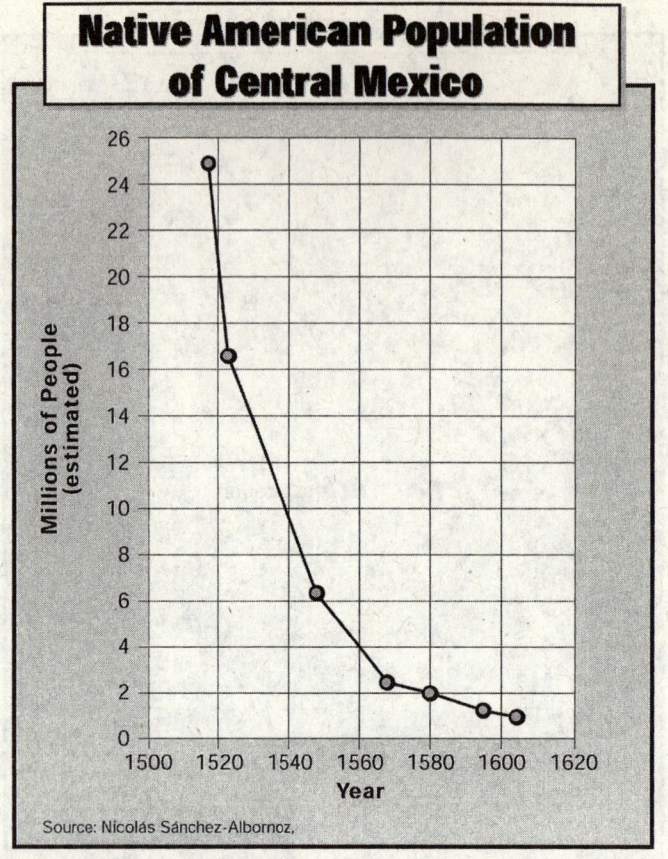

18. What kind of graph is this?
   _____

19. What information is represented on this graph?
   _____

20. About how many Native Americans lived in Central Mexico in 1520?
   _____

21. During which time period did the population decline the most?
   _____

22. Write the letter of the definition next to the media concept. On the lines, explain how knowing these concepts can help you to evaluate the information you get from the media.

   _____ fact   a. a tendency to think in a certain way
   _____ opinion   b. a statement that can be proven to be true
   _____ loaded language   c. a viewpoint that cannot be proven
   _____ bias   d. emotional words used to persuade the viewer or listener

   _____
   _____
   _____
   _____
   _____

Name _____

23. Name an example of the kind of information you get when you examine a piece of artwork.
    _____
    How is this information useful?
    _____

24. Imagine that you have to organize information that compares the qualities of two different juice drinks. Explain how you could display this information using a graphic organizer.
    _____
    _____

25. Why is it useful to organize information visually?
    _____

26. Use the following data to construct a pie chart in the circle below. Include a title for your chart.

    From 1880 to 1900, 59% of the immigrants to the United States came from northern and western Europe; 33% came from eastern and southern Europe; 6% came from the Americas; 1% came from Asia; and 1% came from all other countries.

    ◯

27. What are three examples of basic word-processing formatting features you can use to enhance written work and capture the reader's attention?
    _____

28. Imagine that you wanted to create a multimedia presentation for a report about life in the United States during the Civil War period. Which media would you use to illustrate your report? List two examples on the lines below. Next to each example, write the equipment you would use to present the media.
    _____
    _____

29. Write the letter that shows when you would use a certain type of medium next to the example of the medium.

    ____ slides   a. to display a very small item to an entire group
    ____ overhead projector   b. to have a written version of a story you will videotape
    ____ video shooting script   c. to show a sequence of events in a cartoon strip format
    ____ storyboard   d. to show several paintings so that each can be examined

Name _____

30. Choose a favorite song that you might like to perform for your classmates. On the lines below, write the name of the song. Next to it, identify the mood that you would establish in your performance. Then, briefly describe the costumes, setting, and anything else you would use to create this mood.

_____
_____
_____
_____

Name _____   Date _____

 **Assessment for Chapter 29: Vocabulary and Spelling**

1. Name an example of an activity you could do to develop a wider vocabulary.
   _____

2. Imagine that you come across a word that is unfamiliar to you. Give an example of how you might figure out the meaning of the word.
   _____
   _____

3. The following passage contains five underlined words or phrases. As you read the passage, try to determine a meaning for each word by looking for context clues in the sentence. Then, on the line following each word or phrase, write the meaning as it was used in the passage.

   Janet has always been a (a) harbinger of bad news, insisting that she knows about events before the rest of us. Early last week she insisted that Ms. Ramirez was planning a surprise test. She spoke with such dramatic (b) hyperbole (now we now it was pure exaggeration) that we believed her. We all rushed home to study, never thinking to (d) discount her words as alarmist. The suspense kept us on (d) pins and needles. By Friday afternoon our (e) soaring fears were almost out of control, but we finally found out that we would not have a test after all.

   a. harbinger: _____
   b. hyperbole: _____
   c. discount: _____
   d. pins and needles: _____
   e. soaring: _____

4. Circle the figurative language used in the sentence below. On the line, explain why the circled phrase is an example of figurative language, and write its meaning.

   The drops of sleet fell like daggers on me, sharply pelting my skin with icy moisture.
   _____

5. Circle the idiom used in the sentence below. On the line, explain why the circled phrase is an example of an idiom, and write its meaning.

   Mr. Jackson had a five o'clock appointment with his doctor, but the doctor was behind schedule, so he had to cool his heels for a while.
   _____

6. How can you use a notebook and a glossary to help you study word meanings in content areas such as social studies and science?
   _____
   _____

7. Explain how the Possible Sentences Strategy can help you to increase your vocabulary.
   _____
   _____

Name _____

8. Describe a way in which you can use a vocabulary notebook to learn new words.
   _____
   _____

9. Explain how using flashcards can help you to learn new vocabulary words.
   _____
   _____

10. Give an example of one kind of information you can find in a dictionary, and explain why the information is helpful to readers and writers.
    _____
    _____

11. Describe how the synonym finder in a word-processing program could help a writer in his or her work.
    _____

12. How can learning word roots help you to better understand the meaning of words?
    _____

Read each group of words in questions 13–15. Then, write the root that all the words share. Next to the root, write its meaning.

13. visibility; visual; visionary; invisible
    _____

14. mission, missile, transmit
    _____

15. motor, commotion, motivate
    _____

16. Write the prefix of each word on the line. Then, write the base word.
    a. transmission: _____
    b. rearrange: _____
    c. unnatural: _____
    d. misappropriate: _____
    e. exhale: _____

17. Write the suffix of each word on the line. Then, identify the part of speech of the entire word.
    a. resentment: _____
    b. reflection: _____
    c. remarkable: _____
    d. unkindly: _____
    e. divisible: _____

182 • Chapter 29: Vocabulary and Spelling

Name _____

18. Write the prefixes, roots, and suffixes for the following words in the appropriate columns and spaces. If a word lacks any of these parts, write *none* in the space. Then, write a short definition in the last column.

Word	Prefix	Root	Suffix	Definition
a. invention	_____	_____	_____	_____
b. transmit	_____	_____	_____	_____
c. reversion	_____	_____	_____	_____
d. unlovable	_____	_____	_____	_____
e. vision	_____	_____	_____	_____

19. Give an example of a historical influence on the English language.
_____
_____

20. What is one reason that students should create a personal spelling list?
_____

21. On the lines below, write two derivatives formed from each base word.
   a. real: _____
   b. study: _____
   c. magic: _____

22. Describe each of the following steps for studying spelling words.
   LOOK _____
   SAY _____
   SPELL _____
   COMPARE _____

23. Each of the following sentences contains a spelling error. Find the misspelled word and write it correctly in the space before the sentence.
   a. The cieling collapsed after the hurricane. _____
   b. The king's riegn was long and peaceful. _____
   c. Neither the soldeirs nor their commander knew the territory. _____
   d. We did not recieve the package our neighbors sent. _____
   e. The delicatly embroidered fabric is beautiful. _____

24. Add the suffix in parentheses to each of the following words. Write the new word on the line. Be sure to spell it correctly.
   a. trite (-ly) _____
   b. sturdy (-ness) _____
   c. compete (-ition) _____
   d. defer (-ed) _____
   e. prefer (-ence) _____

Name _____

25. Change each of the following words by adding the word parts indicated. Be sure to spell each new word correctly.

   a. re + iterate = _____

   b. in + disputable = _____

   c. refer + ence = _____

   d. love + able = _____

   e. dis + interested = _____

26. On the line below, write a memory aid to help you spell the following word: *different*.
   _____

27. Explain how other languages and cultures can affect the spelling of English words.
   _____
   _____
   _____
   _____
   _____

28. Write the plural form of each of the following words.

   a. shelf _____

   b. fireman _____

   c. mother-in-law _____

   d. radio _____

   e. clash _____

29. Circle the correct word in each pair in parentheses.
   a. We prepared a (beet, beat) salad for dinner.
   b. Did you bring the horse's (bridal, bridle)?
   c. We followed the (route, root) to the mountain cabin.
   d. I preferred the (plain, plane) dress to the fancy one.
   e. The heavy (steal, steel) beam supports the roof.

30. Proofread the following passage. Circle the misspelled words, and write the correct spellings on the lines below.

   Many of the ponys and horses like to exercise in there pasture near the barn. The ranch hands make sure the animals do not sieze the chance to run away. In the passed, several larger horses jumpped the fence surrounding the pen. For the horses' own protection, the owner of the ranch built a higher fence last spring.

   a. _____
   b. _____
   c. _____
   d. _____
   e. _____

184 • Chapter 29: Vocabulary and Spelling © Prentice-Hall, Inc.

Name _____   Date _____

30 Assessment for Chapter 30: Reading Skills

1. Explain the purpose of an introduction to a chapter in a textbook.
   _____
   _____

2. Write the name of the special section—table of contents; chapter introduction and summary; glossary; or index—that you would use to find the following information.

   a. the meaning of a specialized term in a science textbook _____

   b. a review of the main points of the chapter in a history textbook _____

   c. the page number on which Chapter 4 begins in a literature textbook _____

   d. the history textbook pages on which to find information about the Declaration of Independence _____

3. How do headings and subheadings assist a person who is reading a textbook?
   _____

4. Why is it useful to look over the questions and exercises at the end of a textbook chapter *before* you have started to read the chapter?
   _____
   _____

5. How do pictures help students who are reading a textbook chapter?
   _____

6. Describe the purpose of a caption that might be placed under a picture or photograph in a textbook.
   _____
   _____

7. Write the reading strategy—scanning, skimming, or close reading—that you would use in each of the following situations.

   a. You are trying to find a specific section in a textbook: _____

   b. You are trying to understand all the information in a chapter: _____

   c. You are trying to get a general idea of the chapter content by looking for highlighted or bold type words and topic sentences: _____

8. Write the correct letter of the definition on the line next to the question–answer relationship it describes.

   _____ Right there   a. Answers are not in the text; you rely on your experiences.

   _____ Think and search   b. You relate what the author says to what you know.

   _____ Author and you   c. The answer is in the text, but you have to ponder the question and find evidence to support your answer.

   _____ On your own   d. The answers are in the text in one or two sentences.

Name _____

9. Choose one of the six stages of the SQ4R method—survey; question; read; recite; record; or review—and write it on the line next to the correct definition.

   a. Take notes to reinforce information. _____

   b. Orally or mentally recall questions and their answers. _____

   c. Turn each heading into a question that you ask yourself. _____

   d. Review the material on a regular basis. _____

   e. Preview the material you are going to read. _____

   f. Search for the answers to questions you have posed to yourself. _____

10. In what way can a graphic organizer assist someone who is learning about a new topic?
    _____

11. Imagine that you have to show the various ways in which the American colonists prepared themselves for a revolution. Explain how you might use a graphic organizer to help you show your information.
    _____
    _____

12. Read the following passage. Then, use the Venn diagram below to show the similarities and differences between butterflies and moths. Be sure to label the diagram.

    Butterflies and moths are insects whose bodies are made up of three parts. They both have six legs and four wings. Their wings are often one color on the outside and a different color inside. The butterfly rests at night, while the moth hides in the day. Also, moths are often very hairy while butterflies are not. Butterflies use their colors to find a mate; but male moths find the female by her scent.

13. Why is it important to get in the habit of *paraphrasing* what you read in a nonfiction book such as a textbook?
    _____
    _____

14. What is the difference between main ideas and major details?
    _____
    _____

Name _____

15. Read the following passage from a social studies textbook. Then, answer the questions below.

   In 1840, Lucretia Mott and Elizabeth Cady Stanton decided to hold a convention to draw attention to the problems women faced. Eight years later, in 1848, in Seneca Falls, New York, that convention finally took place. About 200 women and 40 men attended the Seneca Falls Convention. At the meeting, leaders of the women's rights movement presented a Declaration of Sentiments, which was modeled on the Declaration of Independence.

   a. What is the main idea of the passage? _____
   b. What are two main details in the passage? _____
   _____
   c. What is the author's purpose for writing the passage? _____
   d. How does the information in this passage relate to other information that you have studied?
   _____

16. What is the difference between a fact and an opinion?
   _____
   _____

17. Read the sentences below. On the line, identify each as *F* (fact) or *O* (opinion).
   a. ____ Abraham Lincoln was one of the greatest presidents in U.S. history.
   b. ____ Abraham Lincoln issued the Emancipation Proclamation on January 1, 1863.
   c. ____ The Gettysburg Address was delivered on November 19, 1863.
   d. ____ Vice President Andrew Johnson became president after Lincoln's assassination.

18. Write one of the five most common purposes for writing—to inform; to instruct; to offer an opinion; to sell; or to entertain—next to the subject that would best lend itself to the purpose.
   a. the steps to take to build a birdhouse _____
   b. the antics of a group of 5-year-olds at a sleepover party _____
   c. the newest, most exciting product to come on the crispy cereal market _____
   d. the work of Harriet Tubman and the Underground Railroad _____
   e. the reason that people should stop their cars at pedestrian crosswalks _____

19. Read the following sentence. Explain which words helped you to identify the author's purpose.

   In this editorial I will explain my feelings about the new city budget.
   _____

20. Read the sentences. Write either an *inference* or a *generalization* that could be made from reading the sentence.

   Our class is unique: Of the thirty students, three of them are identical to one another.
   _____
   _____

Name _____

21. Explain the difference between *denotation* and *connotation* in writing.
   _____
   _____
   _____
   _____

22. Write the denotation of the underlined word.

   Because of the ice and sleet, the roads were especially <u>hazardous</u>.
   _____

23. Write two sentences that describe an object in your classroom. In the first sentence, convey a positive connotation. In the second sentence, convey a negative connotation.

   a. _____
   _____

   b. _____
   _____

24. Write the meaning of the underlined jargon in the following sentence.

   Due to their fear of <u>cybercrime</u>, some people are afraid to use credit cards to buy products on the Internet.
   _____
   _____

25. Write the letter of the *organizational structure* next to the *purpose* for which it is used in writing.

   _____ to present a series of interrelated events   a. spatial order
   _____ to create a persuasive argument   b. cause and effect
   _____ to arrange events in time   c. chronological order
   _____ to arrange details in space   d. order of importance

26. What is the difference between nonfiction and literary writing?
   _____
   _____
   _____

27. What does it mean to *identify* with a character or a situation in a work of fiction?
   _____
   _____

   Give an example of a character in a work of fiction with whom you have identified, and briefly explain why.
   _____
   _____
   _____

Name _____

28. How can a reader make inferences or draw conclusions to identify the theme of a work?
   _____
   _____
   _____

29. How is drama different from nonfiction?
   _____
   _____
   _____

30. How can a reader make a drama come alive by creating a mental picture of the action?
   _____
   _____
   _____
   _____

31. Name one difference between reading poetry and reading novels or short stories.
   _____
   _____
   _____

32. Describe how identifying the speaker of a poem can help a reader to understand it better.
   _____
   _____
   _____

33. Identify each of the following as a myth, legend, or folk tale. _____
   a. a story about one of the gods or goddesses in Greek mythology. _____
   b. a story about the adventures of Paul Bunyan and his big blue ox. _____
   c. a story about one of the knights at King Arthur's court in medieval England _____

34. Briefly explain why people read newspapers.
   _____
   _____

35. Identify one of these sources—an *application*; an *anthology*; an *electronic text*; or a *newspaper*—that you would use for each of the following purposes:
   a. to find information about a current political issue _____
   b. to apply for a job _____
   c. to find information about your favorite hobby _____
   d. to find short stories by South American writers _____

Name _____   Date _____

 **Assessment for Chapter 31: Study, Reference, and Test-Taking Skills**

1. Give an example of a skill that could be used as part of an overall study plan.
   _____
   _____

2. Fill in the diagram below with a sample daily plan for three of your weekdays. Include daily assignment time; long-term assignments; and sports practice.

SAMPLE STUDY SCHEDULE	
Mon	3:00–4:30
	5:00–6:00
	7:30–8:00
	8:00–8:30
Tue	5:00–6:00
	7:30–8:30
Wed	5:00–6:00
	7:00–8:00
	8:00–8:30

Read the following passage, and use it to answer questions 3–4.

Punishment for Massachusetts

   The British were outraged by what they saw as Boston's lawless behavior. In 1774, Parliament, encouraged by King George III, acted to punish Massachusetts. First, Parliament shut down the port of Boston. No ship could enter or leave the harbor—not even a small boat. The harbor would remain closed until the colonists paid for the tea.
   Second, Parliament forbade colonists to hold town meetings more than once a year without the governor's permission. In the past, colonists had called town meetings whenever they wished.

3. Write a modified outline of the passage. Include the main idea, at least one major detail, and supporting details.
   _____
   _____
   _____
   _____
   _____
   _____
   _____
   _____

4. Write a brief summary of the passage.
   _____
   _____
   _____
   _____

Name _____

5. Give an example of a resource that is available in your school and public libraries.
   _____
   _____

6. How can the library catalog help you find books?
   _____

7. Give a reason that libraries have separate author, title, and subject catalogs.
   _____

8. Suppose you wanted to find out if a book about the solar system was currently available in your public library. Explain which catalog you would use.
   _____
   _____

9. How would you find Fred Gipson's novel *Old Yeller* in your library?
   _____

10. How would you find a nonfiction book about earthquakes?
    _____

11. How would you find a biography of Alfred Hitchcock written by Ken Mogg?
    _____

12. Explain whether you would use a magazine or a book to find the most recent information about U.S. space exploration.
    _____
    _____

13. Explain how you would use a periodical index, such as the *Reader's Guide to Periodical Literature*, to find articles about a favorite sports personality.
    _____
    _____

14. Identify the type of dictionary—*abridged*, *unabridged*, or *specialized*—that you would use to answer each of the following questions:
    - Which dictionary would you use to look up the French term *Au revoir*? _____
    - Which dictionary would you use to check the spelling of a word while you are writing an essay? _____
    - Which dictionary would you use to find all the different meanings of the word *heel*?
    _____

15. Explain how you would look up the word *circumspect* in a printed dictionary and in an electronic dictionary.
    _____
    _____
    _____
    _____

16. What are three elements you find in most dictionary entries?
    _____
    _____

© Prentice-Hall, Inc.

Chapter 31: Study, Reference, and Test-Taking Skills

Name _____

17. Base your answers to these questions on the following dictionary entry.

> **stability** (stə bil′ ə tē) n., *pl.* **-ities** (ME *stablete* < O Fr. *stableté* < L. *stabilitas*)
> 1. steadiness 2. firmness of character or resolution 3. resistance to change

   a. How many syllables are in the word? _____

   b. What part of speech is the word? _____

   c. What is the origin of the word? _____

   d. Write the definition that applies to the use of *stability* in this sentence.
      The man's emotional stability enabled him to survive the crisis.
      _____

18. Give an example of one print or electronic reference that is available in a library.
    _____

19. Write the print or electronic reference—biographical reference; thesaurus; atlas; or almanac—that you would use to find the following information:

   a. the most recent population statistics for all the states in the United States
      _____

   b. the life of President Thomas Jefferson _____

   c. three synonyms and antonyms for *cheerful* _____

   d. general information about Antarctica's climate _____

20. Give an example of one strategy for finding information on the Internet.
    _____
    _____

21. Circle the letter of the best way to preview a test. On the line, explain your answer.
    a. Answer the easy questions first.
    b. Do not change your first answer without a good reason.
    c. Look over the entire test to get an overview.
    d. Proofread your answers.
    _____

22. Circle the letter of the best strategy for answering questions on a test. On the line, explain your answer.
    a. Answer the easy questions first.
    b. Proofread your answers.
    c. Answer the hardest questions first.
    d. Read each question and answer it quickly, trusting your intuition to guide you.
    _____

23. Why is it important to proofread your test answers?
    _____

24. Give an example of a strategy for answering multiple-choice questions, and explain it.
    _____
    _____
    _____
    _____

Name _____

Read the following passage. Use it to answer questions 25–29.

> Puritans were a powerful group in England. Many were well-educated merchants or landowners. Some held seats in the House of Commons. However, Charles I, who became king in 1625, disliked their religious ideas. He took away many Puritan business charters and had Puritans expelled from universities. A few were even jailed.
>
> Some Puritan leaders decided that England had fallen on "evil and declining times." In 1629, they persuaded royal officials to grant them a charter to form the Massachusetts Bay Company. The company's bold plan was to build a new society in New England. The new society would be based on the laws of God as they appeared in the Bible. Far from the watchful eye of the king, Puritans would found their colony and run it as they pleased.

25. Circle the letter of the answer that explains why the Puritans left England. On the line, write the sentence or phrase from the passage that provides this information.
    a. to help the king
    b. to escape religious persecution
    c. to look for land
    d. to look for trade routes

    _____

26. Write *T* on the line if the statement is true. Write *F* if the statement is false.

    a. _____ King Charles I approved of the Puritans' religious ideas.

    b. _____ The charter for the Massachusetts Bay Company was granted in 1629.

    c. _____ The new society would be based on the king's rules.

    d. _____ The Puritans in England had been poor.

27. Complete the following answer by filling in the line.

    Some Puritans held seats in the English _____.

28. In your own words, summarize the reasons that people left England to settle in the Massachusetts Bay Colony.

    _____

    _____

29. On the line, write the letter of the explanation that best explains the term.

    _____ 1. colony   a. a formal document issued by a government that grants rights to organize

    _____ 2. persecution   b. a body of settlers living in an area apart from their country of origin

    _____ 3. charter   c. cruel or unjust treatment

30. Circle the letter of the word that best completes the analogy.
    expel : welcome :: create :
    a. destroy
    b. build
    c. renovate
    d. accept

Answers

Key to Ability Levels: E = Easy; A = Average; C = Challenging

Chapter 1: The Writer in You (p. 3)
1. E *Sample:* class notes, quizzes, phone messages, shopping lists, journal, e-mail messages, letters, poems
2. E *Sample:* People write to communicate across time and space.
3. A b, e, a, f, c, d
4. A *Sample:* You can keep a notebook or journal for interesting facts, observations, or tidbits. You can also keep a learning log to keep track of new information you learn.
5. A *Sample:* You can keep a notebook or journal handy to jot down ideas as they come to you.
6. A 5, 6, 2, 4, 3, 7, 1
7. A *Sample:* quiet, well-organized, neat
8. A *Sample:* pens, pencils, paper
9. A *Sample:* "Budgeting your time" means planning a writing process in stages over time—spreading it out so you don't wait until the last minute.
10. C Students' answers may vary, but they should include adequate time for steps 1, 2, and 3, so they are in the writing stage before the second week begins.
11. A *Sample:* Writers can brainstorm in a group, work cooperatively or collaboratively on a writing project, or peer review each other's writing.
12. A *Sample:* Magazines and periodicals; on-line publications for student writers, or contests
13. C *Sample:* A jazz musician might write liner notes for a recording; a fund-raiser for a homeless shelter might write letters asking for donations; an accountant might write letters to her clients; a health food store owner might write advertisements for her products; a math teacher might write evaluations of his students; a zoo director might write descriptions of the animals he cares for.
14. E Students should be specific about their favorite kind of writing.
15. A Students should address the kind of writing they find most difficult.

Chapter 2: A Walk Through the Writing Process (p. 6)
1. A Reflexive writing is for yourself. Examples are diaries or a friendly letter. Extensive writing is for others, such as a school assignment. Examples are research papers and writing for assessment.
2. A Prewriting, Drafting, Revising, Editing and Proofreading, Publishing and Presenting
3. A *Sample:* Drafting is the first attempt to get ideas on paper, writing sentences in an organized way. Revising is correcting major errors and improving the writing's form and content.
4. E *Sample:* my cat, Mittens; how to take care of a new puppy
5. E *Sample:* Your audience is the people who will read your writing.
    Sample: An appropriate audience for this essay might be a student's family.
6. A *Sample:* Who invented pizza? What ingredients are in pizza? Where is pizza sold in our town? When is the best time to eat pizza? Why do I like pizza so much?
7. A *Sample:* Last night I was literally upside down!
8. A *Sample:* Extension—I have often dreamed of becoming an astronaut.
    Elaboration—Maybe I can pilot a space shuttle that takes many passengers on a vacation to the moon.
9. C *Sample:* Job: to describe the old dog, Duke Qualifications: shows what Duke looks like, shows what Duke does all day, shows what Duke does when he comes home
10. A *Sample:* Even on a rainy day. . .
11. C NASA chooses astronauts for their strength and endurance.
12. A *Sample:* I didn't understand the main idea.
13. A *Sample:* Check spelling, capitalization, and punctuation, grammar and usage.
14. E *Sample:* The appearance of an essay makes an impression on the reader.
15. A *Sample:* A writing portfolio is useful so that writers can look back at their work to see how they've progressed and to get new ideas.

Chapter 3: Paragraphs and Compositions (p. 9)
1. A b, d, a, c
2. A Students should circle the first sentence and underline the other three.
    Sample: You can make people think you're a great baker.
3. A Students should circle "over 1900 miles long."
4. A *Samples:* a. We have a chess club; b. We support a Students for Seniors club; c. Our math team is known around the state.
5. A My family just got a new computer. . .
6. A c, a, d, b
7. E The introduction contains a lead sentence that captures the reader's interest and the thesis statement, the key point in the composition. The body contains several paragraphs that support, explain, and prove the thesis statement. The conclusion restates the thesis statement and sums up the main idea.
8. C *Sample:* It was an incredibly welcome vision. They had food at last!
9. C *Sample:* Functional paragraphs create emphasis, indicate dialogue, or make transitions.

10. A *Sample:* The day was *overcast.* Winter was over. Spring wasn't here yet. Mud was everywhere. Nothing was green. No birds sang. It wasn't *sweltering.* It wasn't *freezing.* I felt bored.
11. A *Sample:* Winter was behind us, but spring hadn't sprung. It was neither hot nor cold, and I felt bored, really bored.
12. E *Sample:* The tone is disapproving. The writer is bored or depressed.
13. A *Sample:* There should be no slang.
14. E The first passage contains contractions and slang expressions.
15. C *Sample:* First we collected some musical recordings, and then we sat and talked at Tony's house.

Chapter 4: Narration/Autobiographical Writing Test 1 (p. 12)
1. E Students' writing will vary but should contain a reference to a celebration, an adventure, or a surprise. They should have the main idea circled.
2. E Students' answers will vary but should name purposes and audiences that are appropriate to the topics they have chosen.
3. E Students' answers will vary but should be specific ideas or events related to their topics. They should add a detail to one of the ideas to form a sentence that can be used in their story.
4. E Students' answers will vary but should be specific and thoughtful and clearly show conflicts.
5. E Students' answers will vary but should express a lesson or an insight.
6. E Students' drafts will vary but should fulfill the assignment and contain details from their prewriting activities.
7. E Students' choices should reflect an understanding of relevant and irrelevant support.
8. E Students' additions will vary but should be correct and appropriate uses of the transition words provided.
9. E stuff
    Sample: hardware and old clothing
10. E Students' answers will vary, but they should replace a vague noun with a more precise noun and rewrite their sentences.
11. E Middletown, Only, I, hour
12. E Students should find and correct capitalization errors.
13. E Students' answers will vary but should reflect an understanding of the rubric.
14. E *Sample:* I could submit my story to a magazine for young readers.
15. E Students' answers will vary but should contain specific references to their drafts.

Chapter 4: Narration/Autobiographical Writing Test 2 (p. 15)
1. A Students' writing will vary but should contain reference to an experience with an animal. They should circle the main idea.
2. A Students' answers will vary but should name purposes and audiences that are appropriate to the topics they have chosen.
3. A Students' answers will vary but should include specific ideas. They should add two details to one of the ideas and create a usable sentence.
4. A Students' answers will vary but should be specific and thoughtful and clearly show conflicts.
5. A Students' answers will vary but should express specific details about the animals they have chosen to write about.
6. A Students' drafts will vary but should fulfill the assignment and contain details from their prewriting activities.
7. A Students should make changes to their drafts, inserting words such as *first, next, then,* or *finally.*
8. A Students' sentences should use words such as *both, similarly,* or *likewise* and should clearly compare an animal and a person.
9. A *Samples:* place/dog house; pet/puppy
10. A Students' answers will vary, but they should circle vague nouns, replace them with more precise nouns, and rewrite their sentences.
11. A Duke, world, Tremont Street, When, I
12. A Students' edits will vary but should reflect an understanding of correct capitalization.
13. A Students' answers will vary but should reflect an understanding of the rubric.
14. A *Sample:* I might try to convey suspenseful events by using a dramatic tone.
15. A Students' answers will vary but should contain specific references to the structuring of an autobiographical account around a conflict.

Chapter 4: Narration/Autobiographical Writing Test 3 (p. 18)
1. C Students' writing will vary but should contain a reference to a personal achievement.
2. C Students' answers will vary but should name purposes and audiences that are appropriate to the topics they have chosen.
3. C Students' answers will vary but should be specific ideas or events related to their topics. They should add a detail to one of the ideas that can be used in their story.
4. C Students' answers will vary but should be specific and thoughtful and clearly show conflicts.
5. C Students' answers will vary but should clearly express an insight.
6. C Students' drafts will vary but should fulfill the assignment and contain details from their prewriting activities.
7. C Students' answers will vary. They should have a summary sentence about their conflicts, and revise supporting sentences as needed.

8. C Students should delete sentences or phrases that are weak or irrelevant.
9. C *Samples:* (sequence) first, then, next, finally; (cause and effect) because, since, as a result of, consequently; (identifies conclusion) consequently, finally
10. C Students should find three vague nouns, replace them, and rewrite the sentences.
11. C I, Six, finish line, Boston Marathon
12. C Students' edits will vary but should reflect an understanding of correct capitalization.
13. C Students' answers will vary but should reflect an understanding of the rubric.
14. C *Sample:* I could submit my story to a magazine for young readers.
15. C Students' answers will vary but should contain specific insights they gained.

Chapter 5: Narration/Short Story
Test 1 (p. 21)
1. E Students' answers will vary but the circled ideas should suggest a story idea.
2. E Students' answers will vary but should list specific details about their purpose.
3. E Students' answers will vary but should list specific details about a vehicle.
4. E Students' answers will vary but should clearly express a problem or conflict.
5. E Students' answers will vary but should contain specific events and use active verbs.
6. E Students' drafts will vary but should fulfill the assignment and contain details from their prewriting activities.
7. E Students should write a sentence that describes a character and add to it to make it more informative about the character's personality or behavior.
8. E *Sample:* Simon went to the store to buy a top hat, but it was too big.
9. E Students' answers will vary but should pick up two short sentences from their own drafts and combine them effectively.
10. E *Sample:* went/ran; said/whispered; saw/spied; took/grabbed
11. E Robert said, "robbery!"
    $449," he chuckled
12. E Students' edits will vary but should reflect an understanding of correct punctuation of dialogue.
13. E Students' answers will vary but should reflect an understanding of the rubric.
14. E *Sample:* I could submit my story to a school literary magazine.
15. E Students' answers will vary but should contain specific references to what they learned about writing a short story.

Chapter 5: Narration/Short Story
Test 2 (p. 24)
1. A Students' answers will vary but should list specific details about a main character.
2. A Students' answers will vary but should list specific details about a specific animal.
3. A Students should identify the conflict in their stories.
4. A Students should identify the audience for their stories.
5. A Students' answers will vary but should contain specific events and use active verbs.
6. A Students' drafts will vary but should fulfill the assignment and contain details from their prewriting activities.
7. A Students' answers will vary but should clearly contain more detailed information than appeared in their original drafts.
8. A *Sample:* Eve saw a balloon man as she walked into the zoo, so she bought a balloon.
9. A Students' answers will vary but should reflect the accurate and clear combination of two shorter sentences from their drafts.
10. A *Sample:* was/hung; left/escaped; ran/dashed
11. A Students should replace two colorless verbs with more vivid verbs.
12. A "Come, Duke!"
    "Goodboy," she said,
    "What would I do without you?"
    Students' edits will vary but should reflect an understanding of correct punctuation of dialogue.
13. A Students' answers will vary but should reflect an understanding of the rubric.
14. A *Sample:* I could submit my story to a magazine for young readers.
15. A Students' answers will vary but should contain specific references to how they will read stories in the future.

Chapter 5: Narration/Short Story
Test 3 (p. 27)
1. C Students' answers will vary but should contain details about the future and an imagined planet, with their most interesting ideas circled.
2. C Students' answers will vary but should list specific details about a main character.
3. C Students' answers will vary but should list specific details about an imaginary setting.
4. C Students' answers will vary but should clearly express a problem or conflict.
5. C Students' answers will vary but should contain specific events and use active verbs.
6. C Students' drafts will vary but should fulfill the assignment and contain details from their prewriting activities.
7. C Students' answers will vary but should clearly contain more detailed information than appeared in their original drafts.
8. C Anna picked up the blue paper, the green yo-yo, and then the small yellow rubber duck.
9. C Students' answers will vary but should reflect the accurate and clear combination of two shorter sentences from their drafts.
10. C *Sample:* looked/gazed; had/possessed; see/view

11. C   Students should replace three verbs with more vivid words.
12. C   "What time are we scheduled for departure?"
"What difference does it make?"
"I just want to be ready,"
His younger brother whispered,
Students' edits will vary but should reflect an understanding of correct punctuation of dialogue.
13. C   Students' answers will vary but should reflect an understanding of the rubric.
14. C   *Sample:* I would practice the different voices of the characters.
15. C   Students' answers will vary but should contain specific references to their new insights.

Chapter 6: Description
Test 1 (p. 30)
1. E   Students' answers will vary but should list three specific places; one will be circled.
2. E   Students' timelines will vary but should contain some suitable descriptive topics.
3. E   Students' answers will vary but should include a variety of specific sensory details.
4. E   *Samples:* sadness, joy, admiration
5. E   Students' drafts will vary but should fulfill the assignment and contain details from their prewriting activities.
6. E   *Samples:* The attic was so big you could stand in it. The garage held three cars.
7. E   Students' answers will vary but should contain the sentence with the main impression and another detailed sentence to strengthen it.
8. E   The attic was usually warm and musty. There were lots of cobwebs in the corners.
9. E   Students should look carefully for run-on sentences and correct them using conjunctions, sentence combining, or separation into two sentences.
10. E   *Sample:* small/tiniest; room/attic; loud/screeching
11. E   musty, warm attic
elementary school papers
our holiday decorations
12. E   Students' edits will vary but should reflect an understanding of correct use of commas with adjectives.
13. E   Students' answers will vary but should reflect an understanding of the rubric.
14. E   *Sample:* I would use a photograph of a special piece of furniture in the attic, such as my old baby crib.
15. E   Students' answers will vary but should contain specific references to the revision strategies they used.

Chapter 6: Description
Test 2 (p. 33)
1. A   Students' answers will vary but should list two specific events; one will be circled.
2. A   Students' answers will vary but should be a more focused treatment of the event than in the answer above.
3. A   Students' answers will vary but should include thoughtful and creative responses to the three prompts.
4. A   *Samples:* sadness, joy, excitement, fear
5. A   Students' drafts will vary but should fulfill the assignment and contain details from their prewriting activities.
6. A   *Sample:* My footsteps echoed in the deserted hall.
7. A   Students should write their main impression sentences and another sentence that strengthens the main impression with additional details.
8. A   The juggler tossed four flaming torches into the air. Then he threw in a fifth and a sixth. I couldn't believe my eyes.
9. A   Students should look carefully for run-on sentences and correct them using conjunctions, sentence combining, or separation into two sentences.
10. A   *Sample:* nice/charming; little/miniature; old/antique
11. A   many upturned faces
fiery lit
cold night air
12. A   Students' edits will vary but should reflect an understanding of correct use of commas with adjectives.
13. A   Students' answers will vary but should reflect an understanding of the rubric.
14. A   *Sample:* I could submit this essay to our local newspaper.
15. A   Students' answers will vary but should contain specific and thoughtful references to what they learned.

Chapter 6: Description
Test 3 (p. 36)
1. C   Students' timelines will vary but should include six specific events in chronological order.
2. C   Students' answers will vary but should be a more specific treatment of the event than in the answer above.
3. C   Students' answers will vary but should include thoughtful and creative responses to the six prompts.
4. C   *Samples:* sorrow, excitement, wonder, nostalgia
5. C   Students' drafts will vary but should fulfill the assignment and contain details from their prewriting activities.
6. C   I lay on the sand, panting and crying. I had nearly drowned.
7. C   Students should look carefully for run-on sentences and correct them using conjunctions, sentence combining, or separation into two sentences.
8. C   *Sample:* small/tiniest; room/attic; bad/criminal; scary/terrifying
9. C   *Sample:* I think he or she will like the middle, because it is the most exciting part.
10. C   *Sample:* I could add more details to support the main idea of the weak paragraph.

11. C dry, stony
       distant, rumbling
       quick, much-needed
12. C Students' edits will vary but should reflect an understanding of correct use of commas with adjectives.
13. C Students' answers will vary but should reflect an understanding of the rubric.
14. C *Sample:* I could include sounds of crashing waves.
15. C Students' answers will vary but should contain specific, thoughtful references to the insights they gained.

Chapter 7: Persuasive Essay
Test 1 (p. 39)
1. E Students' sentences will vary but should address a reasonable change in the family routine.
2. E Students' answers will vary but should be a more focused treatment of the topic than in answer 1.
3. E Students' thesis statements should express the gist of the argument, not specific details.
4. E Students' outlines should reflect serious and thoughtful attempts to include all main points.
5. E Students' drafts will vary but should fulfill the assignment and contain details from their prewriting activities.
6. E Students should write a concise, thoughtful main point.
7. E Students should write a detailed, precisely worded sentence that supports their main points.
8. E Students should revise the sentence from the previous question so that it is stronger.
9. E Students' answers will vary but should reflect the accurate and clear combination of two shorter sentences from their drafts.
10. E *Samples:* loud/clanging; bright/blinding
11. E privacy.
       neat?
       certainly
12. E Students' edits will vary but should reflect an understanding of correct use of ending punctuation.
13. E Students' answers will vary but should reflect an understanding of the rubric.
14. E *Sample:* I would use more informal language.
15. E *Sample:* I learned that I needed a lot of details to be truly persuasive.

Chapter 7: Persuasive Essay
Test 2 (p. 42)
1. A Students' charts should contain a clearly stated opinion and thoughtful and relevant pros and cons.
2. A Students' answers will vary but should be thoughtful and specific to the topic of recycling.
3. A Students' thesis statements should express broad opinions about the recycling center, not specific details.
4. A Students' outlines should reflect serious and thoughtful attempts to include all main points.
5. A Students' drafts will vary but should fulfill the assignment and contain details from their prewriting activities.
6. A Students should write a concise, thoughtful main point.
7. A Students should write a detailed, precisely worded sentence that supports their main point.
8. A Students should revise the sentence from the previous question so that it is stronger.
9. A Students answers will vary but should reflect the accurate and clear combination of two shorter sentences from their drafts.
10. A *Samples:* better/more efficient; wrong/less effective; bigger/broader
11. A family
       per week.
       each month.
       imagine
       clogging
       landfill!
12. A Students' edits will vary but should reflect an understanding of correct use of ending punctuation.
13. A Students' answers will vary but should reflect an understanding of the rubric.
14. A *Sample:* I hope you will consider publishing the enclosed editorial. It concerns a subject that is important to our community.
15. A *Sample:* I had to think about ways to convince people that we need to take action.

Chapter 7: Persuasive Essay
Test 3 (p. 45)
1. C Students' charts should contain a clearly stated opinion and thoughtful and relevant pros and cons.
2. C Students' answers will vary but should be thoughtful and specific to the topic of bicycle helmets.
3. C Students' thesis statements should express broad opinions about the use of bicycle helmets, not specific details.
4. C Students' outlines should reflect serious and thoughtful attempts to include all main points.
5. C Students' drafts will vary but should fulfill the assignment and contain details from their prewriting activities.
6. C Students should write a concise, thoughtful main point.
7. C Students should write a detailed, precisely worded sentence that supports their main point.
8. C Students should revise the sentence from the previous question so that it is stronger.
9. C Students answers will vary but should reflect the accurate and clear combination of two shorter sentences from their drafts.
10. C Students should rewrite a sentence so that it is more powerful and persuasive.

11. C expensive?
       Compared
       bargain.
       annual
       Skatefest.
12. C Students' edits will vary but should reflect an understanding of correct use of ending punctuation.
13. C Students' answers will vary but should reflect an understanding of the rubric.
14. C *Samples:* Sites that focus on bicycle safety or parents' concerns
15. C *Sample:* It was challenging to write for peers who might not think my topic was a serious issue.

Chapter 8: Exposition/Comparison-and-Contrast
Test 1 (p. 48)
1. E Students' charts should include at least two specific similarities and two specific differences that are relevant to the topic they have chosen.
2. E *Sample:* how reading a book is like and unlike taking a vacation
3. E Students should write a sentence that clearly expresses their main idea.
4. E Students should extend their main idea by restating it in other words.
5. E Students' drafts will vary but should fulfill the assignment and contain details from their prewriting activities.
6. E Students' leads should be more thoughtful and creative than those in their drafts.
7. E Students' conclusions should be more thoughtful and creative than those in their drafts.
8. E Students' restated topic sentences should elaborate on their ideas by explaining them in different words.
9. E An almanac and the Internet are good sources of up-to-date information.
10. E Students' answers will vary but should reflect the accurate and clear combination of two short sentences from their drafts.
11. E Spelling errors: ticket; before
       Agreement errors: When people read . . .
12. E Students' edits will vary but should reflect an understanding of correct pronoun-antecedent agreement and spelling.
13. E Students' answers will vary but should reflect an understanding of the rubric.
14. E *Sample:* I might bring in photographs of a garden and a fireworks display.
15. E Students' answers will vary but should contain specific references to how they used the revising strategies to improve their drafts.

Chapter 8: Exposition/Comparison-and-Contrast
Test 2 (p. 51)
1. A Students' diagrams should contain thoughtful and specific details that show similarities (in the middle) and differences (on each side).
2. A *Sample:* show how *Malcolm in the Middle* is similar to and different from *The Simpsons*.
3. A *Sample:* Block Method
       A. *Malcolm in the Middle*
       1. comical side of family life
       2. four boys
       B. *The Simpsons*
       1. comical side of family life
       2. two girls and one boy
4. A Students' drafts will vary but should fulfill the assignment and contain details from their prewriting activities.
5. A Students should mark each sentence of their drafts with a *T*, *R*, or *I*. They should have at least one *I* for every *T*.
6. A *Sample: Old Yeller* and *Call of the Wild* can be seen as sad stories.
7. A *Old Yeller* is a sad story of a boy who discovers and then loses his best friend.
8. A Students' sentences should use the conjunction *and* to combine subjects.
9. A *Sample:* Peers might say the two subjects are both sad.
10. A *Sample:* Peers might say the differences between the two subjects are that they are about different animals in unique situations.
11. A Spelling errors: exciting; wonderful
       Agreement errors: They were exciting books . . .
12. A Students' edits will vary but should reflect an understanding of correct pronoun-antecedent agreement and spelling.
13. A Students' answers will vary but should reflect an understanding of the rubric.
14. A Students might suggest an entertainment magazine or the arts section of a newspaper.
15. A Students' answers will vary but should contain specific references to a change in their understanding of their topics.

Chapter 8: Exposition/Comparison-and-Contrast
Test 3 (p. 54)
1. C Students' diagrams should contain thoughtful and specific details that show similarities (in the middle) and differences (on each side).
2. C *Sample:* My essay will show how Pedro Martinez and Roger Clemens are alike and different.
3. C *Sample:* Block Method
       A. Pedro Martinez
       1. power, fastball pitcher
       2. from Dominican Republic
       B. Roger Clemens
       1. power, fastball pitcher
       2. from Texas
4. C Students' drafts will vary but should fulfill the assignment and contain details from their prewriting activities.
5. C Students should mark each sentence of their drafts with a *T*, *R*, or *I*. They should have at least one *I* for every *T*.
6. C Students' sentences should use the conjunction *and* to combine subjects.

7. C   The second occurrence of *Adults* should be *They*.
8. C   Students should find repetitive words and eliminate them or change them to more interesting words.
9. C   *Sample:* Peers might say the two subjects are both exciting and talented.
10. C *Sample:* Peers might say the subjects differ in terms of their backgrounds and their experiences as professional players.
11. C Spelling errors: terrific; incredible; audience
       Agreement errors:
       They can capture . . .
12. C Students' edits will vary but should reflect an understanding of correct pronoun-antecedent agreement and spelling.
13. C Students' answers will vary but should reflect an understanding of the rubric.
14. C *Sample:* My information might be useful to fans of major league baseball. I might publish it in a sports magazine or the sports section of a newspaper.
15. C Students' answers will vary but should contain specific references to how they used the revising strategies to improve their drafts.

Chapter 9: Exposition/Cause-and-Effect
Test 1 (p. 57)

1. E   The language might be a combination of both. The purpose is to inform the readers about the school garden.
2. E   The audience is made up of the people who read the newspaper.
3. E   Students' flowcharts should contain distinct and specific steps in chronological order.
4. E   *Sample:* We planted sunflowers, zinnias, and marigolds, and they grew into a living mural of yellow, green, pink, and orange.
5. E   Students' drafts will vary but should fulfill the assignment and contain details from their prewriting activities.
6. E   If you want to paint . . . ; Take a medium grade . . . ; Use a brush . . . ; Now the wood . . .
7. E   Students' drafts should be revised to reflect accurate chronological order.
8. E   *Sample:* As a result of their meeting with the principal, the students were given the "go ahead" to plant the garden.
9. E   Students should identify and correct unnecessary changes in tense.
10. E *Sample:* put/planted; made/designed
11. E Spelling errors: April; there
       Preposition errors: on a high ledge; moved them into the ground
12. E Students' edits will vary but should reflect an understanding of correct spelling and the correct use of prepositions.
13. E Students' answers will vary but should reflect an understanding of the rubric.
14. E *Sample:* A layout of how the finished garden will look would be a good visual aid.
15. E Students' answers will vary but should mention a specific writing strategy and explain why they found it useful.

Chapter 9: Exposition/Cause-and-Effect
Test 2 (p. 60)

1. A   The language might be a combination of both. The purpose is to inform readers about the teacher who was elected mayor.
2. A   The audience is made up of people who read the newspaper.
3. A   Students' flowcharts should contain distinct and specific steps in chronological order.
4. A   *Samples:* When Mr. Martin promised to rebuild the town playground, he received a standing ovation.
       Election day was sunny and warm, so 85% of the town's voters went to the polls.
5. A   Students' drafts will vary but should fulfill the assignment and contain details from their prewriting activities.
6. A   Students' drafts should be revised to reflect accurate chronological order.
7. A   Students' openings will vary, but they should contain the main ideas and be written in a way that grabs the attention of the reader.
8. A   *Sample:* Seventy-two percent of the town voted for Mr. Martin. Consequently, he's our next mayor!
9. A   Students' answers will vary. Their verbs should all be in a consistent tense.
10. A *Samples:* got/earned; said/announced; went/traveled
11. A Spelling errors: build; history
       Preposition errors: off the charts; appear in the headlines
12. A Students' edits will vary but should reflect an understanding of correct spelling and the correct use of prepositions.
13. A Students' answers will vary but should reflect an understanding of the rubric.
14. A *Sample:* A photograph of Mr. Martin at his victory party would be a good addition.
15. A Students' answers will vary but should contain specific references to an interesting piece of information.

Chapter 9: Exposition/Cause-and-Effect
Test 3 (p. 63)

1. C   The audience is made up of the readers of the school newspaper.
2. C   Students' charts should include clearly expressed topics and at least two causes and two effects.
3. C   *Sample:* Since students are learning keyboarding skills early, they can easily become computer proficient in middle school.
4. C   *Samples:* When the schools added keyboarding to the curricula, about 50% of the teachers needed to take additional classes in computer skills.
       Last year, the district spent about $10,000 on computer maintenance and repair.

5. C Students' drafts will vary but should fulfill the assignment and contain details from their prewriting activities.
6. C Students' "tug" sentences should use vivid language that grabs the attention of the reader.
7. C *Sample:* The program is necessary because it will help students use computers faster and more easily.
8. C Students should correctly identify the dominant verb tense in their essays.
9. C The three verbs should be in the dominant tense.
10. C *Samples:* ran/dashed; sat/landed; talked/conversed
11. C Spelling errors: separate; elementary; expense
Preposition errors: for each student; budget of many schools
12. C Students' edits will vary but should reflect an understanding of correct spelling and the correct use of prepositions.
13. C Students' answers will vary but should reflect an understanding of the rubric.
14. C *Sample:* A chart showing what computer skills are taught at each grade would be a helpful addition.
15. C Students' answers will vary but should contain specific references to the writing strategy they found most useful, and explain why.

Chapter 10: Exposition/How-to Essay
Test 1 (p. 66)
1. E Students should explain clearly that their purpose is to teach their readers more about a given subject.
2. E Students should identify their audience and describe what they would or would not know about the subject.
3. E Sample left box: Scramble eggs, squeeze oranges, toast whole wheat bread, slice apples, serve and enjoy!
Sample right box: break two fresh eggs; whip with whisk; cook over medium heat; add a little cheese, add salt and pepper to taste
4. E *Sample:* toast bread for 2–3 minutes, spread lightly with margarine, cut into triangles
5. E Students' drafts will vary but should fulfill the assignment and contain details from their prewriting activities.
6. E Students' leads should contain vivid words and images.
7. E Students' drafts should include at least two of the connecting words from the list.
8. E *Samples:* For/To have; You have to/First you have to; Then pass out/Next, pass out; For extra/ Finally, for extra
9. E Students should make at least one change to their drafts to increase the variety in their sentence beginnings.
10. E Students' answers will vary. They should carefully choose a word that they have repeated at least three times, and replace it with a more interesting substitute.
11. E Spelling errors: break, grated
Comma errors: grated cheddar cheese, a pinch of salt, and pepper to taste; toast the rye bread, slice the strawberries, and make the hot chocolate
12. E Students' edits will vary but should reflect an understanding of correct spelling and the correct use of commas with items in a series.
13. E Students' answers will vary but should reflect an understanding of the rubric.
14. E *Sample:* I might get a hot plate and ingredients and actually cook an omelet.
15. E Students' answers will vary but should contain specific references to what they learned about the activity by explaining it to someone else.

Chapter 10: Exposition/How-to Essay
Test 2 (p. 69)
1. A Students should explain clearly that their purpose is to teach their readers more about a given subject.
2. A Students should identify their audience and describe what they would or would not know about the subject.
3. A Sample left box: find a computer you can use regularly; practice every day; once a week, add a new skill; find a good teacher; use the computer for homework and projects
Sample right box 1: find a good reference book; copy the table of contents; check off the skills you already know; circle the skills you want to learn
Sample right box 2: write reports on the computer; keep a journal; set up a data base for something you collect
4. A *Sample:* find a good reference book or textbook
5. A *Sample:* look in library; talk to a computer teacher; take a computer class
6. A Students' drafts will vary but should fulfill the assignment and contain details from their prewriting activities.
7. A Students' answers will vary. Their leads should contain vivid words and images.
8. A Students' drafts should include at least two of the connecting words from the list.
9. A Students should make at least one change to their drafts to increase the variety in their sentence beginnings.
10. A *Sample:* get; obtain, locate, acquire, attain
11. A Spelling errors: mystery; articles
Comma errors: read, read, and read some more; mystery novels, computer magazines, newspaper articles, and video game directions
12. A Students' edits will vary but should reflect an understanding of correct spelling and the correct use of commas with items in a series.
13. A Students' answers will vary but should reflect an understanding of the rubric.
14. A *Sample:* My poster would have steps listed in different boxes.

15. A Students' answers will vary but should address any steps that are especially complicated.

Chapter 10: Exposition/How-to Essay
Test 3 (p. 72)
1. C Students should explain clearly that their purpose is to teach their readers more about a given subject.
2. C Students should identify their audience and describe what they would or would not know about the subject. They should list specific skills that their audience would have.
3. C Sample left box: list the foods you eat in three days; circle ones that are "healthy"; look at balance; visit a health food store; substitute according to taste
Sample right box 1: list all foods, including snacks; list amounts; list brand names if food is packaged
Sample right box 2: look in yellow pages for stores; spend time browsing; ask questions; try one new item
4. C *Sample:* drink more water
5. C *Sample:* drink 6–8 glasses a day; carry water with you; mix with ice in hot weather
6. C Students' drafts will vary but should fulfill the assignment and contain details from their prewriting activities.
7. C Students' answers will vary. Their leads should contain vivid words and images.
8. C Students' drafts should include at least three of the connecting words from the list.
9. C Students should make at least one change to their drafts to increase the variety in their sentence beginnings.
10. C *Sample:* eat; experiment, try, explore, discover, nibble, gobble, guzzle
11. C Spelling errors: organize; miscellaneous; applications
Comma errors: letters to family, finished work, miscellaneous documents, or college application materials
12. C Students' edits will vary but should reflect an understanding of correct spelling and the correct use of commas with items in a series.
13. C Students' answers will vary but should reflect an understanding of the rubric.
14. C *Sample:* I might bring in samples of the products I am discussing.
15. C Students' answers will vary but should contain specific references to two new things they learned about their activity by explaining it to someone else.

Chapter 11: Research Report
Test 1 (p. 75)
1. E Note card #1; it includes quotation marks.
2. E Kevin forgot to include the author and the date of publication.
3. E Note card #3 comes from a Web site.
4. E Michael Jordan has achieved greatness in many ways. *Sample:* This general idea can be proven and supported with details from the research.
5. E Ordering by Type. The thesis statement and the note cards don't really tell a story or a process; they are about categories of "greatness."
6. E Section II
7. E Section IV
8. E Section III
9. E *Sample:* In addition, Jordan challenges himself in areas beyond basketball—he challenges himself to help others, too.
10. E *Sample:* Jordan supports a lot of charities. For example, he donates money to . . .
11. E Paragraph 1: Jordan is an important part of the Wizards.
Paragraph 2: Jordan has interests other than basketball, such as supporting charities.
12. E Herbert
13. E *Sports Illustrated*
14. E *Sample:* A photograph of Michael Jordan would be a good visual aid.
15. E Students' answers will vary but should contain specific references to the revising strategy they found most useful.

Chapter 11: Research Report
Test 2 (p. 78)
1. A Note card #1; it includes quotation marks.
2. A Sarah forgot to include the date of publication.
3. A Note card #3 comes from a Web site.
4. A Throughout her life, Eleanor Roosevelt was a leader and a pioneer. *Sample:* This general idea can be proven and supported with details from the research.
5. A Chronological Order. The thesis statement and the note cards tell the story of a woman's life through time.
6. A Section IV
7. A Section III
8. A Section VI
9. A *Sample:* That life began on October 11, 1884, in New York City. Born to wealthy parents . . . (circle "that life" as "glue" to "Roosevelt's life" in previous sentence)
10. A She could add a short sentence for punch and emphasis. For example, she could make "She was a lot more" an independent sentence to emphasize its idea.
11. A Eleanor Roosevelt was not just the president's wife.
12. A Miller, Roosevelt, Skarmeas
13. A *Eleanor Roosevelt: A Photobiography;* "Eleanor, My Heroine"
14. A *Sample:* famous first lady and crusader for human rights
15. A Students' answers will vary but should contain specific references to the revising strategy they found most useful.

Chapter 11: Research Report
Test 3 (p. 81)
1. C Note card #1; it includes quotation marks.
2. C Erin forgot to include the page number.
3. C Note card #4 does not include the name of the publisher.
4. C The Battle of Gettysburg was the turning point of the Civil War. *Sample:* This general idea can be proven and supported with details from the research.
5. C Chronological Order. The thesis statement and the note cards tell the story of the Battle of Gettysburg from beginning to end.
6. C Section II
7. C Section V
8. C Section III
9. C *Sample:* After the Battle of Gettysburg, General Lee offered to resign.
10. C She could add a short sentence for punch and emphasis. For example, she could make "Jefferson Davis refused," an independent sentence.
11. C *Samples:* Paragraph 1: The wagon train of Confederate wounded was a gruesome sight.
Paragraph 2: David refused Lee's resignation offer.
12. C Beller, Catton, McPherson
13. C *The Battle of Gettysburg, To Hold this Ground*
14. C *Sample:* Photographs of Gettysburg would be striking images.
15. C *Samples:* Readers will learn details about the wounded and about General Lee's fighting skill.

Chapter 12: Response to Literature
Test 1 (p. 84)
1. E *Sample:* Actor: "a very old man," or the "keeper of life." Acts: He swings a watch in front of an infant and then lets it run down. Scene: an infant's room. Agency: We don't really learn how it's done. Purpose: First, the old man wants to amuse the infant. Then, he "becomes tired."
2. E *Sample:* The toy begins to swing more slowly.
3. E *Sample:* The infant reminds me of my baby brother; the old man reminds me of my grandfather.
4. E *Sample:* Circle infant, old man, and watch. Summary: The poem suggests the cycle of life, using an old man swinging a watch in front of an infant.
5. E *Sample:* I like the poem because it is easy to picture what is going on.
6. E *Sample:* The watch is a clear symbol of the passing of time. The contrasting images of the baby and the old man also clearly show the passing of time.
7. E Students' drafts will vary but should fulfill the assignment and contain details from their prewriting activities.
8. E Answers will vary, but students should focus on an important part of the poem.
9. E *Sample:* Since the old man is bored and tired, he begins to let the watch run down.
10. E says/describes; nice/simple
11. E Spelling errors: writes; meaning
Punctuation errors: "My universe key,"; "a treasure."
12. E Students' edits will vary but should reflect an understanding of correct spelling and the correct use of punctuation in quotations.
13. E Students' answers will vary but should reflect an understanding of the rubric.
14. E Students might suggest writing to the publisher or looking on the Internet.
15. E Students' answers will vary but should contain specific references to their increased understanding of the poem.

Chapter 12: Response to Literature
Test 2 (p. 87)
1. A *Sample:* Actor: The speaker and a hippopotamus. Acts: They both look at each other and laugh and wonder. Scene: Maybe a zoo? Agency: The actions are mostly lighthearted, except for the one that is "dark and grim." Purpose: Both are curious about the other.
2. A *Sample:* Students may say they're writing for children because the subject and the words are humorous.
3. A *Sample:* The poet uses rhyme and word play.
4. A *Sample:* This poem is about trying to understand creatures (or people) who are different from you.
5. A Students should support their opinions with two specific details from the poem.
6. A *Sample:* The hippopotamus in this poem gets "delight" by looking at others of his kind.
7. A Students' drafts will vary but should fulfill the assignment and contain details from their prewriting activities.
8. A *Sample:* The poem shows that we shouldn't criticize how others look.
9. A *Sample:* As a result of thinking about life from the hippopotamus's view, the speaker learns something about judging others based on their looks.
10. A good/humorous; big/important
11. A Spelling errors: speech; several; delightful
Punctuation errors: 'You are doubtless very big,' "; "Neither can you crack a nut."
12. A Students' edits will vary but should reflect an understanding of correct spelling and the correct use of punctuation in quotations.
13. A Students' answers will vary but should reflect an understanding of the rubric.
14. A *Sample:* I might make a collage of cartoon-type hippopotami.
15. A Students' answers will vary but should contain references to humorous aspects of the poem.

© Prentice-Hall, Inc.

Chapter 12: Response to Literature
Test 3 (p. 90)

1. C *Samples:* Related Experience: I once went horseback riding. I read more books in the winter than in the summer. Summary: "Stopping by Woods" is about a man who stops in a snowy woods one night and thinks about his life. "Winter" is about the way we prepare for winter. What I Liked or Didn't Like: I like the rhyme and the music of Frost's poem. I like the simple images in "Winter." Similarities to Other Works: "Woods" reminds me of a song or lullaby. "Winter" reminds me of a nursery rhyme. Author's Technique: Both poems use winter as a symbol of quiet reflection. Themes: "Woods"—It's good to stop and think in the midst of life's journey. "Winter"—It's good to take time to prepare for what's ahead.
2. C *Sample:* Both speakers use the first-person point of view. The voice in "Stopping" is very serious, but the voice in "Winter" is more lighthearted.
3. C Students' drafts will vary but should fulfill the assignment, contain details from their prewriting activities, and include quotations.
4. C *Sample:* Both speakers look ahead to the future.
5. C *Sample:* The speaker in the poem needs to keep moving, because he has many things to do in his life; he can't stop.
6. C *Sample:* good/important; nice/peaceful; do/prepare
7. C Spelling errors: remain; beauty; beginnings
Punctuation errors: "sweet plum blossoms,"; "fragment blossoms remain."
Students' edits should reflect an understanding of correct spelling and the correct use of punctuation in quotations.
8. C Students' answers will vary but should reflect an understanding of the rubric.
9. C *Sample:* Literary magazines or newspapers with book-review columns might publish my essay.
10. C *Sample:* Comparing and contrasting the poems made me make more detailed observations about both.

Chapter 13: Writing for Assessment
Test 1 (p. 93)

1. E d.
2. E *Sample:* circle *explain, long division, steps*; The purpose is to explain the steps in a long-division problem.
3. E d.
4. E Students should copy the long-division problem and solve it, making notes about their steps.
5. E *Sample:* divide 37 by 7 and get 5; multiply 5 times 7 (35) and write it below the 37; subtract and get 2; bring down the 9 and divide 29 by 7 and write 4 on top; multiply 4 by 7 and write 28 under the 29; subtract to get 1; this is the remainder.
6. E Students' drafts will vary but should fulfill the assignment and contain details from their prewriting activities.
7. E Students' openings will vary, but they should contain their main ideas and be written in a way that will grab the attention of readers.
8. E Students' conclusions will vary but they should present a final, summarizing thought that restates their explanations.
9. E Students should write sentences that included *then, next, after,* or *finally* to show the connections between steps.
10. E *Samples:* put/write; get/multiply
11. E *Sample:* Bring the next number, 9, down by the side.
12. E Students' edits will vary but should reflect an understanding of complete sentences.
13. E Students' answers will vary but should reflect an understanding of the rubric.
14. E *Sample:* The hardest part is working against the clock. I get nervous.
15. E Students' answers will vary but should contain specific references to a writing strategy in this chapter.

Chapter 13: Writing for Assessment
Test 2 (p. 96)

1. A d.
2. A *Sample:* circle *explain, rules, basketball*; the purpose is to explain the rules of basketball or another team sport.
3. A d.
4. A Students should list details about playing basketball, such as number of players, object of the game, and rules of the game.
5. A *Sample:* 2 teams, 5 per team; score 2 points by making baskets; play against the clock; passing, dribbling, and shooting; possession; fouls
6. A Students' drafts will vary but should fulfill the assignment and contain details from their prewriting activities.
7. A Students' openings will vary, but they should contain their main ideas and be written in a way that will grab the attention of readers.
8. A Students' conclusions will vary, but they should present a final thought that restates their explanations.
9. A Students should circle transition words or write sentences using them to clearly show transitions from one stage to another.
10. A *Samples:* go/dash; put/shoot; take/steal
11. A *Sample:* An action-packed sport, soccer is played by two teams of eleven players each.
12. A Students' edits will vary but should reflect an understanding of complete sentences.

13. A Students' answers will vary but should reflect an understanding of the rubric.
14. A *Sample:* The hardest part is working against the clock. I get nervous.
15. A Students' answers will vary but should contain specific references to a writing strategy in this chapter.

Chapter 13: Writing for Assessment
Test 3 (p. 99)
1. C d.
2. C *Sample:* circle *explain, caterpillar, turns into, butterfly*; the purpose is to explain how a caterpillar becomes a butterfly.
3. C d.
4. C Students should list details they know about this metamorphosis, or draw an example of the process.
5. C *Sample:* eggs laid; caterpillars emerge; spend life eating and growing; may shed skin; spins itself a pupa; attaches to twig; shell cracks; adult emerges
6. C Students' drafts will vary but should fulfill the assignment and contain details from their prewriting activities.
7. C Students' openings will vary, but they should contain their main ideas and be written in a way that will grab the attention of readers.
8. C Students' answers will vary, but each paragraph should include a main idea and at least one specific detail to support it.
9. C Transition words may include *when, after, during, first, then, next,* or *finally*. Students should write sentences that use these transition words to show the connections between steps.
10. C *Samples:* make/spin; go/crawl; come out/emerge
11. C *Sample:* After the larvae grow big enough, they break out of their shells.
12. C Students' edits will vary but should reflect an understanding of complete sentences.
13. C Students' answers will vary but should reflect an understanding of the rubric.
14. C Students' answers will vary but should contain specific references to a writing strategy in this chapter.
15. C *Sample:* I might circle key words in writing assignments to make sure I understand the purpose of the essay.

Grammar, Usage, and Mechanics: Cumulative Diagnostic Test (p. 105)
The numbers in brackets indicate the chapter and section of the skills being tested.
1. E verb [15.2]
2. E conjunction [18.1]
3. A verb [15.1]
4. E preposition [17.1]
5. C adverb [16.2]
6. A noun [14.1]
7. E adjective [16.1]
8. A pronoun [14.2]
9. E adjective [16.1]
10. E interjection [18.2]
11. A predicate noun [19.5]
12. A fragment [19.1]
13. C complete predicate [19.2]
14. A direct object [19.5]
15. C complete subject [19.2]
16. A complete subject [19.2]
17. E complete predicate [19.2]
18. C predicate adjective [19.5]
19. E sentence [19.1]
20. C indirect object [19.5]
21. C participial phrase [20.1]
22. A appositive phrase [20.1]
23. A independent clause [20.2]
24. C adjective clause [20.2]
25. E participle [20.1]
26. E appositive [20.1]
27. C adverb clause [20.2]
28. A prepositional phrase used as an adverb [20.1]
29. A prepositional phrase used as an adjective [20.1]
30. E infinitive [20.1]
31. E interrogative sentence [21.1]
32. A Jerome and Monica are doing reports on poison dart frogs. [21.2]
33. E Frogs croak and leap. [21.2]
34. A Heather bought a bright blue frog and a yellow frog. [21.2]
35. C *Sample:* Frogs in tropical climates may be active all year, but many species breed only in certain seasons. [21.2]
36. E Jason bought three poison dart frogs; he keeps them in an aquarium in his room. [21.2]
37. C *Sample:* Because Todd takes good care of his collection of frogs, the frogs are very healthy. [21.2]
38. C missing a predicate; *Sample:* Frogs in their natural surroundings enjoy their lives. [21.4]
39. C *Sample:* Leaping many times its own body length, the frog amazed Rob with its ability. [21.4]
40. C *Sample:* Janice didn't have any blue frogs in her collection because she couldn't find any. [21.4]
41. A past participle [22.1]
42. E present participle [22.1]
43. A Tasmania is separated from the rest of Australia by a strait. [22.1]
44. C Have you spoken to your Australian friend lately? [22.1]
45. C Before 1856, people had known Tasmania as Van Diemen's Land. [22.2]
46. C By the end of our trip, we will have visited four of Australia's states. [22.2]
47. C Jake has been studying the history of Australia. [22.2]
48. E Suzie wrote to her Australian pen pal. [22.2]
49. E We tried to join the tour group, but they had already gone. [22.3]
50. A correct [22.3]
51. A she, nominative [23]
52. E nominative [23]
53. E objective [23]
54. C It, subject of a verb [23]
55. A he, predicate pronoun [23]
56. E *Sample:* We, subject of a verb [23]

57. E *Sample:* She, subject of a verb [23]
58. C them, object of a preposition [23]
59. C me, indirect object [23]
60. A its, possessive [23]
61. E are [24.1]
62. E gets [24.1]
63. A cover [24.1]
64. A are [24.1]
65. A Sea snakes, like every other water reptile, have lungs, not gills. [24.1]
66. A snakes are [24.1]
67. A come [24.1]
68. E *Sample:* live [24.1]
69. A her [24.2]
70. A their [24.2]
71. E faster, fastest [25.1]
72. A more sweetly, most sweetly [25.1]
73. E Alligators are smaller than crocodiles. [25.1]
74. A A crocodile's snout is more pointed than an alligator's snout. [25.1]
75. A superlative [25.1]
76. A A cottonmouth is more dangerous than the northern water snake. [25.1]
77. C Of all the reptiles, only the turtle has a shell. [25.2]
78. A If you are bitten by a cottonmouth, you will undoubtedly react badly. [25.2]
79. C Allison has just one turtle in her aquarium. [25.2]
80. A correct [25.2]
81. E Fish can breathe underwater, but water reptiles must swim to the surface to breathe. [26.2]
82. E Water reptiles include alligators, turtles, and certain kinds of snakes. [26.2]
83. A Most reptiles have long, low bodies. [26.2]
84. C Because a sea turtle cannot pull its head, legs, and tail into its shell, it cannot protect itself easily. [26.2]
85. C Listen, Carmen, while I tell you about crocodiles, alligators, green turtles, and snapping turtles. [26.2]
86. E The green turtle, in my opinion, should be protected from its human enemies. [26.2]
87. A I bought my pet turtle on June 18, 2001, and my iguana arrived one month later. [26.2]
88. C "Snapping turtles," said Ed, "are omnivores, which means they eat plants as well as animals." [26.4]
89. A correct [26.4]
90. A On his scuba-diving trip, Dan saw fifty-two green turtles. [26.5]
91. E Have you ever seen a marine iguana? [27]
92. E The marine iguana, I understand, is the only lizard that lives both in the sea and on the land. [27]
93. E My friends Richard and Sandra are helping me with a report on lizards. [27]
94. A Marine iguanas are found only on the Galápagos Islands in the Pacific Ocean. [27]
95. C Alligators can be found in the southern part of the United States and in China. [27]
96. E In this cookbook for French food, I found a good recipe for turtle soup. [27]
97. C According to the article "Alligators and Crocodiles," American crocodiles are about twelve feet long. [27]
98. A My dentist, Dr. Sam Mallory, has two iguanas at home on Fourth Street. [27]
99. C Dave asked, "Have you ever touched an iguana, Mom?" [27]
100. C We read about reptiles in my biology class last January. [27]

Chapter 14: Nouns and Pronouns (p. 113)
1. E Mount Fuji—proper noun; volcano—common noun; Japan—proper noun
2. A mountain, province—common nouns; Honshu—proper noun; distance—common noun; Pacific Ocean—proper noun
3. C Japanese—proper noun; shape, silhouette, symbol, beauty—common nouns
4. E peak—common noun; Fuji—proper noun; snow, part, year—common nouns
5. E slopes, mountain, vegetation—common nouns
6. A traveler—common noun; John Morris, Mount Fuji—proper nouns; time—common noun
7. C Englishman—proper noun; start—common noun; World War II—proper noun
8. E time, peak, sea, dawn—common nouns
9. A Mr. Morris—proper noun; cone—common noun
10. A light, morning—common nouns; Morris, Fuji—proper nouns; sky—common noun
11. C group—collective; sightseers, Mount Fuji—compound
12. E couple—collective; lifetime—compound
13. A sunrise—compound; team—collective
14. E crowd—collective; countryside—compound
15. C class—collective; Mount Fuji, earthquake—compound
16. A Outpourings—compound; pair—collective
17. A family—collective; Mount Fuji, great-grandmother—compound
18. C background—compound; herd—collective; foreground—compound
19. A committee—collective; landscape—compound
20. C Mount Fuji—compound; club—collective; sunset—compound
21. E Which—interrogative
22. A it—personal, singular, third person
23. A we—personal, plural, first person
24. C you—personal, singular, second person
25. E Who—interrogative
26. A they—personal, plural, third person
27. E This—demonstrative, singular
28. E These—demonstrative, plural
29. C something—indefinite, singular
30. C Anybody—indefinite, singular
31. C This—picture
32. C It—picture
33. C He—Katsushika Hokusai
34. A you—Sharon
35. C We—Spencer and Sharon, I—Spencer, this—information about the picture

36. A him—Spencer, I, my—Sharon
37. C yours—Spencer('s)
38. A Mine—Spencer('s), her—Sharon
39. E My—Spencer, we—Spencer and Harry
40. E we—Spencer and Harry
41. C B
42. E F
43. A C
44. C J
45. E A
46. A H
47. E D
48. C G
49. C A
50. A J

Chapter 15: Verbs (p. 117)
1. E form, transitive, center
2. C lead, intransitive
3. A thrive, intransitive
4. E took, transitive, him
5. A entered, transitive, ocean
6. A lasted, intransitive
7. C covered, transitive, miles
8. A saw, transitive, Hawaiian Islands
9. A traveled, intransitive
10. A encountered, transitive, Hawaiian Islands
11. E was, arrow connecting Kamehameha I and ruler
12. E became, arrow connecting Honolulu and port
13. C had been, arrow connecting Kamehameha and wise
14. A grew, arrow connecting Honolulu and important
15. A has remained, arrow connecting city and busy
16. E felt, arrow connecting Kamehameha and comfortable
17. A had become, arrow connecting he and man
18. E seemed, arrow connecting island and suitable
19. E was, arrow connecting son and ready
20. A grew, arrow connecting son and ill
21. E had visited, underline visited, circle had
22. C must have been exposed, underline exposed, circle must have been
23. C might have survived, underline survived, circle might have
24. C could be done, underline done, circle could be
25. A was succeeded, underline succeeded, circle was
26. A would have been, underline been, circle would have
27. E did rule, underline rule, circle did
28. A would remain, underline remain, circle would
29. C could permit, underline permit, circle could
30. C would lead, underline lead, circle would
31. E linking
32. A action, visible
33. E linking
34. C action, mental
35. A linking
36. C action, mental
37. C action, mental

38. A action, visible
39. E action, visible
40. C action, mental
41. E C
42. A J
43. A D
44. E F
45. A D
46. A F
47. C B
48. C H
49. A A
50. E J

Chapter 16: Adjectives and Adverbs (p. 120)
1. E Friendly, arrow to relationships; cave-dwelling, arrow to times; cave-dwelling, compound
2. A modern, arrow to society; most, arrow to dogs; family, arrow to pets
3. E main, arrow to reason; special, arrow to work
4. A recent, arrow to times; many, arrow to breeds
5. C German, arrow to shepherd; excellent, arrow to shepherd; guard, arrow to dog; German, proper
6. E My, arrow to friend; good, arrow to friend; Irish, arrow to setter; Scottish, arrow to terrier; Irish, proper; Scottish, proper
7. A sight-impaired, arrow to person; some, arrow to breeds; sight-impaired, compound
8. C Many, arrow to people; purebred, arrow to dog; purebred, compound
9. C mixed-breed, arrow to dog; suitable, arrow to dog; other, arrow to people; mixed-breed, compound
10. A Humane, arrow to societies; rescue, arrow to groups; free, arrow to dogs; good, arrow to homes
11. E adjective, dog
12. A pronoun
13. A adjective, kind
14. A pronoun
15. E adjective, backyard
16. A adjective, yard
17. A adjective, personality
18. E adjective, dog
19. A pronoun
20. C adjective, dog
21. E very, arrow to curious
22. A more, arrow to active; enthusiastically, arrow to wags
23. C less, arrow to lively; more, arrow to timidly; timidly, arrow to behaves
24. C frequently, arrow to Feed; about, arrow to six
25. A steadily, arrow to should grow
26. E commercially, arrow to produce
27. C mainly, arrows to are produced
28. C also, arrow to are included
29. C usually, arrow to will play; vigorously, arrow to will play; then, arrow to nap
30. A easily, arrow to learn; instinctively, arrow to learn
31. A adverb
32. A adjective
33. A adverb

34.	A	adjective
35.	A	adverb
36.	E	adjective
37.	A	adverb
38.	A	adjective
39.	E	adjective
40.	C	adverb
41.	E	C
42.	A	M
43.	A	B
44.	E	J
45.	C	B
46.	A	K
47.	E	C
48.	E	M
49.	A	B
50.	A	M

Chapter 17: Prepositions (p. 123)

1. C of Florida, circle of, arrow to Much; by forests, circle by, arrow to is covered
2. E in southern Florida, circle in, arrow to thrive
3. A of America's species, circle of, arrow to half; of trees, circle of, arrow to species; in Florida, circle in, arrow to grow
4. A of Florida's plants, circle of, arrow to Many; into the state, circle into, arrow to were imported
5. A about the soggy environment, circle about, arrow to spoke; of the Everglades region, circle of, arrow to environment
6. E across the swamp, circle across, arrow to looked
7. A along the coast, circle along, arrow to swim; of Florida, circle of, arrow to coast
8. C near Florida's shores, circle near, arrow to leap; in fishing nets, circle in, arrow to land
9. C for the protection, circle for, arrow to maintains; of migratory birds, circle of, arrow to protection
10. E on a golf course, circle on, arrow to alligator
11. E out of; *Sample:* In ancient times, people came from the north and entered Florida.
12. C According to; *Sample:* By some reports, this was about 10,000 years ago.
13. C In addition to; *Sample:* Along with fishing, some of these early groups began farming.
14. A by means of; *Sample:* They also survived by hunting and gathering.
15. E on account of; *Sample:* By 1750, these Native Americans suffered because of many factors.
16. C Because of; *Sample:* On account of disease and other difficulties, they were virtually destroyed.
17. C In place of; *Sample:* Instead of the dwindling native population, Europeans soon inhabited Florida.
18. A Aside from; *Sample:* In addition to the Spanish settlements, there were also large Italian groups.
19. A As of; *Sample:* By 1819, Florida was part of the United States.
20. A instead of; *Sample:* Older, retired people who want heat in place of cold often come to Florida.
21. A preposition, adverb
22. A adverb, preposition
23. C adverb, preposition
24. A preposition, adverb
25. A preposition, adverb
26. A adverb, preposition
27. A adverb, preposition
28. A adverb, preposition
29. A preposition, adverb
30. A adverb, preposition
31. A *Sample:* There were boxes within boxes.
32. A *Sample:* Look up.
33. C *Sample:* Besides the two boys, there are eight girls who came for me.
34. C *Sample:* Because of you I went to the park instead of to the movies.
35. C *Sample:* Before the end of the movie, you will begin to wonder if you have seen it before.
36. E *Sample:* We drove through Florida.
37. C *Sample:* Instead of a sleigh ride, an indoor game enabled us to stay inside the warm house.
38. A *Sample:* I wore my blue jacket instead of my red sweater.
39. A *Sample:* I went to the store with my sister and bought a gift for you.
40. E *Sample:* According to Bob, it takes two hours to get there.
41. E C
42. A F
43. E D
44. C G
45. A A
46. C J
47. A A
48. E G
49. A C
50. E F

Chapter 18: Conjunctions and Interjections (p. 127)

1. E underline and; circle smooth; circle flat
2. A underline but; circle They knew the ocean was deep; circle they did not realize it also had mountains
3. A underline nor; circle the ocean's deep trenches; circle its many plains
4. A underline so; circle More recently, scientists wanted a map of the ocean floor; circle they used sonar
5. A underline for; circle It was a long process; circle each sound wave had to be timed
6. C underline and; circle bounce sound off the bottom; circle wait until its echo returned
7. E underline or; circle long; circle short
8. A underline and; circle A long wait for an echo indicated greater depth; circle a short wait indicated less depth
9. A underline yet; circle tedious; circle exciting
10. A underline and; circle bats; circle whales
11. A underline both; circle heat from the tropics; underline and; circle cold from the polar regions
12. A underline neither; circle too hot; underline nor; circle too cold

13. E underline either; circle warm; underline or; circle cool
14. A underline not only; circle as a source of food; underline but also; circle as a highway for trade and exploration
15. A underline not only; circle near the shore; underline but also; circle in the deepest trenches
16. C underline Whether; circle you fish in the deep sea; underline or; circle you stay near the shore
17. E underline either; circle salmon; underline or; circle tuna
18. A underline whether; circle he catches anything; underline or; circle he comes back empty-handed
19. E underline neither; circle bored; underline nor; circle tired
20. E underline both; circle fun; underline and; circle relaxing
21. E and, coordinating
22. A but, coordinating
23. A not only . . . but also, correlative
24. C both . . . and, correlative
25. A Whether . . . or, correlative
26. C nor, coordinating
27. A Either . . . or, correlative
28. E yet, coordinating
29. A not only . . . but also, correlative
30. A but, coordinating
31. E A
32. A H
33. E B
34. A J
35. A C
36. E H
37. A B
38. A F
39. A C
40. E J

Chapter 19: Basic Sentence Parts (p. 130)
1. A <u>Sarah Breedlove</u> | <u>was born in 1867 on the Burney family plantation in Louisiana</u>.
2. E <u>Sarah</u> | <u>married a Mr. McWilliams in 1881</u>.
3. A <u>Mr. McWilliams</u> | <u>died six years later</u>.
4. C <u>Sarah and her daughter, A'Lelia,</u> | <u>moved to St. Louis, Missouri</u>.
5. A <u>Sarah's job as a washerwoman</u> | <u>paid the bills until 1905</u>.
6. E <u>Sarah</u> | <u>married Charles J. Walker, a newspaperman, in 1906</u>.
7. A <u>Madame C.J. Walker</u> | <u>developed some beauty products</u>.
8. A <u>Her method of straightening curly hair</u> | <u>was very popular</u>.
9. E <u>Her agents</u> | <u>sold the hair treatments door-to-door</u>.
10. C <u>Her company</u> | <u>eventually employed 3,000 people</u>.
11. E fragment
12. E sentence
13. A sentence
14. E fragment
15. A sentence
16. E sentence
17. C fragment
18. A fragment
19. E sentence
20. A fragment
21. A *Sample:* sold
22. E *Sample:* Maureen
23. A *Sample:* study
24. A *Sample:* Internet
25. C *Sample:* edit
26. C *Sample:* print
27. E *Sample:* Bill
28. A *Sample:* class
29. A *Sample:* operated
30. C *Sample:* enjoyed
31. C Madame C. J. Walker
32. A (You)
33. A information
34. A improvements
35. C Madame C. J. Walker
36. C Madame Walker
37. E you
38. C scholarships
39. A people
40. A users
41. A *Sample:* shampoo, direct object
42. E *Sample:* curly, predicate adjective
43. A *Sample:* combs, direct object
44. A *Sample:* some money, direct object
45. A *Sample:* a new product, direct object
46. A *Sample:* black skirts, direct object
47. A *Sample:* a question, direct object
48. A *Sample:* patient woman, predicate noun
49. E *Sample:* conditioner, direct object
50. A *Sample:* effective, predicate adjective
51. A C
52. A F
53. C A
54. A H
55. C B
56. A G
57. E D
58. C J
59. A A
60. A H

Chapter 20: Phrases and Clauses (p. 134)
1. A prepositional phrase used as an adjective
2. E infinitive phrase
3. A participial phrase
4. E infinitive
5. E participle
6. E infinitive phrase
7. C prepositional phrase used as an adverb
8. C participial phrase
9. A prepositional phrase used as an adjective
10. C prepositional phrase used as an adverb
11. E the oldest national park in the United States—renames Yellowstone
12. E the most famous geyser in Yellowstone—renames Old Faithful
13. A those vapor-emitting holes in the earth—renames Fumaroles
14. A the shiny black volcanic glass—renames obsidian
15. A the Giantess—renames Another geyser near Old Faithful

16. E a multicolored terrace with hot water cascades—renames Minerva
17. C the trumpeter swan—renames bird
18. A a colorful gorge—renames The Grand Canyon of the Yellowstone River
19. A an eighty-mile scenic roadway—renames The John D. Rockefeller Jr. Memorial Parkway
20. A a Rocky Mountain pine tree—renames Lodgepole pine
21. E who was born in Scotland in 1838—adjective clause, modifies John Muir
22. A After he attended college—adverb clause, modifies worked
23. C when an industrial accident almost cost him an eye—adjective clause, modifies 1867
24. C which became his life's work—adjective clause, modifies nature
25. C While keeping a journal—adverb clause, modifies walked
26. E which was published in 1916—adjective clause, modifies journal
27. A which she has read four times—adjective clause, modifies book
28. A that became so important in his life—adjective clause, modifies valley
29. C Whenever I am in Yosemite—adverb clause, modifies feel
30. C Because of John Muir's efforts—adverb clause, modifies has been protected
31. A simple
32. E simple
33. C complex
34. A compound
35. A simple
36. A complex
37. A simple
38. A compound
39. A complex
40. C compound
41. A *Sample:* El Capitan, which rises from the floor of Yosemite Valley, is a plain mass of granite 3,300 feet high.
42. A *Sample:* Half Dome, the most imposing rock in Yosemite, is 4,740 feet high.
43. C *Sample:* Vernal Fall, which is easier to reach than the other waterfalls, is a favorite with visitors.
44. E *Sample:* The tallest pines in Yosemite are more than 200 feet high. Some of the oaks have trunks of eight feet in diameter.
45. A *Sample:* No one but Native Americans saw the valley until 1851, but by 1856, regular tourist travel had begun.
46. A *Sample:* Yosemite's first permanent settler, who moved there in 1860, built a cabin in the upper end of the valley.
47. E *Sample:* The first permanent settler planted gardens. He also planted orchards.
48. A *Sample:* Violets, lilies, and goldenrods grow in Yosemite, and wild roses and azaleas also flourish in the park.
49. A *Sample:* The climate of Yosemite, which is surprisingly mild, creates excellent growing conditions for the vegetation.
50. C In its beauty and grandeur, Yosemite has no rivals; however, there are many other valleys of the same type.
51. A B
52. E F
53. A C
54. C J
55. A A
56. A H
57. C D
58. A G
59. A A
60. C J

Chapter 21: Effective Sentences (p. 139)
1. E . declarative
2. E . declarative
3. A ? interrogative
4. C ! exclamatory
5. E . declarative
6. A . declarative
7. C . imperative
8. A ! exclamatory
9. E . declarative
10. A ? interrogative
11. A *Sample:* In 1838, Queen Victoria saw and enjoyed Van Amburgh's circus act.
12. C *Sample:* She contacted the artist Edwin Landseer, who made her a portrait of the American circus performer.
13. A *Sample:* Many circus performers practice long hours and give their audiences excellent performances.
14. C *Sample:* The performers present the animals, which are still wild, as obedient, playful pets.
15. A *Sample:* Marsha, my best friend, saw a circus performance last week.
16. C *Sample:* Elephants, which have been in circuses since the 1830's, are to many people the very symbol of the circus.
17. E *Sample:* Elephants are really quite dangerous; some have been known to turn on their trainers.
18. A *Sample:* The flying trapeze was invented in 1859 by a French acrobat.
19. C *Sample:* The French acrobat's name, J. Léotard, gave us our word *leotard*.
20. E *Sample:* The circus presents people at their best in physical achievement and coordination.
21. E *Sample:* Human circus performers do balancing acts on high wires. They also do acts with wild animals.
22. C *Sample:* The skilled and disciplined trapeze artist performs a thrilling feat.
23. A *Sample:* Predictably, the audience is almost silent as the artist performs the dangerous act.
24. A *Sample:* The life of a circus performer would be difficult for many people.
25. C *Sample:* To work in a circus, other people would do almost anything.
26. E *Sample:* Circus performers may work with animal or human partners.
27. C *Sample:* Into the center ring walked the clown.

28. E *Sample:* Some clowns wear elegant costumes and paint their faces white. Others wear shabby clothes and use colorful makeup.
29. A *Sample:* The black bear rode on the bicycle.
30. A *Sample:* Surprisingly, some circus animals are uncaged, even though they can be dangerous.
31. E correct
32. C *Sample:* Wearing a very small amount of makeup, Oleg performed his act.
33. E *Sample:* Oleg became well known not only in the Soviet Union but throughout Europe and also in the United States.
34. C *Sample:* Pretending to copy the acts of the regular circus performers, he would almost succeed.
35. A *Sample:* The circus band set the pace.
36. E correct
37. A *Sample:* Animals are not always a part of circus acts.
38. A *Sample:* Two-ring circuses began in 1872; three-ring circuses began in 1881.
39. E correct
40. C *Sample:* One big top covered more than two acres.
41. A *Sample:* Depicting exciting times in the Old West, Wild West shows drew large crowds.
42. A correct
43. C *Sample:* Annie Oakley gained fame as "Little Miss Sureshot" in Wild West shows throughout the United States.
44. C *Sample:* Walking down the midway, I thought that the carnival seemed a lot like a circus.
45. C *Sample:* A woman who told the future was wearing fifteen rings and a tall turban.
46. A *Sample:* The reason I won the prize is that I have very good aim.
47. A Carrying my prizes, I realized that the car was farther away than I had thought.
48. E Tony said, "I want to give you a little bit of advice."
49. A Tony's words had a negative effect on my mood.
50. E *Sample:* He told me not to spend any more money on carnival tickets.
51. A B
52. E H
53. A A
54. E J
55. A A
56. A G
57. A D
58. A H
59. E A
60. C H

Chapter 22: Using Verbs (p. 144)
1. E present, irregular
2. A past participle, regular
3. E present, irregular
4. A past participle, regular
5. A past, regular
6. A past, regular
7. C past participle, irregular
8. A present participle, regular
9. A past participle, regular
10. E present, regular
11. E varies
12. A walking
13. E move
14. A drawn
15. C spread
16. A made
17. E converted
18. A scratched
19. A feeling
20. A taken
21. A The cat is expressing its feelings to you.
22. A The cat has given you a look of annoyance.
23. E That particular vocal sound indicates that the cat is content.
24. A The cat knew that you were getting ready to pet it.
25. A The Persian cat had rubbed its head against the couch.
26. E Cats will smell their food before they eat it.
27. E Cats' ears contain thirty muscles, compared to the six in humans.
28. A A cat will have heard sounds that you never will.
29. C Before our last earthquake, the cat had been acting very oddly.
30. C I have been wondering why the cat was so nervous.
31. C By next week, we will have immunized our cats.
32. A I will have taken them for their shots by then.
33. C Kittens often will be racing crazily through the house.
34. E Wild behavior in cats has many causes.
35. E Before domestication, cats actively hunted around dawn and dusk.
36. A Our white cat has groomed not only herself but our other cat as well.
37. C The white cat had been feeling affection for the other cat.
38. C By the time we get home, the cat will have been sleeping for two hours.
39. A I will be training the cats to use scratching posts.
40. A The cat was adjusting to our new home.
41. C Every afternoon, that cat lies on the couch and naps.
42. E It is not (or isn't) acceptable for the cat to scratch the furniture.
43. A I like to sit in the rocker and pet the cat.
44. E The cats have gone outside to lie in the sun.
45. E I did (or have done) some reading about the care and feeding of cats.
46. A I should have chosen a Siamese cat instead of this Persian.
47. E I saw (or have seen) a beautiful Burmese cat at the pet store.
48. A correct
49. E That cat did (or has done) something very unusual.
50. C The short-haired cat is lying on the windowsill.
51. E B

52.	E	J	9.	A	hangs
53.	C	B	10.	C	swallows
54.	E	J	11.	E	Sample answer: Some whales are larger . . .
55.	E	C			
56.	A	M	12.	E	Sample answer: . . . and it weighs more . . .
57.	A	B			
58.	E	J	13.	E	Sample answer: Baleen whales obtain their . . .
59.	E	A			
60.	C	M	14.	C	Sample answer: . . . fishes, breathe air. . .

Chapter 23: Using Pronouns (p. 148)

1. C you, nominative
2. C she, nominative
3. E her, objective
4. E her, objective
5. A hers, possessive
6. A them, objective
7. E I, nominative
8. E them, objective
9. C they, nominative
10. A Theirs, possessive
11. C nominative, subject of a verb
12. C objective, indirect object
13. E objective, object of a preposition
14. A nominative, subject of a verb
15. A possessive
16. A objective, object of a preposition
17. C objective, indirect object
18. A objective, direct object
19. A possessive
20. C nominative, predicate nominative
21. A John and I have always wanted to talk to Mary Shields.
22. A correct
23. C We know that she and Lolly Medley were the only two women in the 1974 Iditarod.
24. A Their courage and determination helped them finish the race.
25. C The story is inspiring to John and me.
26. A He and I want to ask Mary Shields how she did it.
27. A If I met her, I would ask, "How did you train your dogs?"
28. E correct
29. C It's interesting to talk to winners of such a race, with all its difficulties.
30. E I always wonder how much of the glory is really theirs and how much belongs to the dogs.
31. E B
32. E F
33. C D
34. A H
35. E B
36. A F
37. A C
38. C J
39. E A
40. C G

Chapter 24: Making Words Agree (p. 151)

1. E are
2. C includes
3. A fall
4. E do
5. E are divided
6. A has
7. C feeds
8. A supply

15. E Sample answer: . . . whales are helpless.
16. E Sample answer: It is impossible . . .
17. A Sample answer: Whales inhabit all . . .
18. C Sample answer: . . . social—travel in groups . . .
19. C Sample answer: . . . sound are made by whales.
20. A Sample answer: Whales use barks . . .
21. A his
22. A them
23. E it
24. E he
25. C his or her
26. C her
27. A their
28. E its
29. C his or her
30. C their
31. A Researchers in Antarctica launch more than 9,000 balloons each year, hoping that they will learn more.
32. E These balloons range greatly in size, and their purposes are varied.
33. A Some of them are weather balloons about six feet in diameter.
34. E Others stretch to an enormous size.
35. A Some of these balloons are big enough to hold three jumbo jets set inside them.
36. A The helium inside them expands as the balloons rise.
37. A Eventually, the gas bursts the balloons.
38. E Their plastic skins then drift slowly back to earth, landing on the ice or on the oceans.
39. C You might think that a scientist who sends up a balloon would go out to retrieve it, but often he or she does not.
40. C Any whale that cruises the ocean in that area faces great danger if it happens to eat the plastic.
41. E B
42. A F
43. E C
44. C J
45. A A
46. C H
47. A D
48. A G
49. E A
50. A J

Chapter 25: Using Modifiers (p. 155)

1. E dimmer, dimmest
2. A happy, happiest
3. E soon, sooner
4. C wonderful, most wonderful
5. C more coldly, most coldly
6. C tenderly, more tenderly
7. C better, best

8. C   bad (or badly), worst
9. E   afraid, more afraid
10. A more efficient, most efficient
11. C more steadily, most steadily
12. C few, fewest
13. A rapidly, more rapidly
14. E loud, louder
15. A icier, iciest
16. A expensive, least expensive
17. A more interesting, most interesting
18. E sharp, sharpest
19. E young, younger
20. C far, furthest
21. C best, superlative; good, better
22. A more exciting, comparative; exciting, most exciting
23. E strong, positive; stronger, strongest
24. C clumsier, comparative; clumsy, clumsiest
25. A graceful, positive; more graceful, most graceful
26. C higher, comparative; high, highest
27. A best, superlative; good, better
28. A most delicate, superlative; delicate, more delicate
29. E younger, comparative; young, youngest
30. A more elaborate, comparative; elaborate, most elaborate
31. C Have you ever seen a ballet?
32. C The only one Bob saw was <u>Swan Lake</u>.
33. A From the dancers to the orchestra, everyone performed really well.
34. E <u>Swan Lake</u> is one of the most famous of all ballets.
35. C Whenever I attend a ballet, I feel good afterward.
36. A The last one I saw had the most extraordinary costumes ever!
37. E The dancers performed the most amazing steps I have ever seen.
38. E That dancer is the most graceful dancer on the stage today.
39. A correct
40. A Tonight's performance was better than last night's.
41. C B
42. C H
43. E A
44. E J
45. A B
46. E G
47. E D
48. C F
49. A C
50. A H

Chapter 26: Punctuation (p. 158)
1. E . . . farm.
2. E . . . plantation.
3. A . . . lived.
4. C . . . area!
5. A . . . cooking?
6. E When the Civil War ended, Booker T. Washington was nine years old.
7. C Newly freed by the Emancipation Proclamation, Washington, his mother, and his brother moved to West Virginia.
8. A Mrs. Viola Ruffner, a New England woman, hired Washington as a houseboy.
9. E Recognizing Washington's eagerness to learn, Mrs. Ruffner encouraged his studies.
10. C Eventually, he enrolled in a vocational school, and after three years, Washington graduated with honors.
11. A Soon after graduation, in fact, Booker T. Washington became a teacher at the same school.
12. A On July 4, 1881, Washington opened the school for which he is famous, Tuskegee Institute.
13. A In November 1915, while in New York City on business, Washington became ill.
14. C He had often said, "I was born in the South, have lived all my life in the South, and expect to die and be buried in the South."
15. E A few hours before he died on November 14, 1915, Washington arrived by train in Alabama.
16. C Booker T. Washington wrote two volumes of autobiography: <u>The Story of My Life and Work</u> and <u>Up From Slavery</u>.
17. A Langston Hughes called <u>Up From Slavery</u> "one of America's most revealing books."
18. A Washington was given an interesting nickname: the "Wizard of Tuskegee."
19. E Washington dined with President Theodore Roosevelt; they discussed politics.
20. C Education, industriousness, and racial solidarity: These were Washington's goals for African Americans.
21. E Maria asked, "Have you ever been to Alabama?"
22. A Henry told her that he had never been there but would like to go.
23. E "If you were in Alabama," he asked, "would you visit Tuskegee Institute?"
24. C "Absolutely!" exclaimed Maria. "I wouldn't miss it."
25. E Henry asked, "What else would you do in Alabama?"
26. A "Well," said Maria, "I'm not sure. What would you suggest?"
27. C "We should look in a guidebook," said Henry, "to find out about points of interest."
28. C The first chapter of <u>Up From Slavery</u> is called "A Slave Among Slaves."
29. E correct
30. A Washington was praised in the magazine the <u>North American Review</u>.
31. A Thirty-one people started Tuskegee Institute: one teacher and thirty students.
32. E One of Booker T. Washington's goals was to educate former slaves.
33. C Washington wanted to give students real-world skills.
34. A He wanted to train them for teaching, trades, and farm-related work.
35. E At first, Washington didn't know how he would pay for Tuskegee.
36. C Two Boston women's contribution to Tuskegee was six thousand dollars a year.

37. A   Booker T. Washington gave a speech on farm production in mid-June.
38.   correct
39. A   A graduate of Tuskegee grew two hundred and sixty-six bushels per acre.
40. E   A self-employed farmer could make a good living.
41. E   C
42. E   F
43. A   B
44. A   F
45. A   D
46. C   G
47. A   D
48. C   G
49. A   A
50. C   H
51. A   C
52. A   J
53. A   A
54. E   H
55. A   A

Chapter 27: Capitalization (p. 162)
1. E   One
2. E   The
3. E   The
4. A   Not, I
5. A   One, I
6. E   Henry Ford's parents were named William and Mary.
7. A   Ford was born during the Civil War.
8. E   At the time, Abraham Lincoln was in office.
9. C   There were only twenty-four states in the Union.
10. A   In the Confederacy, there were eleven states.
11. A   That was a terrible time in American history.
12. A   The Civil War ended, and the United States went back to work.
13. E   In 1888, Ford married a woman named Clara Bryant.
14. E   In 1893, they had their only child, Edsel Bryant Ford.
15. A   Many years later, a car in the Ford line would be named the Edsel.
16. A   The Edsel was never as popular as other Ford cars, such as the Mustang.
17. A   Ford thought that more Americans should have cars.
18. C   In October 1908, Ford announced the birth of the Model T.
19. A   This car was produced in Ford's new plant in Highland Park, Michigan.
20. C   The American sales of this car far exceeded Canadian and British sales.
21. A   In 1899, Ford formed the Detroit Automobile Company.
22. C   My uncle says this company later became the Henry Ford Company.
23. A   Did you know that Uncle Dan once collected vintage cars?
24. A   What kind of car did President Eisenhower drive?
25. C   I heard that my mother's great-grandfather once owned a Model A.
26. A   I remember Aunt Alice showing me a picture of one of her old cars.
27. A   correct
28. A   The movie Bonnie and Clyde had some interesting old cars in it.
29. A   Donald would rather work on old cars than study for his English class.
30. A   I once wrote a story called "Clara and the Clunky Old Car."
31. E   B
32. A   F
33. C   D
34. E   H
35. C   B
36. C   F
37. C   C
38. A   J
39. A   A
40. A   G

Grammar, Usage, and Mechanics: Cumulative Mastery Test (p. 165)
The numbers in brackets indicate the chapter and section of the skills being tested.
1. A   adjective [16.1]
2. E   verb [15.1]
3. E   preposition [17.1]
4. E   noun [14.1]
5. A   noun [14.1]
6. C   adverb [16.2]
7. A   adjective [16.1]
8. E   pronoun [14.2]
9. E   conjunction [18.1]
10. E   interjection [18.2]
11. C   predicate noun [19.5]
12. A   fragment [19.1]
13. A   complete predicate [19.2]
14. E   complete subject [19.2]
15. A   complete subject [19.2]
16. A   direct object [19.5]
17. A   complete predicate [19.2]
18. A   predicate adjective [19.5]
19. C   sentence [19.1]
20. C   indirect object [19.5]
21. A   participial phrase [20.1]
22. A   appositive phrase [20.1]
23. A   independent clause [20.2]
24. C   adjective clause [20.2]
25. E   participle [20.1]
26. A   appositive [20.1]
27. C   adverb clause [20.2]
28. A   prepositional phrase used as an adjective [20.1]
29. A   infinitive [20.1]
30. C   prepositional phrase used as an adverb [20.2]
31. E   interrogative sentence [21.1]
32. C   Irish famine victims and many German immigrants came to America in the late 1840's. [21.2]
33. A   Most immigrant residences were crowded and had poor air circulation. [21.2]
34. E   The winning design improved air circulation and light. [21.2]
35. E   A new kind of housing was built to solve New York's housing problem; it was called the tenement. [21.2]

36. A *Sample:* The tenements were soon overcrowded, so the people inside were not very comfortable. [21.2]
37. C *Sample:* Sandra's ancestors lived in a New York tenement building that has since been torn down. [21.2]
38. A *Sample:* They wanted to move out of the overcrowded building. [21.4]
39. C *Sample:* Hoping to win the contest, the designer included an air shaft in the center of several buildings. [21.4]
40. C *Sample:* The family had no choice but to accept the offer to live in the crowded building. [21.4]
41. A past; irregular [22.1]
42. A present participle; regular [22.1]
43. E In 1903, officials had ruled that all boundary lines on a basketball court must be straight. [22.1]
44. A Before 1903, teams were drawing the lines around existing obstructions such as pillars, stairways, or offices. [22.1]
45. C Max had shown us pictures of some old basketball teams. [22.2]
46. C By the end of the night, our basketball team surely will have won the championship. [22.2]
47. C Don has been practicing some of his basketball moves. [22.2]
48. E Donna saw the game last night. [22.2]
49. C correct [22.3]
50. C As Todd watched the game, his dog lay on the floor by the couch. [22.3]
51. E nominative [23]
52. A possessive [23]
53. E objective [23]
54. E We—subject of a verb [23]
55. A they—subject of a verb [23]
56. E I—subject of a verb [23]
57. C he—predicate nominative [23]
58. C them—indirect object [23]
59. C it—direct object [23]
60. A its—possessive [23]
61. A was [24.1]
62. E is [24.1]
63. A play [24.1]
64. C joins [24.1]
65. E The Revolution now over, Sam Wilson moves to Troy, New York. [24.1]
66. A story is [24.1]
67. A begin [24.1]
68. A *Sample:* gets [24.1]
69. C his [24.2]
70. C they [24.2]
71. E more patriotically, most patriotically [25.1]
72. A more unclear, most unclear [25.1]
73. A Today's drawings of Uncle Sam are more colorful than the early sketches in black and white. [25.1]
74. C The best images of Uncle Sam today are in red, white, and blue. [25.1]
75. E superlative [25.1]
76. C After the flag, the image of Uncle Sam is probably the most familiar of all American symbols. [25.1]
77. C At the antique show, I want to buy only an original World War I poster of Uncle Sam. [25.2]
78. A After I found the antique poster, I felt really good. [25.2]
79. C I need just one more poster to complete my collection. [25.2]
80. C correct [25.2]
81. E illustrations, for [26.2]
82. A The first Uncle Sam illustrations did not show the figure as tall, thin, and hollow-cheeked. [26.2]
83. C correct [26.2]
84. C During Andrew Jackson's presidency, the bright red pants were added to the figure of Uncle Sam. [26.2]
85. A Look, Jane, at this interesting old poster of Uncle Sam. [26.2]
86. E This poster, I believe, will go up in value within the next five years. [26.2]
87. A Frances found this poster on April 24, 2001, and she paid only fifty dollars for it. [26.2]
88. C "It starts with every one of us giving a little more," said Sam Wilson, "instead of only taking and getting all the time." [26.4]
89. A correct [26.4]
90. A Sam Wilson, owner of a meat-packing company, died in 1854 at the age of eighty-eight. [26.5]
91. E Many people think that there was no real-life Uncle Sam. [27]
92. E In fact, I used to think that the figure was just a myth. [27]
93. A A historian named Thomas Gerson discovered an old newspaper dated May 12, 1830. [27]
94. C The article talked about Pheodorus Bailey, a postmaster in New York City. [27]
95. A It said that Mr. Bailey went to Sam Wilson's meat-packing plant in October of 1812. [27]
96. A Mr. Bailey confirms that one of the workers said that *U.S.* meant "Uncle Sam." [27]
97. A Samuel Wilson is buried at Oakwood Cemetery in Troy, New York. [27]
98. C My favorite cousin, Dr. Alice May, visited that cemetery last year. [27]
99. C Sylvia asked, "Do you like my new poster, Dad?" [27]
100. A I did a presentation on historical posters for my history class last month. [27]

Chapter 28: Speaking, Listening, Viewing, and Representing (p. 175)
1. E *Samples:* Do the homework and reading so you are well prepared.
2. A *Samples:* Think through directions before you speak; speak slowly and clearly.
3. A *Sample:* Use the person's full name and give some background about each person.
4. A explanatory—c
    persuasive—b
    entertaining—a
5. A persuasive
6. A explanatory

7. A to persuade the city council to save the garden
8. E members of the city council
9. A Students' answers will vary but should include a clear outline specific to the city garden topic, with two main points and details.
10. A The note card should be in an informal outline format with details standing out in capital letters (or underlined).
11. A d. Nonverbal language can add to, or take away from, the effect of a speech.
12. A b. Taking notes helps the listener to focus on the speaker's message.
13. E *Sample:* to decide what information you want to remember after the speech
14. A *Samples:* labels, topography, captions, distances
15. A so you can focus your mind on the specific information you are looking for
16. A to show products made in the southern colonies
17. A lumber, grain, cattle, rice, tobacco, indigo
18. E line graph
19. C Native American population of Central America from 1500–1620
20. A 20 million
21. C 1520–1550
22. A fact—b
opinion—c
loaded language—d
bias—a
23. E *Samples:* colors, moods
The information is useful because it adds to people's abilities to think creatively.
24. A *Sample:* You could use a comparison-and-contrast chart, with two columns.
25. C It helps present difficult or technical information in an easy-to-understand form.
26. A Sections of student graphs should be clearly labeled, and their sizes should correspond to the values they represent. Possible title: Immigrants to the U.S., 1880–1900.
27. A *Samples:* boldface, italics, capital letters, bulleted lists
28. C *Samples:* music from the period, played on a cassette; photographs from the period displayed on an overhead projector
29. A slides—d
overhead projector—a
video shooting script—b
storyboard—c
30. E Students should identify the title of the song and the mood. They should describe appropriate costumes and setting, with specific details.

Chapter 29: Vocabulary and Spelling (p. 181)
1. E *Samples:* converse, read more
2. E *Samples:* Look it up in the dictionary; try to figure it out with context clues.
3. A a. sign or indication of what is to come
b. exaggeration
c. ignore or disbelieve
d. in suspense
e. rising

4. C fell like daggers
It is figurative, because daggers didn't actually fall.
Its meaning is that the falling sleet was sharp.
5. A cool his heels
It is an idiom, because heels are not actually literally cooled.
Its meaning is that he had to wait.
6. A A notebook can be used to record unfamiliar words. A glossary can be used to find meanings of new words.
7. C You can try out unfamiliar words in new sentences, and then check them in a dictionary to see if they are correct.
8. A You can study new words that you have recorded.
9. E You can use flashcards to practice the meaning of new words.
10. A *Sample:* pronunciation of words *Samples:* Readers need dictionaries for finding word meanings; writers use them to find substitutes for words in their writing.
11. A A writer could use it to find substitutes for other words, in order to avoid repetition.
12. A The root is the base of the word. Knowing its meaning helps you figure out the meaning of related words.
13. A -vis-; to see
14. C -mis- or -mit-; to send
15. C -mot-; to move
16. A a. trans; mission
b. re; arrange
c. un; natural
d. mis; appropriate
e. ex; hale
17. A a. -ment; noun
b. -ion; noun
c. -able; adjective
d. -ly, adverb
e. -ible; adjective
18. C a. in; ven; tion; something that is invented
b. trans; mit; none; to send
c. re; vers; ion; a turning away
d. un; lov; able; not able to be loved
e. none; vis; ion; sight
19. A *Samples:* Countries conquered England; people traveled.
20. E to help them learn to spell words they have had trouble with in the past
21. A *Samples:*
a. reality; realistic
b. studious; student
c. magical; magician
22. A LOOK—Examine the word for patterns.
SAY—Pronounce each syllable of the word.
SPELL—Spell the word on paper.
COMPARE—See whether your spelling is correct, and fix it if you need to.
23. A a. ceiling
b. reign
c. soldiers
d. receive
e. delicately

24. C a. tritely
       b. sturdiness
       c. competition
       d. deferred
       e. preference
25. C a. reiterate
       b. indisputable
       c. reference
       d. lovable
       e. disinterested
26. A *Sample:* Things that diff<u>er</u> are diff<u>er</u>ent.
27. A English borrows spellings from other languages.
28. A a. shelves
       b. firemen
       c. mothers-in-law
       d. radios
       e. clashes
29. C a. beet
       b. bridle
       c. route
       d. plain
       e. steel
30. C a. ponies
       b. their
       c. seize
       d. past
       e. jumped

Chapter 30: Reading Skills (p. 185)
1. E to introduce the reader to key ideas in a chapter
2. A a. glossary
       b. chapter introduction and summary
       c. table of contents
       d. index
3. A They break up information into more manageable pieces of text.
4. A It helps you to focus your reading.
5. E They supplement the meaning of the text.
6. E A caption can explain the content of a picture or cartoon.
7. A a. scanning
       b. close reading
       c. skimming
8. A Right there—d
       Think and search—c
       Author and you—b
       On your own—a
9. C a. record
       b. recite
       c. question
       d. review
       e. survey
       f. read
10. A It can visually explain a complex topic.
11. C *Sample:* You might use a sunburst diagram titled "Preparation for Revolution," with offshoots of the sun labeled with the ways in which colonists prepared themselves.
12. A Under Butterfly: rests at night, not hairy, uses colors to find mate
       Under Moth: hides during day, hairy, uses scent to find mate
       Under "Both": insects, three-part bodies, six legs and four wings, wings are often two colors

13. A *Samples:* to interpret what you have read; to check your understanding
14. C Main ideas represent the author's key points. Major details support the main ideas.
15. A *Samples:*
       a. The Seneca Falls Convention focused attention on women's problems.
       b. Two hundred women and 40 men attended; a Declaration of Sentiments was presented
       c. to provide information about the event
       d. It relates to other developments in women's progress through history
16. E Facts can always be proven by using an authority or evidence. Opinions represent a person's feelings or judgments and cannot always be supported.
17. A a. opinion
       b. fact
       c. fact
       d. fact
18. A a. to instruct
       b. to entertain
       c. to sell
       d. to inform
       e. to offer an opinion
19. A The author's purpose is to offer an opinion, as evidenced by *explain my feelings*.
20. C Inference: There are triplets in the class. Generalization: This is the only class in school with triplets.
21. C *Denotation* refers to literal meaning. *Connotation* refers to implied meaning.
22. A dangerous
23. A *Samples:*
       a. The blackboard was chock full of written information.
       b. The blackboard was covered with densely written, unreadable words.
24. A computer crime; crime on the Internet
25. A to present a series . . . —b
       to create a persuasive argument—d
       to arrange events in time—c
       to arrange details in space—a
26. E Nonfiction is based on facts. Literary writing, such as short stories, novels, or drama, is not literally factual, although it can be based on facts or historical events.
27. A to experience the action through their thoughts and feelings
       Sample: In *To Kill a Mockingbird*, I identified with Scout, because she was curious about the world and its injustices.
28. A *Samples:* You can makes inferences based on characters' comments or actions.
29. A It is not literally factual, although it can be loosely based on facts.
30. A *Sample:* A reader can read the work aloud to better envision the action.
31. A *Sample:* Poetry is shorter, and elements such as sound, rhythm, and imagery play a more important role. Poetry also lends itself more to being read aloud.
32. A Identifying the speaker can help the reader to imagine the speaker's point of view and the purpose of the poem.

33. E a. myth
       b. folk tale
       c. legend
34. E *Sample:* People read newspapers to stay current with the events of the world.
35. A a. newspaper
       b. application
       c. an electronic text
       d. an anthology

Chapter 31: Study, Reference, and Test-Taking Skills (p. 190)

1. E *Sample:* Choose a study area that is neat and well lit; create a study schedule; keep an assignment book.
2. A Students should fill in diagram with specific and clear activities such as daily homework assignments, long-term reports, and athletic activities.
3. C *Samples:*
      Main idea: In 1774, the British punished Massachusetts.
      Major detail: Parliament shut down the Boston port.
      Supporting details: No ships could enter or leave; The harbor stayed closed until the colonists paid for the tea.
4. C *Sample:* The British decided to punish the colonists of Massachusetts. Parliament shut down the port of Boston and restricted colonists' right to hold meetings.
5. E *Samples:* nonfiction books, biographies, novels, atlases
6. A *Sample:* You can look up a book, get its call number, and locate it on the shelf.
7. A *Sample:* It can help you find books by subject, if you don't know the title or author of a book.
8. C The electronic catalog would be the most useful way to determine whether the book was in the library.
9. A On the shelves, look in *G* for *Gipson* (novels are shelved alphabetically by author).
10. A In the catalog, look up the subject "earthquakes" to get the call number for the section.
11. C On the shelves, look in *H* for *Hitchcock* (biographies are shelved alphabetically by subject).
12. A A magazine would have more current information.
13. A You can look up the person's name in the index to find names and dates of periodicals that have articles about the person.
14. A specialized
       abridged
       unabridged
15. A Print dictionary: Use the thumb index or guide words.
       Electronic dictionary: Type in the word, and the computer will check its database.
16. A *Samples:* pronunciation, etymology, part of speech, definition, derived words

17. A a. 4
       b. noun
       c. It comes from Middle English and Old French.
       d. firmness of character
18. A *Samples:* CD-ROM encyclopedias and atlases; electronic databases
19. A a. almanac
       b. biographical reference
       c. thesaurus
       d. atlas
20. A *Sample:* Do a general search for a key word using a search engine.
21. E c. The other answers do not refer to previewing a test.
22. E a. Answering the easy questions first allows the most time to think about the harder ones.
23. E to make sure that you have followed directions and answered every question
24. A *Sample:* One strategy is to eliminate the obviously incorrect answers, in order to narrow the possible answers.
25. A b. "He took away many Puritan business charters . . ."
26. E a. F
       b. T
       c. F
       d. F
27. E House of Commons
28. C *Sample:* People left for both religious and economic reasons. They wanted the freedom to run their own affairs, based on their biblical beliefs.
29. A 1. b
       2. c
       3. a
30. A a. (destroy)